Series Editors:

Alan Ware (University of Oxford) and
Vincent Hoffmann–Martinot (Sciences Po Bordeaux)

joining political organisations

institutions, mobilisation and participation in western democracies

Laura Morales

First published by the ECPR Press in 2009

The ECPR Press is the publishing imprint of the European Consortium for Political Research (ECPR), an independent, scholarly association, which supports and encourages the training, research and cross–national cooperation of political scientists in institutions throughout Europe and beyond. The ECPR's Central Services are located at the University of Essex, Wivenhoe Park, Colchester, CO4 3SQ, UK

Typeset in Times 10pt by the ECPR Press
Printed and bound in the UK by the University of Essex Print Centre

British Library Cataloguing in Publication Data
A catalogue record for this book is available from the British Library

ISBN 13: 978–0–9552488–9–4

The ECPR Monographs series is published by the ECPR Press, the publishing imprint of the European Consortium for Political Research (ECPR).

The ECPR is an independent, scholarly association, established in 1970. It supports and encourages the training, research and cross-national co-operation of political scientists throughout Europe and beyond. The ECPR currently has nearly 350 European institutional members and associate members in over 40 countries, from as far afield as New Zealand and Japan. These members together form a network of thousands of individual political scientists, international relations and European studies specialists.

The ECPR Monographs series publishes major new research in all sub-disciplines of political science and includes work from both senior and younger members of the profession and trans-lations of important new research not yet published in English.

contents

acknowledgements

This book is the product of an extended period of research that started with my PhD dissertation. Therefore, a long list of persons and institutions should be acknowledged for their support and scholarly input to this work and, unfortunately, I can only name a few. I, thus, want to express my sincere appreciation to everyone who helped me along the way.

My research for this book was financially supported by numerous institutions. The Juan March Institute provided the initial funding and academic support that made this piece of research possible. The British Council and the La Caixa Foundation supported a year of study and research at the London School of Economics that proved crucial for the methodological development of the core sections of this book. Additional funding for research and data collection was provided by the Spanish Ministry of Education and Science through project grants SEC95-1007, SEC 2000-0758-C02, SEC2002-03364; as well as from the Education Council of the Regional Government of Madrid through project grant 06/0087/2002. A Fulbright/MEC postdoctoral fellowship at Columbia University provided valuable time free from teaching obligations to transform the dissertation into a book, and for this I am very grateful.

I wish to sincerely acknowledge the many useful comments I have received to chapters and portions of this book by Eva Anduiza, Miguel Caínzos, Jan van Deth, Joan Font, María Jiménez, Hanspeter Kriesi, José María Maravall, José Ramón Montero, Jan Teorell, and Alan Ware. The roll call of colleagues and scholars to whom I am intellectually indebted is too long to list but it is very present in my mind. A special note of appreciation is due to Svante Ersson, who gave me extremely useful suggestions for the creation of some of the indicators presented in Chapter six; to Hanspeter Kriesi, who gave me access to the dataset on protest events, the results of which are published in Kriesi *et al.* (1995); and to Ron Francisco for enabling public access to the collection of datasets on protest events and coercion in Europe. I would also like to sincerely thank Rebecca Knappett and Alan Ware at the ECPR Press for all their support and patience during the various stages of production of this book, and to the ECPR for their institutional support to young scholars all along the way.

None of this would have ever been possible without the love, the constant support, and the joy that my family has brought to my life. This book is dedicated to my mother, Nieves, and my partner, Luis, for their unconditional belief in me. Not a day goes by without me thinking 'Gosh! I am so lucky to have you!'

introduction

Political associations are large free schools, where all members of the community go to learn the general theory of association.
(Alexis de Tocqueville 2000 [1835]: 492)

Political participation is one of the defining features of democratic government. If a democratic society is one where '... ordinary citizens exert a relatively high degree of control over leaders' (Dahl 1956: 3), then effective citizen participation is the only real mechanism for exerting such a control and holding governing elites accountable. So, why then do some people participate in politics while others do not? Why is the citizenry of certain democracies more active in politics than that of other nations with similar levels of socio-economic development? Why do we find democracies with low levels of electoral turnout but high levels of political membership and those in which it's the other way around? Why are the British much less engaged in political associations than, for example, Americans; or Germans more than Italians? How does gaining a more detailed knowledge of the political context help us understand cross-national differences in political membership? Are certain institutional settings particularly advantageous or beneficial for citizens' engagement in politics?

The main goal of this book is to provide some answers to these questions. This study focuses on a specific form of political participation: political membership. Throughout the volume, I identify some of the factors that help explain why citizens join political organisations – or fail to do so. The main contribution of this investigation is its systematic analysis of the effects of the political context on individual decisions to participate in organisations. Building on the analytical contribution of the new social movements field, this study particularly focuses on the effects of two different dimensions of the political context: institutional configurations related to political opportunity structures and patterns of political mobilisation. Throughout the volume, the results of this research show that, institutional structures and configurations, as well as mobilisation efforts, shape citizens' participation patterns in important ways.

As we will see, western democracies differ notably in the extent to which their citizens engage in political associations. However, rarely does research on individual political behaviour systematically include in its analyses the effect of the political context. In order to improve our current understanding of political participation, this study incorporates and combines several theoretical and analytical approaches that, too frequently, talk past each other. The core elements of this investigation develop from more traditional approaches to individual political behaviour and participation, which stress the relevance of citizens' resources and orientations when explaining their political actions. Accordingly, the methodological strategy of this study relies mainly on the use of cross-national survey data for more than eighteen western democracies, extracted from the World Values Survey, the Eurobarometers and the European Social Survey. Yet, the results presented in this book also underline the considerable limitations of the approaches that exclusively focus on individual attributes for explaining political behaviour. Consequently, this study systematically considers two types of aspects that have been central in past research on social movements and collective action: institutional configurations – more specifically, those connected to the notion of political opportunity structures – and mobilisation patterns.

Bringing the mobilisation and institutional contexts into the study of individual political behaviour provides clearer answers to the main questions of this investigation. The institutional configuration of democracies, as well as the mobilisation strategies pursued by political organisations, explain to a large degree why in some western nations citizens join political groups in considerable numbers while in others they very rarely do. These aspects of the political context clarify as well why this happens even across western democracies, which are rather similar in social and economic terms. For example, by taking institutional configurations and mobilisation patterns into account, we can learn that party fragmentation and corporatist and consensual arrangements of interest representation substantially foster citizens' engagement in political organisations. We can also learn that it is, precisely, in those countries with less open political opportunity structures that social inequalities are more commonly transformed into inequalities in political voice and representation.

But why should we care who joins political organisations and how many they are? And, why does it matter that citizens join political groups more often in some countries and much less in others? Put simply, because these matters have important effects on how democracies actually work.[1]

First and foremost, political membership is a form of political action and, as such, it has an impact on political processes. Democratic decision-making processes are extremely complex and so is demand- and preference-aggregation. Unless citizens make their preferences – and the intensity with which they hold them – known to politicians, demand-aggregation will very likely fail to be responsive to preferences.[2]

Electoral participation is one of the main means to hold governments accountable and make politicians responsive to citizen demands. However, voting is not

precisely the form of political participation best suited to expressing unambigu-
ously citizens' preferences. During electoral campaigns, not all relevant issues are
subject to public debate. Yet, very frequently, politicians face unforeseen circumstances and issues during their terms that require decisions for which no electoral
mandate can be claimed.[3] The ballot provides very little information about citizens'
preferences. At best, one can infer broad ideological considerations about how
voters want governments to act but no real input as to what specific orientation
public policies and decisions should take is manifest in the act of voting for one
party or candidate.

Thus, voting is a limited – albeit crucial – way to control politicians. In contrast, political activity between elections conveys much clearer messages about
participants' preferences, since these forms of political action are usually directed
at influencing specific decisions at a given layer of government and at a certain
stage in the policy process. In some instances, non-electoral participation provides
public visibility to citizens' reactions to governmental actions; in other cases,
these forms of political action are proactive rather than reactive; and they are
aimed at the introduction of new issues into the agenda. In both cases, participation between elections helps to bind the set of options among which politicians
finally choose (Rosenau 1974: 10).

Additionally, non-electoral political action contributes to the public debate of
the issues involved and, hence, forces politicians to position themselves on those
issues. Often, as well, this public saliency entails that the entire decision-making
process will be more transparent to citizens, since information about it will flow
both from the media and from the organisations and groups that made the issue
salient. And information, in turn, is fundamental if politicians are to be held
accountable for their records.

In short, participation between elections has a crucial impact on democratic
governance. Its impact derives from its capacity to shape political decisions
through three main mechanisms: communication of citizens' preferences over specific issues; setting the political agenda; and contributing to clarifying politicians'
policy positions and making the decision-making process more transparent.

Of course, political membership is not the only option citizens have to make
themselves heard between elections. The repertoire of political action is ever
widening and citizens can choose among a broad array of participation forms.
Nonetheless, political action is rarely truly spontaneous, although it may sometimes seem to be so.[4] In most cases, citizens are mobilised into action by groups
and organisations.[5] As Wilson (1995: 7) put it, 'passions can be aroused and for
the moment directed; they cannot be sustained. Organization provides continuity
and predictability to social processes that would otherwise be episodic and uncer-
tain'. Thus, although engagement in political associations is not the only way to
influence decision-making processes between elections, it is certainly a good way
to have a say, to the extent that these organisations perform an intermediation
function through demand-aggregation and -creation.

In this sense, the members of political organisations have a certain influence, albeit sometimes limited, on the decisions their organisations make: they frequently choose leaders and they have some say – more or less, depending on the circumstances – on the courses of action they take. At a minimum, their membership fees serve to fund the activities of political associations and, hence, their contribution will have a substantial impact if the latter are successful in achieving their goals. Additionally, joining a political organisation entails supporting, intentionally or otherwise, the organisation's political activities.

Given that political membership usually responds to political motivations and has political consequences, a second and fundamental reason for studying this type of behaviour lies in its implications for the equality of citizens' representation. Since political organisations have an independent impact on how and what politicians decide, political equality is no longer granted by the 'one person, one vote' principle. This is more the case if we take into account that any given citizen can join several political organisations at a time. Political membership, thus, contributes to the over-representation of the most active citizens, who tend, invariably, to be more resourceful and wealthier. Thus, the more privileged social groups are able to organise their interests adequately in order to influence political decisions effectively, while the less well off – who tend to have fewer organisational resources – are limited to resort to sporadic protest (Hardin 1991). Additionally, although some scholars argue that political associations contribute to representing citizens' preferences adequately,[6] several studies have shown that special interests face fewer barriers to collective action than public interests do, thus considerably biasing the process of interest representation (Olson 1965 and 1982, Schlozman 1984, and Gray & Lowery 1993).

If political membership and political organisations increase political inequalities, then greater numbers of political members and political associations are probably the only way to restore equality.[7] Verba, Nie & Kim (1978) recognised that organisational membership is probably the only chance for the less privileged to level with the resourceful. Participation in political associations, especially when these organisations actively seek to mobilise the less advantaged groups in society, allows citizens with few socio-economic resources and little political motivation and involvement to obtain additional resources for political action. Hence, increasing levels of political membership can contribute to equalising political influence. Inversely, democracies with few political members will very likely reproduce – or even increase – social inequalities in the representation of political preferences. Getting to know how many citizens join political organisations provides valuable insight into the possible biases of the democratic process. However, even if it did not matter how many people join political organisations, it certainly matters who does.

Finally, the empirical study of political membership may contribute to the debates on the quality of democracy, which are some times linked to levels of effective political participation.[8] In this regard, political membership is relevant for several aspects of procedural notions of democratic quality. On the one hand, political organisations foster democratic accountability and control through both organisational and individual mechanisms. Political associations are attentive to the performance of politicians and they mobilise their members and the public when they want to lobby officials. This monitoring role is further enhanced by the increasing participation of various sorts of organisations in the decision-making processes and structures, such as advisory councils and legislative committees. Moreover, political associations help improve democratic controls by transmitting information to citizens, who will, thus, be better equipped to monitor and hold politicians accountable through voting and other forms of political action. Therefore, political associations provide their members, and the public, with valuable information on new political issues, as well as to framing existing issues through different perspectives. They fulfil a fundamental role of information-provision, reducing action costs; and information is essential if citizens are to hold politicians accountable (Manin, Przeworski & Stokes 1999b). Furthermore, political associations provide individuals with useful skills and social resources that can be transferred into other forms of political participation. As Alexis de Tocqueville (2000: 492) already noted, political associations act as privileged schools for democracy, since their members learn in them how to make collective decisions, how to accommodate their will to that of others, and how to coordinate their individual efforts to obtain common goods.[9]

On the other hand, studying political membership gives us useful clues about the effective inclusion of the citizenry in the democratic process. Membership of political associations frequently introduces social biases into political representation but these biases are very likely to diminish when associational involvement extends to all sorts of citizens. Studying what contextual factors favour or hinder political membership will also help identify institutional and mobilisation settings that might promote greater citizen involvement and, thus, greater political equality.

Finally, political associations play an important role in improving the quality of democracy to the extent that they provide politicians with information on the preferences and demands of their members and, frequently, of the public.[10] If a high proportion of the citizenry joins political organisations, the flow in the communication of citizens' preferences to governing officials will be more intense and direct. This, in turn, will allow governments to be more responsive to these preferences and demands.[11]

In summary, studying political membership will advance our understanding of the way contemporary democracies work, of how the process of communication between citizens and governments is shaped, and of which social groups are in a better situation to achieve their goals.

AN OVERVIEW OF THE BOOK

The main objective of this study is to answer the following questions. How can we explain political membership? Especially, how can we explain the substantial variations that we find in the levels of political membership across democracies that are, otherwise, similar? The main contention of this investigation is rather simple: to account properly for this type of political behaviour and, in particular, for the significant differences we find across western democracies, we need to consider adequately and systematically the political context in which citizens, as well as the organisations, make their decisions.

Certainly, individual characteristics matter. Socio-economic resources and attributes have an important impact on citizens' ability to join political organisations. Political attitudes and orientations provide (or fail to provide) the motivation to join a political group. However, these individual traits do not necessarily shape political inequalities similarly in all societies, nor do they have the same impact. The social and political context in which citizens make decisions about their public engagement interacts with individual features to trigger or neutralise their political impact.

Furthermore, the social and political context that surrounds citizens does also have an independent impact on their political behaviour. A number of aspects of the political context might be relevant for understanding citizens' political action. However, in this study we will specifically assess the impact of two broad aspects of the political context: mobilisation patterns and institutional configurations related to political opportunity structures. Political institutions and mobilisation patterns are vital determinants of political membership because they structure the opportunities citizens actually have for participation. Some democratic polities have developed political institutions that facilitate political membership while others have not. In some western countries, citizens are mobilised into political associations very frequently; in others they are not. And, as we will see, these differences in institutional configurations and mobilisation do shape, to a great extent, citizens' tendency to join political organisations. Countries that have more 'open' institutional configurations, and where organisations are more active and embedded in society, are also typically the nations where citizens join political associations in greater numbers.

This study is, therefore, an attempt to incorporate systematically 'politics' and 'institutions' into an analysis of individual political behaviour. The need to do so emerges from the explanatory limitations of the individual factors that motivate or have an impact on citizens' political participation. As we shall see in the first chapter, the classical studies of political participation have contributed to furthering our knowledge of how socio-economic inequalities transform into participatory inequalities. However, this tradition of research into political participation pays little or no attention to exactly how political institutions and the varying aspects of democratic governance shape citizens' participation, and its interaction with social inequalities. Few would dispute that citizens' political behaviour results from the interaction between the political realm and the individuals, between the political context and citizens. Both types of factors are interdependent: trying to understand citizens' political behaviour while ignoring politics and institutions leaves a big part of the process unexplained.

Consequently, the analytical framework of this investigation relies on previous research within the field of political participation – most notably, those of Verba and his colleagues in the last three decades[12] – and systematically incorporates the three elements that explain political participation (or its absence): motivation, resources, and opportunities. However, this study aims to improving some past research, primarily as regards the specification and analysis of opportunities. In traditional analyses of political participation, the consideration of opportunities is frequently limited to processes of intentional recruitment. With the exception of some studies on electoral participation, research on individual political behaviour rarely takes into account other factors that structure citizens' opportunities for participation.

As we will see in Chapter one, this study considers the three different levels that shape the real opportunities to participate that an individual has (see Figure 1). Firstly, individuals are embedded in networks of social relations with other persons with whom they interact in various environments – family, neighbourhood, workplace, educational institutions, etc. These networks are the *micro-context* where citizens receive – or fail to receive – information about the public realm. Some times, they are invited – explicitly or implicitly – to participate in political actions or to join political organisations. As a result, the nature of this micro-context and its degree of politicisation will shape the opportunities of participation the individual has.

Secondly, citizens are surrounded – even if they are unaware of it – by a network of organisations active in public and political issues: neighbourhood or community groups, political parties, trade unions, environmental organisations, other advocacy

Figure 1: The analytical framework: levels of analysis

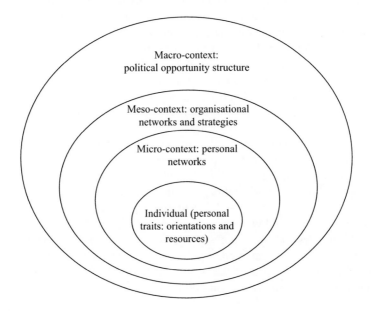

Macro-context:
political opportunity structure

Meso-context: organisational
networks and strategies

Micro-context: personal
networks

Individual (personal
traits: orientations and
resources)

groups, etc. These organisational networks can be either dense and visible or weak and relatively invisible and they form the *meso-context* in which citizens act and make decisions about their political engagement. In some societies, organisations are very active and aggressive in their attempt to recruit new members; in others, they rarely organise activities or they do not invest heavily in attracting people. Moreover, in some places, organisations establish wide alliances and co-operative bonds that contribute to membership sharing; in others, organisations are isolated and seldom collaborate. Thus, the structure and the strategies of political organisations shape recruitment processes and information flows and, therefore, they largely determine the opportunities citizens have to join them.

Finally, individuals are placed in a web of institutions and rules of the game that outline the opportunities and incentives they have to participate in politics. These *macro-contexts* have both direct and indirect impacts on participation opportunities. Directly, the set of institutions and rules determine the specific channels citizens may use to participate in the democratic process. Indirectly, the macro-context moulds the creation of political organisations, as well as their recruitment strategies and mobilisation patterns, since these institutions and rules of the game determine the incentive structure that guides their behaviour.

Accordingly, this study will take into account several levels of analysis and multiple explanatory factors, both individual and contextual. Constraining the investigation to individual attributes would offer only partial explanations of citizens' political behaviour and, especially, it would prevent us from explaining important cross-national variations among western democracies. In this sense, research undertaken during decades in the field of social movements will be shown to be particularly helpful for combining contextual analyses – primarily *meso* and *macro* – into an integrated model of individual political membership. As we will illustrate in this study (especially in Chapters five and six), it is very unfortunate that researchers in the social movements and the individual political participation fields tend to talk past each other. And, yet, this book shows that incorporating the analytical lenses and tools of social movement research into analyses of individual behaviour is fruitful. More specifically, the notion of political opportunity structures is rather helpful, as it provides an adequate frame for analysing the specific institutional features that provide (or fail to provide) incentives and opportunities for individual political membership.

Finally, this study challenges some theses about individual political behaviour that are increasingly popular with political scientists. On the one hand, our results question the central role reserved to the 'political culture' of a society – especially political attitudes and orientations – in the explanation of all types of political participation and of cross-national differences in participatory levels. As we shall see in Chapter three, individuals' socio-economic resources are much more relevant than attitudes and orientations to account properly for cross-national variations in levels of political membership across western democracies. In other words, fundamental aspects of the social structure of these nations have a much greater impact than the set of factors linked to citizens' political culture.[13] And, most certainly, the political culture of the various western democracies included in this study is not even close to explaining the vast differences that we find in levels of political membership across them.

The book is structured as follows. Chapter one presents the main analytical framework of the whole research and provides some important definitions. The theoretical and analytical approach of the study develops around the main aspects that contribute to understand what makes citizens join political organisations: their willingness or inclination to participate, their ability and capacity to do so, the opportunities they are granted for getting involved in political affairs, and the recruitment and mobilisation cues they receive to become involved. Accordingly, the study is organised around the core set of factors that define those various aspects: attitudes, resources, institutional opportunities and organisational mobilisation. Further to framing the main analytical approach, the chapter offers the main definitions that are at the foundation of the study: what are 'political' associations, what counts as 'membership', and how to distinguish between different kinds of membership of organisations.

Chapter two turns to a detailed description of the cross-national and longitudinal patterns of political membership in western democracies and, at the same time, discusses some important methodological issues in the study of political membership. As we will see, cross-national variations in levels of political membership in western countries are wide and long lasting. Moreover, this chapter shows that there are three distinctive patterns of engagement in associations in western democracies. One is typical of North American countries and some central-European countries, and is characterised by relatively high to moderate levels of membership and activism. A second pattern, usual in Scandinavian and North European countries, entails extensive but fundamentally passive memberships. And a third pattern, common to South European countries is characterised by a marginal number of members but with very intense levels of activism. However, this chapter also shows that political membership is – to a great extent – a matter of passive involvement and yet cross-national variations are considerable. It is, in fact, because these are relatively effortless contributions that these wide differences across western democracies in political membership become even more interesting and puzzling.

Chapters three to seven build up, gradually, the explanatory model of political membership of this study. Chapter three focuses exclusively on individual characteristics and it discusses the extent to which individuals' resources and social position are transformed into political inequalities. This chapter provides empirical evidence of the relatively minor relevance of most political attitudes and orientations in the explanation of political membership and, especially, of its cross-national variations. Finally, the chapter shows that, although essential to any understanding of political membership, individual-level factors are insufficient to explain this type of political participation within and across western democracies.

Chapter four discusses in greater detail than was possible in Chapter one the theoretical and empirical implications of contextual approaches to individual political behaviour. Its main purpose is to present fully the various hypotheses and mechanisms that connect macro-level factors and variables with micro-level political behaviour. After outlining the micro–macro mechanisms, the last section explores the impact of micro-contexts – especially, the politicisation of family ties – on political membership. Stemming from this analytical standpoint, Chapters five to seven move on to test the multi-level model of political membership that incorporates the two core sets of factors of the political context considered in this study: mobilisation patterns and structures and institutional settings related to the openness of political opportunity structures.

Chapter five analyses how mobilisation processes (meso-contexts) affect political membership. It discusses the concept of mobilisation and presents bivariate and multivariate analyses that show the link between structures and patterns of mobilisation and levels of individual political membership. The results demonstrate that the patterns and structures of political mobilisation that prevail in each nation are closely connected to the propensity of their citizens to join political associations. The three dimensions of mobilisation that we consider – structural, cognitive, and historical – are relevant, and they importantly contribute to reduce the unexplained variation in levels of political membership across western democracies.

Chapter six, then, examines whether institutional factors (macro-contexts) have any significant impact on citizens' political behaviour. The results support the conclusion that the institutional features of western democracies that relate to the openness of political systems to the demands of their citizenry have a significant impact on individual political membership. In particular, the importance of corporatist arrangements and of levels of elite fragmentation is clearly unveiled by the results.

Finally, Chapter seven tests the whole model,[14] by combining all individual- and contextual-level factors and, thus, evaluates the independent and net effect of the political context on individual political behaviour. The results show that certain institutional characteristics represent powerful incentives for associative political participation. In addition, the chapter also discusses how the type and magnitude of mobilisation by political organisations determine the extent to which citizens join political associations as well as the type of organisations they choose to join. Mobilisation structures and patterns also have discernible – albeit more moderate – effects on the various forms of political membership. The main finding of the chapter – and of the study – is that 'open' political systems provide similar opportunities for influence to citizens with unequal socio-economic resources. Open political opportunity structures have important equalising effects by boosting the engagement of the less well off in the population.

The concluding chapter summarises the main findings, highlights the main contributions of the book, and discusses the main implications for the study of democratic processes.

NOTES

1   The underlying vision of democracy of the discussion that follows mainly corresponds to the 'responsive' model of democracy, as described and discussed by Teorell (2006). Nevertheless, it does also take into account some of the central concerns of deliberative theories of democracy.

2   In fact, as Manin, Przeworski & Stokes (1999b: 9) note, 'the concept of responsiveness is predicated on the prior emission of messages by citizens'.

3   In most cases, not even clear electoral mandates exist for many issues, since electoral platforms, promises and campaigns tend to be full of vague proposals and commitments. Yet, on other occasions, the problem is just the opposite: new information and circumstances force politicians to act against their mandates and electoral platforms (Stokes 1999).

4   This conclusion is shared even within the field of social movement research, where organisations are conceived of as the instruments that confer stability to collective action (McAdam, McCarthy & Zald 1996: 13).

5   See Rosenau (1974: 409) and Parry, Moyser & Day (1992: 86–8) for some evidence.

6   Individuals are more likely to form groups when their interests are threatened (Truman 1951 and Hansen 1985).

7   Rousseau (cited in Pateman 1970: 24) also viewed the multiplication and, therefore, equalisation of power of organisations and associations as the 'least bad' solution, if their creation cannot be avoided.

8   Diamond & Morlino (2004) define the notion of the quality of democracy by three elements: the type of democratic procedures, the outputs of democratic decision-making and citizens' satisfaction with democracy.

9   Putnam (2000) assigns these properties to all associations.

10 Nevertheless, political organisations may distort their members' (or the citizens') preferences in the process of aggregation and transmission, just as governments frequently distort the electorate's preferences when making political decisions.

11 The risk is, however, one of system overload (Olson 1982).

12 Almond & Verba (1989), Verba, Nie & Kim (1971), Verba & Nie (1972), Verba, Nie & Kim (1978), and Verba, Schlozman & Brady (1995).

13 This is not to deny the role of attitudes in any explanation of political participation; it just calls for a reconsideration of their role as the main explanatory factor for all forms of participation alike.

14 With the sole exception of micro-contexts, due to data limitations.

chapter one | political participation and political membership: an analytical model

ATTITUDES, RESOURCES, OPPORTUNITIES AND MOBILISATION: AN EXPLANATORY MODEL OF POLITICAL MEMBERSHIP

How can we explain political membership? What factors help us better understand why some citizens join political associations and others do not? What can account for the huge variations in levels of political membership across western democracies? This study proposes a framework that combines individual and contextual variables in the explanation of this form of political participation by taking into account four different sets of factors: attitudes, resources, institutional opportunities and organisational mobilisation.

When trying to analyse any type of political activity, there are several aspects we need to consider: citizens' willingness or inclination to participate, their ability and capacity to do so, the opportunities they are granted for acting, and the recruitment and mobilisation cues they receive to become involved.[1] As we will see in the next sections, when focusing specifically on political membership, this entails considering four types of factors: citizens' attitudes, their resources, the opportunities for participation granted by the institutional context, and the patterns of mobilisation and recruitment in which organisations engage.

Motivated to participate?

In democratic societies, the voluntary nature of citizens' political participation means that anyone who does not wish to participate will not. Thus, in most cases, having the motivation or the inclination to participate would seem as a crucial factor. Positive attitudes and orientations towards politics and participation in public affairs contribute to citizens' engagement, negative feelings usually prevent it.

A lack of motivation to participate in public affairs may be due to very different reasons.[2] Citizens may display a clear lack of interest in anything related to politics and the community and prefer to look after their own personal and family affairs. Apathy may be due to a fear of the negative consequences of politics, to its consideration as something useless or irrelevant, or simply to satisfaction with the status quo (Rosenberg 1954). Lack of interest in politics might be conscious or unconscious; very frequently it is linked to a lack of information and a limited understanding of what happens in the public realm. In this regard, possessing minimal levels of information and interest in public affairs is almost a prerequisite for engaging in political action. Without political information citizens will be unlikely to find reasons to join a political organisation and they will probably ignore the various options among which they can choose.[3]

However, how much information on political organisations is necessary for individuals to decide to join them is more difficult to establish. Rothenberg (1988, 1989 and 1992) offers data which suggest that not much information is necessary because citizens generally dedicate few resources – time or money – to their contribution. The information held regarding the organisation seems, however, to be much more decisive when their commitment is to be maintained over a long period of time. Therefore, individuals use information for their 'experiential search': given that joining a group comes at a very low cost, individuals join political groups to acquire more information on their objectives and how they operate; if they are convinced, they stay with the group; if not, they leave.[4]

Thus, having an interest in public affairs will partly determine the degree of exposure to sources of political information; it will also determine willingness to devote always limited resources to engaging in political associations. But, in addition to information and an interest in public affairs, citizens also need to grant effectiveness to organised action. They need to feel capable of acting politically and they must also believe that the organisation to which they will contribute their time and/or money will be able to obtain the desired goal.[5]

Feelings of effectiveness are frequently crucial for overcoming the collective-action dilemma, as citizens invariably tend to overestimate the importance of their individual contribution to the achievement of the collective good pursued (Moe 1980a and b). Political organisations also contribute to this overestimation by stressing the importance of each individual contribution in their recruitment messages. For example, Amnesty International systematically emphasises the value of individual contributions in its human-rights campaigns and for membership recruitment.[6] The section 'Join' in their website highlights the phrase 'You can make a difference'. And Greenpeace uses a very similar motto: 'Your support will make all the difference'. The more political organisations are affected by the collective-action dilemma, the more we should expect them to over-emphasise the impact of individual contribution. Equally, political organisations less capable of providing 'hard' selective incentives will need more to assure potential recruits of their effectiveness in achieving the desired collective good.

Nevertheless, for many individuals, having an interest in politics, possessing sufficient amounts of political information, and feeling politically effective is not enough to motivate them to participate and join political organisations. Many individuals act as free-riders, while others choose to co-operate even if facing the same cost and benefit structures. One possible explanation is that some citizens display altruistic preference structures or, rather, that some individuals combine two utility functions: one that maximises group interest and another that maximises personal interest (Margolis 1982). Individuals act altruistically when they incorporate the effects of their actions on others (the group) and their course of action is such that their strictly personal benefit would have been greater had they ignored those effects.[7] Perhaps, then, citizens who do not participate in politics purely because they do not 'want' to are the ones who only maximise the utility function of their personal interest. In other words, not only political attitudes and orientations matter: preferences and the structure of values (i.e. the utilities) are also relevant for understanding why citizens might be willing to engage in public affairs.

Beyond political interest, feelings of efficacy, information and value preferences, the role of other political and civic orientations in influencing citizens' associational behaviour is much less clear. The growing literature on social capital pays great attention to the relationship between trust in other citizens, social co-operation and membership. In some cases trust is even identified with the very concept of social capital and, in others, both trust and membership are indicators of the existence or absence of it. In most cases it is assumed that the relationship between interpersonal trust and membership is clear and direct; but empirical backing for this thesis is still scarce.

The causal mechanism between interpersonal trust and participation in associations is, thus far, somewhat unclear. Some scholars have argued that, contrary to what Putnam (1993, 1995a and b, 2000) seems to claim, associations that pursue collective goods may contribute more to the creation of social capital than those associations whose goal is to obtain private goods, such as leisure or sports associations.[8]

In addition to social trust, research on political behaviour has shown that citizens with post-materialist or libertarian values are much more prone to engaging in organisations linked to the NSMs.[9] But it is much less clear that this type of value preference leads to a general inclination to join political associations.

In short, joining political organisations requires some minimal level of motivation in the form of interest, information, feelings of efficacy, or value preferences. If non-participation is mainly due to citizens' unwillingness or lack of motivation to participate in politics, any intervention aimed at increasing levels of participation would need to change these individual attitudes and preferences. However, as we will discuss in the following section, in many cases citizens refrain from participating not out of unwillingness or a lack of motivation but because they lack the resources or the opportunities to get involved.

Enabling participation: individual resources

In addition to motivation, citizens need to be able to participate: they need resources for political action. Political action is costly and participants, therefore, need resources – whether economic, social, cognitive or time-related. In fact, early studies of political participation emphasised the relevance of individual resources – as well as the mediating role of attitudes.[10] And one of the main limitations of the classical model of political participation developed initially by Verba, Nie and their various colleagues is precisely the reduction of the explanation of variations in political participation to factors related to the individual – in particular resources and orientations.[11]

However, which resources will be relevant for explaining political membership is not self-evident. The cost structure of action varies depending on the form of participation. For example, the cost structure of co-ordinated actions (e.g. protests) is very different to that of co-operative actions (e.g. contributing to or joining an organisation): whilst in the former case the costs decrease with the number of participants, the costs of co-operative action remain constant (Hardin 1991: 366–8). In other words, the resources needed for political action importantly vary depending on the cost structure of the activity.

In general terms, we should expect that people with more resources and a more privileged social and economic position will be more likely to join political organisations, either because they are more aware of their ability to defend their interests; because they are more exposed to political socialisation experiences that favour involvement; because their life experiences build up greater cognitive resources; or because they are more often the target of mobilisation efforts by political organisations.[12]

Given that social, economic and cognitive resources have an impact in the cost structure of citizens' political activity, individuals with varying stocks of these resources will most likely have different propensities to join political organisations. For example, citizens with higher incomes face lower costs for contributing financially to political associations than lower-income individuals; citizens with little free time available confront higher opportunity costs for actively engaging in an organisation than someone who has some free time; and citizens with few educational and cognitive resources face greater information costs than those who have them in abundance. Thus, not surprisingly, citizens with greater resources usually tend to join political associations more frequently and in greater numbers and this pattern is likely to be common in most western democracies.

Still, even with motivation and with resources, many individuals will not participate. In many cases, citizens will need to have specific participation opportunities before engaging in politics. Opportunities for participation – provided by the institutional context and recruitment efforts – will very frequently facilitate citizens' political action.

Facilitating political action: opportunities for participation

In many ways, opportunities for participation can be viewed as facilitating political participation. Citizens do not act in a vacuum: most political activities are collective in nature and require co-ordination and/or co-operation between a number of citizens. Rosenau (1973) has already warned of the excessive importance that studies of political participation attribute to personal initiative when explaining how and why citizens participate in politics. This bias in behavioural approaches has recurrently meant neglecting the fact that citizens' participation occurs in interactive situations and that it tends to be activated by some agent – individual or organisational.

Thus, the political activity of any one individual also depends on various facilitating factors that are beyond his or her control: other people's actions, organisational recruitment strategies and the institutional opportunities afforded for citizens to have a say. Sometimes, the presence or absence of these opportunities to become engaged will even determine the capacity (or not) to act politically in certain fashions at all. For example, if referenda are not allowed (or are rarely used), direct democratic actions and a certain array of conventional forms of participation linked to these ballots will not be frequent forms of political expression.

In this sense, opportunities for participating in political associations are, to a large extent, a function of the political and social context. In fact, we should refer to 'contexts', as we should distinguish between the immediate context or *micro-context* of citizens (their personal networks), the organisational context or *meso-context* (the organisational networks around them) and, lastly, the political and institutional context or *macro-context*. The first two levels shape the direct and indirect contacts individuals will have with organisations and, therefore, the extent to which they are the targets of recruitment for these. The macro-context does also have an indirect impact on citizens' opportunities for joining political organisations: on the one hand it determines the institutional boundaries of political action; and on the other it conditions the structure of opportunities that political associations face, thereby determining their recruitment and mobilisation strategies. We will briefly discuss the impact of these types of contexts on political membership separately.

Personal and organisational networks
As Verba, Schlozman and Brady (1995) put it, many citizens do not engage in political activities simply because nobody asked them. As they emphasise, recruitment and mobilisation initiatives are crucial for our understanding of political participation. In particular, one important aspect of recruitment and mobilisation processes is that they frequently interact with individual resources. In fact, past research has shown that organisational strategies for political mobilisation are clearly selective: the effectiveness of the mobilising action is maximised by aiming it at people who are most likely to respond positively (Rosenstone & Hansen 1993). This implies that opportunities for participation deriving from the processes of explicit recruitment are often extremely unequal amongst people of different economic strata, employment and occupational background, race and age.

For the specific case of political membership, the exposure to personal or organisational networks that facilitate contacts with and recruitment by political associations is fundamental. The tasks of contact and recruitment – either directly by organisations or through personal contacts and intermediaries – contribute to the substantial reduction of information costs implicit in the decision to join an organisation. Several studies have shown that citizens who are asked to join a political organisation are always more likely to become members,[13] and Johnson (1998: 60) even claims that 'collective interests do not explain group membership – recruitment activity does'. It is often not sufficient to have reasons, inclination and resources to join a political organisation; most people will simply not take the initiative. Organisations need to devote resources and effort to recruiting and informing people of their existence and objectives. Indeed, Hansen (1985) provides evidence that most of the changes in levels of interest-group membership in the United States reflect the changing mobilisation practices of organisations.

Consequently, micro and meso-contexts are of vital importance in understanding why some citizens participate in political associations and others do not, as social and organisational contacts and recruitment efforts are not distributed uniformly amongst all individuals. Citizens' social networks determine whether one is in contact with other people who engage in associations or not. Similarly, these networks condition the likelihood of being approached by organisations to request one's support. This has been termed the 'mobilisation bias'. People with fewer socio-economic resources tend to live surrounded by other people who rarely participate in public affairs, which means that the chances of an acquaintance encouraging them to participate in political organisations are far lower. Likewise, organisations carefully target the type of public they want to reach and they concentrate their efforts on the type of citizens that are most likely to contribute resources or time to their cause.

Hence, the information costs of joining a political association are clearly non-randomly distributed, simply because organisational efforts in mobilising citizens are not random either. Mobilisation is crucial, therefore, because citizens are more likely to join political associations if they are asked to do so and, additionally, because it increases organisational visibility, awareness of organisations' goals and perceptions of organisations' effectiveness. Thus, we need to consider the role of personal networks and organisational mobilisation in our models of political membership.

Macro-contexts: institutional opportunities
Whereas the role of factors related to recruitment and mobilisation has received some attention – especially in studies of social movements and of interest groups,[14] the incorporation of contextual factors related to institutional configurations has been mostly limited to electoral participation and behaviour.[15] Some scholars mention the importance of these opportunities for all forms of participation, although in many cases this has been limited to merely theoretical or speculative approaches, or to general expressions of ideal research programmes.[16] Only recently have some researchers made limited attempts to include very general aspects of the political configuration of democracies in their analyses of membership in all types of voluntary associations (Curtis, Baer & Grabb 2001 and Schofer & Fourcade-Gourinchas 2001).[17]

However, the opportunities for action afforded by specific political configurations are very likely to be relevant for explaining cross-national variations in patterns of political membership. In this line, Hardin (1991: 370) argues that states which most ably respond to citizens' reformist demands increase the incentives for collective action to adopt the form of group organisation (co-operation) as opposed to forms of protest (co-ordination).[18] If political institutions and authorities are receptive to citizens' demands, the probabilities of success will be, on average, greater. This means that institutional opportunities are likely to affect the anticipated costs and benefits of political action, thus modifying the incentive structures for co-operative action and for joining political organisations.

Moreover, the institutional opportunities for participation that citizens have are also important because they frequently affect different types of individuals differently.[19] Given that citizens do not reserve a 'fixed quota' of resources (time, money, effort, etc.) to dedicate to participation or any other form of altruism, the amount they eventually invest to maximise collective utility will depend on the opportunities for participation they are presented with (Margolis 1982: 24).[20]

Macro-contexts – mainly institutions and political processes – shape the incentive structure of individual action through various mechanisms. On the one hand, the political context might have effects associated with changes in circumstances. For example, changes in the economic cycle have an impact on perceptions of threat held by specific social groups and frequently provoke distress. This, in turn, frequently stirs political associations to emerge and mobilise in order to voice those feelings of threat and distress. Hansen (1985) and King & Walker (1992) show how situations that threaten group interests contribute to individuals being more likely to join organisations that pursue collective goods. Amongst other reasons, greater mobilisation of organisations during periods of conflict increases the amount of information individuals receive regarding the potential benefits of action (and the potential losses of inaction) at the same time that they are prepared to take more risks.[21]

A final effect of the varying political situation is related to subsidies and funds for the creation of political organisations, which could be available from various sources but come primarily from governmental agencies. The availability of 'seed' money for the creation and maintenance of organisations varies substantially from one period to another and is very dependent on the political priorities set by public institutions or private funders.[22] This impact on the organisations 'in supply' is fundamental because supply creates its own demand (Hansen 1985: 94); and without an adequate supply of organisations demand will have fewer opportunities to develop – given the limits on co-operation imposed by the logic of collective action. Thus, individual decisions to join organisations reflect, in part, opportunities available to do so: even if individuals feel politically or economically threatened, they cannot join groups that do not exist.

Yet, beyond the impact of changes in circumstance in the macro-context, the latter also imposes structural constraints for both the creation of political associations and individuals' decisions to join them. Firstly, the availability of institutions and organisations able and willing to act as patrons in the creation and consolidation of organisations with political goals varies across democracies. A society's capacity for 'patronage' fundamentally affects the opportunities to form political organisations and to join them. Research in the field of social movements has repeatedly demonstrated the importance of inter-organisational networks in understanding the emergence of new groups and political actors.[23] 'Patrons' and inter-organisational networks provide material resources (money, infrastructures, etc.) and social resources (experience, contacts, leadership, etc.) that contribute to the creation of new organisations. Logically, the existence of these patrons and organisational networks provides the initial investment necessary for creating new political associations.

On the other hand, the institutional configuration of each political system conditions the channels of participation available and these channels then structure the incentives for joining political associations. The political opportunity structure (POS)[24] determines whether the political system is more or less receptive to citizens' demands as voiced by associations. If political structures are open to the accommodation of interests expressed through organisations, citizens will have greater incentives to join them. If the political system is, on the contrary, closed and hostile to the demands of citizen organisations, the effectiveness of collective action will be limited and citizens will find few reasons to bear the costs of co-operation in organisations. Additionally, these costs will increase, given that it will be necessary to devote greater efforts to achieve the desired goals. Hence, the POS affects both the benefit and cost structures of co-operative action.

Consequently, this study takes into account three aspects that, largely, define the level of openness of a political system: the level of accessibility; the degree of fragmentation of the political elites; and the porosity of the bureaucratic decision-making system.[25]

Firstly, the level of decentralisation of the government and the availability of institutions of direct democracy determine how accessible the political system is for citizen organisations. Several studies have discussed the relevance of the decentralisation of political structures as an incentive for participation. Hansen (1985: 81), for example, argues that decentralisation affects the probability that the collective good will not be provided if the individual does not co-operate. The greater the decentralisation of the government's political functions, the smaller the size of the population affected by the latter and the greater the impact of individual action on the final result of collective action. For her part, Nanetti (1980) considers that the introduction of decentralised structures in local politics favours citizen participation because it contributes to making issues more visible and to focusing the efforts of local associations on specific actions whilst, at the same time, increasing the feeling of effectiveness of the political action.

Additionally, decentralised, federalist or de-concentrated political systems encourage the creation of political organisations due to the fragmentation of power in different bodies and at different levels of government. Thus, by multiplying the opportunities to affect democratic decision-making processes, they encourage the formation of organisations. Yet, this multiplying effect might also be due to much simpler reasons: federalist and decentralised states provide a hierarchical structure that organisations can effectively mimic for their own organising (Skocpol, Ganz & Munzon 2000).

The availability of institutions of direct democracy also seems to contribute to the proliferation of political associations and groups, by offering additional opportunities for citizen organisations to participate in the political decision-making process and by providing an alternative means for traditional lobbying activities (Boehmke 2000 and 2002). In addition, these institutional mechanisms reduce the cost of co-operation – as they are regulated and conventional processes – and they noticeably increase the visibility of organisations, thus reducing information costs (Kriesi & Wisler 1996).

Secondly, the fragmentation of elites might favour political membership by increasing political pluralism, contributing to greater political competition between parties and increasing the political vulnerability of those in power. When the political elites are fragmented, citizen organisations are better able to establish political alliances with political actors who intervene in decision-making processes (e.g. governing or opposition parties) and thus will more frequently achieve their goals.[26]

Finally, the degree of porosity of the interest-intermediation system also contributes to structure the incentives for co-operative collective action. Research on social movements has traditionally considered that pluralist intermediation systems and 'weak' administrative systems have a greater channelling capacity for the demands of organised citizens, since interest groups have more chances to influence the decision-making processes (Kitschelt 1986, Kriesi et al. 1995: 31). In addition, pluralist systems tend to allow the incorporation of a greater number of different demands, as no group enjoys a privileged or monopolist situation. However, other aspects of interest-intermediation systems are also relevant, in particular the level of conflict. Consensual intermediation traditions and patterns of conflict-resolution include negotiation systems and structures that allow the incorporation of different demands from citizen organisations, while conflictual systems very often give rise to zero-sum games and the exclusion of certain preferences and demands. Clearly, the expected benefits of organised action will be, on average, greater in the former than in the latter systems of interest-intermediation.

The analytical model
In accordance with the framework discussed in previous pages, this investigation approaches the study of political membership with an analytical model that attempts to explain this type of participation by taking into account the impact of four main types of factors (Figure 1.1).[27] On the one hand, factors related to individual attributes: citizens' political motivation and resources. On the other hand, factors related to the context in which citizens decide and act: the opportunities for participation granted by political structures, and the patterns and processes of mobilisation and recruitment into organisations around them.

Political attitudes and orientations such as feelings of efficacy, an interest in politics, political information, and post-materialist value structures, will shape expectations about the impact of the individual contribution to the achievement of the political goal, as well as the expected returns from the activities of the political organisation. In turn, individual resources have a clear impact on the relative magnitude of the costs citizens will have to bear for joining political associations. Thus, individuals with greater political motivation and greater resources are expected to be more likely to join political associations in all western nations.

But these individual-level factors are not sufficient if we are to understand why, in some western democracies, citizens are much more likely to join political organisations than in otherwise similar societies. In order to explain cross-national differences among western countries, we need to identify to what extent the institutional and mobilisation context fosters or hinders their citizens' participation in political organisations.

The institutional and mobilisation contexts are expected to have a direct impact on individuals' behaviour and to account – at least partially – for cross-national variations in political membership. Political opportunities structures will mould the cost-benefit structure of joining: open political systems are expected to reduce the costs of action and to increase the expected returns of organised activity. Organisational mobilisation and structures will affect expectations of individual impact – by reinforcing feelings of efficacy through mobilisational cues; perceptions of the degree of support by other citizens and the expected costs of action – primarily by reducing information costs.

However, both sets of factors are also expected to have an interactive effect on certain groups of individuals, in such a way that they promote or discourage, in varying degrees, the participation of individuals who have different levels of resources. This potential interactive effect is of the utmost importance, as it would mean that the political context, and political institutions in particular, impinge on the way social inequalities are transformed into political inequalities. Thus, it is particularly interesting to explore the extent to which institutional opportunities and mobilisation patterns by organisations increase (or diminish) participatory inequalities stemming from social inequalities in education, income or gender.

Finally, the model will also consider – although to a much more limited extent, due to the lack of suitable network data – the impact of recruitment efforts within personal networks. The different types of personal networks to which citizens are exposed are expected to shape individuals' political orientations and attitudes: having acquaintances already engaged in politics will contribute to more positive dispositions, through the effect of socialisation processes. But having active 'alters' will also reinforce positive expectations about others contributing to the political goal, based on the experience that others do actually also join political organisations. Finally, citizens embedded in networks of active 'others' will have to bear lower costs in order to engage in political groups, as they are more frequently exposed to recruitment and mobilisation efforts.

If we are to achieve a more complete understanding of the decisions citizens make with regard to political participation, we need to adopt more systematic and encompassing models of analysis. Limiting our studies to individual attributes or to contextual factors alone is unsatisfactory. We need, therefore, to combine different levels of analysis if we are to better understand individuals' political behaviour. And this study aims at moving a step forward in that direction.

Figure 1.1: The analytical model

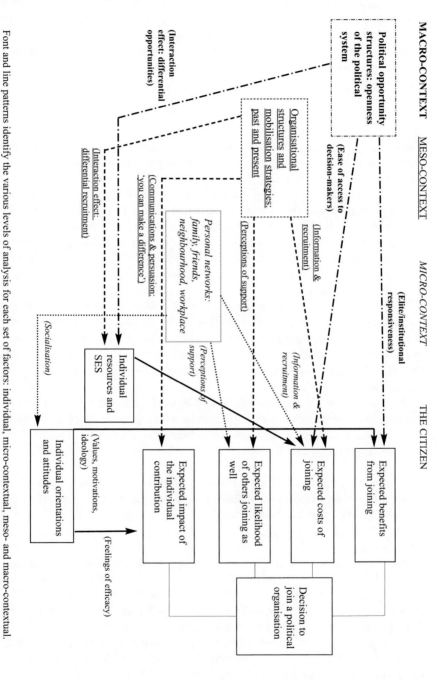

The next section will discuss some definitional issues that are relevant for the research design that will be developed in the remaining parts of this book. Its main goal is to address the following questions: how can we distinguish 'political' from 'non-political' associational involvement? What exactly is an association and how do we distinguish associations from other social institutions and organisations? What is 'membership'?

POLITICAL MEMBERSHIP: SOME DEFINITIONS

This study will, therefore, focus its attention on a specific form of political participation: political membership. But, what do we mean exactly by political participation and political membership?

Our starting point is a somewhat modified version of the well known definition of political participation proposed by Verba, Nie & Kim (1971: 9), partially developed from Milbrath's (1965). Political participation is, thus, defined here as *the acts by private citizens[28] that are more or less directly aimed at influencing the selection of governmental personnel and the actions they take, including new issues on the agenda, and/or changing values and preferences directly linked to political decision-making.*

This definition excludes the requirement that these acts must be legal and incorporates activities aimed at including issues on the political agenda and changing social values and preferences. This takes into account activities intended not to influence the selection of governmental personnel but to attempt to redefine what should be considered of public concern and, therefore, subject to political debate.

However, given that this research deals with political membership as a specific type of political participation, we need to provide a definition of political associations and to make explicit what distinguishes them from other associations. The definition of associations proposed by Knoke (1986: 2) is extremely useful for this study:

> A minimum definition of association is a formally organized named group most of whose members – whether persons or organizations – are not financially recompensed for their participation.

Knoke's definition is useful in distinguishing associations from other social and political institutions such as the family, groups of friends, and other organisations,[29] which are frequently included in notions regarding the 'third sector'.[30] On the one hand, associations are distinct from other organisations, such as foundations or government agencies, in that very few individuals receive payment for their activities in the former (Knoke & Prensky 1984). On the other hand, associations are different from economic organisations such as companies, in that they are institutions that seek solutions to individual or collective problems that are different from those of the market (Knoke 1990b: 5).

Within the entire set of organisations we call associations we can distinguish a subset formed by those aimed mainly at political action: political associations. Yet, the problem lies in defining the political nature of an organisation. In what sense is an organisation 'political'? Lane (1965: 75) contends that there are notable differences between a political and a non-political organisation[31] and links political organisations to their effects on (1) the political process, and (2) the political interests and motivations of their individual members. Likewise, Knoke (1990b) considers the distinction between political and non-political associations to be crucial from many different angles. First of all, although associations often have mixed goals, some associations emphasise their political objectives more. Simultaneously, these differences in goals have important consequences for aspects such as the associations' sources of funding and their budget priorities (79–81). Secondly, the reasons, motivations and interests that lead citizens to join political groups are fundamentally different from those which lead them to join non-political associations. The provision of services, material benefits and social incentives are much more important in the latter than in the former. For members of political associations, motivations which are related to the collective good pursued by the associations they join are much greater. Additionally, the motivations of members of political associations are much more varied (132–5).

Therefore, the definition of political associations used in this study employs similar defining criteria as displayed in the concept of political participation. Hence, political associations[32] are defined as *those formally organised groups that seek collective goods (whether pure public goods or another type of collective goods) and which have as their main goal to influence political decision-making processes, either by trying to influence the selection of governmental personnel or their activities, to include issues on the agenda, or to change the values and preferences that guide the decision-making process.*[33]

This definition of political associations is similar to that provided by Knoke (1986: 2) with regard to interest groups: 'when associations attempt to influence government decisions, they are acting as an interest group'.[34] Nevertheless, the fundamental problem of the concept of interest group is that it tends to exclude political parties, as they (or their elected officials) are usually – with bureaucrats – the object of pressure from these groups. For this reason, in this study, the more general concept of political associations is preferred.[35] Lastly, and with the aim of distinguishing political associations from social movements or citizen protests, this definition requires some level of formal interaction between individuals within the group. In other words, this investigation is primarily concerned with associations and organised groups, although their level of organisational formalisation may vary from one case to another.

Additionally, the definition proposed in this study stresses the relevance of goals as the main defining criterion. Members may have very different reasons to join an association, and these might even differ substantially among individuals in any given association. Thus, the crucial aspect is not so much exactly what citizens look for when they join a political association but what are the collective goals that the organisation seeks to achieve. Clearly, any individual might join a political party or an environmental organisation just to make friends but this misses the point. What is most relevant, and what forms the basis of the definition employed in this study, is what organisations do with the capital – financial, human, and social – they have. In this sense – as we will discuss later – trade unions and business organisations are clearly to be regarded as political organisations, as some of their primary goals are to exert influence on political decision-making processes, on the selection of governmental personnel, and on the political agenda.

Nevertheless, the problem is not solely, nor fundamentally, to define what a political association is from a theoretical or analytical point of view. The more challenging aspect is to distinguish political from non-political organisations when addressing the data available on associations and membership. Finding a satisfactory operational definition of which associations should be classified as political is difficult. As Verba, Schlozman & Brady (1995: 58–9) very correctly point out, technical decisions on how to measure the political nature of an association have very significant substantive implications.

As will be discussed in greater detail in Chapter two, various alternatives exist for distinguishing between political and non-political associations when we are using survey data of representative samples of a population of individuals. We can use as the main definitional criterion the level of political activity the association engages in, obtaining this information either from survey respondents' perceptions[36] or from the type of activities respondents claim to engage in within the organisation.[37] When we cannot get this type of information on associations' political activities, we might classify them according to some theoretical criterion and the analyst's best judgment.

In this study, in most cases, there is no other option but to resort to the latter type of operational classification between political and non-political associations. The cross-national survey data employed throughout the volume does not include explicit questions regarding associations' political activities. Thus, the theoretical definition of political associations presented on previous pages is used to classify organisations, judging from the type of primary goals they can be assumed to pursue.

In addition to the distinction between political and non-political associations, in some parts of this study I analyse what type of political organisations western citizens join. More specifically, some attention is paid to the distinction between 'traditional' and 'new' political associations, a differentiation which has already been used in other research related to political membership[38] and, certainly, in a long list of studies of new social movements (NSMs).

Much has been written on what distinguishes 'old' from 'new' politics, particularly when comparing political parties and social movements. Some scholars have highlighted that traditional political organisations differ from new ones in their ideology and the values they defend. While the former build their ideological frameworks around distributive values, the latter are characterised by their defence of libertarian values.[39] Others highlight the different logics of participation – instrumental in traditional organisations and expressive in those related to the NSMs[40]; their contrasting organisational structures (decentralised and participative in the case of the NSMs, centralised and hierarchical in traditional political associations);[41] or the forms of action that are more characteristic of each type of political associations (leaning more towards protest in the case of NSM organisations as opposed to the more institutionalised forms of traditional political organisations).[42]

Nevertheless, these aspects are not particularly useful when establishing a criterion for classifying specific organisations and groups into the categories of 'new' or 'traditional' political associations. Some of them are even challenged by specialists in the NSMs subfield. Rucht (1990) rejects the validity of the distinction based on the different logics of action (expressive as opposed to instrumental) because both logics are present in all NSMs, although one may prevail in certain periods. In fact, Rucht demonstrates how the majority of NSMs are either ambivalent or power-oriented (instrumental) as regards the logics of action they pursue. A similar problem arises from the distinction based on their organisational structure. Although in many cases 'new' politics organisations adopt loose, decentralised structures, and make much use of participatory democracy, this is not always the case. Some organisations which undoubtedly are related to 'new' politics show organisational traits that are extremely hierarchical and have few or no mechanisms of participatory democracy – particularly all the big multinational organisations, such as Greenpeace or Amnesty International. In contrast, some political parties are adopting more decentralised and participatory structures and rules (most notably, Green parties and left-wing libertarians). This very argument is also valid for forms of action: although 'new' politics is very much related to protest and non-conventional forms of participation, this is not exclusive to new organisations, nor is it the only form of action in their repertoire. Therefore, most of the differentiating characteristics between 'old' and 'new' politics put forward in the literature on NSMs are not glaringly obvious in practice and many are common to both types of politics and organisations.

What might be, then, a suitable criterion for differentiating one type of political organisation from another? The alternative proposed in this study is to employ as the distinctive characteristic what we could call the *nature of the representative link*. 'New' political organisations are characterised by their lack of a representative link with specific sectors of the population; in other words, with a specific constituency. On the one hand, these organisations do not engage in the representative mechanisms that would link them to constituencies: they do not run for elections, and they cannot claim representative mandates for any subset of citizens. On the other hand, their demands, the issues they stand for, are universalist in their aims: when environmental, peace or human rights organisations defend their causes, they are not claiming to represent a specific constituency; rather they defend these issues in the name of all (human) beings.

In contrast, traditional political organisations (political parties, unions, and special interest groups) are the political actors *par excellence* in the representation of the interests and demands of specific sectors of society. On the one hand, traditional political associations are directly involved in electoral politics in different fields, which creates representative links to specific constituencies. Political parties represent their voters, unions represent the workers who vote for them – and, stretching the representative link, the set of workers in their economic sector – and interest groups represent the professionals or the industries whose interests they defend.

Additionally, one of the main objectives of 'traditional' organisations is to gain representative power within the political system. 'New' political organisations, however, do not consider themselves intermediary organisations and do not seek to play this role within political institutions:[43] representation of a constituency is not the goal of these organisations. Thus, there is no representative link between these associations and specific constituencies, either formal or self-proclaimed. Furthermore, representing a constituency implies negotiating with the representatives of other constituencies and the demands of these 'new' groups are not negotiable (Offe 1988).

However, of most importance is not how they portray themselves or what their intentions or platforms are but the dynamics by which traditional and new political organisations defend their goals. These different dynamics are related not so much to the type of interests or demands they stand for as to the representative linkages they have (or fail to have). Being an agent of representation for a constituency requires competing with other agents for that representative status. 'New' political organisations are free from this type of competition. This does not mean that they do not compete on other fields: 'new' political organisations do compete for social and human resources, for patronage, for economic support, for media coverage and, to a certain extent, for political opportunities. However, they do not compete for representative status and neither is one of their main organisational goals to perform well in the competition for representation.

The distinction between 'traditional' and 'new' political organisations proposed in this study partly stems from the typology proposed by Kriesi (1996: 152–4), who distinguishes social movement organisations (SMOs) from traditional political organisations (parties and interest groups) depending on the level of direct participation of the *constituency* in its political actions.[44] However, the distinction used in this study, based on the representative link, goes slightly beyond Kriesi's proposal by arguing that the different forms of political action undertaken by 'traditional' and 'new' organisations are due to the different nature of their relationships with organisations of the same type, with citizens, and to the issues they defend. It is not just that NSM organisations tend to mobilise their members directly whilst traditional political organisations do so to a much lesser extent; rather that the type of issues they stand for (universalist) and the way in which they put these forward (outside of representative institutions) requires this type of political action. In the absence of representative links to constituencies, political action must take the form of mobilisation, almost by necessity.

In this regard, it is very illuminating that when 'new' political organisations get into the dynamics of 'traditional' ones, there is little to distinguish between them.

Thus, when environmental movements create Green parties, engagement in representative politics almost completely transforms them into a different 'species'. And frequently this will mean getting into trouble with their origins and grassroots, especially because representative politics requires negotiation and the trading-off of some goals for others.

Finally, a few words are needed about the political behaviour that will be the primary focus of this study: engagement in political associations. Different concepts can be used when defining engagement in organisations: militancy, activism, affiliation, and membership. By simply listing them, we detect their connection to varying levels of activity within the organisation. Yet, it is not essential to be particularly active in a political association in order to be a political participant: merely joining or paying fees supports the organisation in its attempt to influence the political process. Therefore, the concepts of affiliation and membership would most suitably define the type of behaviour we are interested in. The term affiliation, however, implies a formal process of registration with the association, but many political groups have a formal organisation that is looser than this but should still be included in this study. Hence, the concept of membership is the best suited for this investigation.[45]

A last definitional issue is the need to distinguish between members and nonmembers. The definitions of membership, and the requirements that individuals must fulfil to be considered members vary from one organisation to another and it is therefore impossible to offer a single operational definition of political membership. This, of course, introduces difficulties for measurement. These are solved in this study pragmatically, as we will see in greater length in Chapter two, and entail using survey respondents' claims of membership as the only criterion.

Chapter two spells out in greater detail the methodological implications of these definitions and also provides a comprehensive description of the object of analysis: political membership.

NOTES

1   Verba, Schlozman and Brady (1995) provide a very complete conceptual and analytical framework for tackling the central issue of why citizens (do not) participate. They offer three distinct types of response, which are not mutually exclusive: citizens do not participate because they do not want to, because they can not, or because nobody has asked them to. This study builds upon Verba, Schlozman & Brady's framework and tries to improve it through the further development of explanatory elements neglected in their study: institutional opportunities.

2   The lack of motivation for participating in public affairs is, generally, not independent from socioeconomic resources and socialisation. Its separate discussion is only for argumentative purposes.

3   In this sense, political information is better conceived as a cognitive resource rather than as an attitude. However, given its close link with political interest it is probably better to discuss and analyse it together with attitudes and orientations.

4   Johnson's study (1998: 45) supports Rothenberg's model on the 'experiential' search for membership of political groups, as the turnover rate in the environmental groups studied by Johnson is very high (around 30 per cent) and everything seems to indicate that it is much higher among new members (around 50 per cent). However, one problem with Rothenberg's proposal is that, in keeping with his rationalist approach, he presents the situation of joining a group as an express intentional act of the individual. The citizen 'seeks' an organisation to join and this search process is 'experiential'. In this study, however, a somewhat less ratio-nalist approach is favoured; as Rothenberg himself would term it, a more 'sociological' approach. In many cases, the process which leads citizens to join a political association is the result of coincidences, social contacts and inertias which, as we shall see, are related to their social environment or *micro-context*.

5   Past research has shown that perceptions of effectiveness are very important for citizens' motivations to participate, both in terms of the ability of political action to change things or achieve its objectives (external efficacy) and in terms of the individual's personal capacity to contribute significantly (internal efficacy) to the course of action. Nevertheless, it seems that internal efficacy has a more decisive effect on political action than external efficacy (Madsen 1987, Parry, Moyser & Day 1992).

6   After the successful 2002 campaign to save Safiya Hussaini's life from being stoned to death in Nigeria, the Spanish branch of Amnesty International launched another campaign to save Amina Lawal's life from a similar death penalty. The campaign was entitled 'Thanks to you', and went on to argue that thanks to individual contributions and actions Hussaini's life had been saved. Clearly the goal was to emphasise the effectiveness of individual action even to affect political decisions in regions that may seem remote to many western citizens.

7   Ahn, Ostrom & Walker (2003) prefer to model this individual not as an altruistic one but as one with heterogeneous motivations – the 'inequity-averse'. While altruists have utility functions that combine their own payoffs with payoffs received by others, the inequity-averse would respond to utility functions that incorporate the aggregated result of (in)equality of income.

8   Critical comments on Putnam's theses in this regard can be found in Tarrow (1996), and Boix & Posner (1996).

9   See, for example, Flanagan (1987), Inglehart (1990 and 1997), and the articles in Müller-Rommel & Poguntke (1995) and in Clark & Rempel (1997).

10 See, for example, Verba & Nie (1972), and Verba, Nie & Kim (1978).

11 Many have criticised this 'atomisation' of the individual when studying participation, as it neglects the fact that many forms of political action require co-operation with other people or depend on social interaction (see, for example, Przeworski 1974, Knoke 1990c, Huckfeldt & Sprague 1993, Leighley 1995).

12 Empirical evidence on some or various of these claims can be found in Verba and Nie (1972), Verba, Nie and Kim (1978), Rothenberg (1988, 1989 and 1992), Parry, Moyser and Day (1992), Rosenstone and Hansen (1993), Leighley (1995), Verba, Schlozman and Brady (1995), Johnson (1998), and Burns, Schlozman and Verba (2001).

13 See, among others, Pollock (1982), Klandermans and Oegema (1987), Kriesi (1988), Huckfeldt and Sprague (1993), Rosenstone and Hansen (1993), Verba, Schlozman and Brady (1995), and Leighley (1995).

14 Some examples are to be found in Snow, Zurcher & Ekland-Olson (1980), McFarland (1984), Kriesi (1988), Rothenberg (1988 and 1992), Knoke (1990c: 69–73), Oegema (1991), McAdam and Paulsen (1993), Jordan and Maloney (1997), Johnson (1998). Logically, there are some exceptions within the scope of the more classical research on political or associational participation. See, for example, Booth & Babchuk (1969), Rosenstone & Hansen (1993), Verba, Schlozman & Brady (1995: chapter 5), Knoke (1990b and 1990c), and Leighley (2001).

15 The use of contextual approaches is quite extended in the analysis of electoral behaviour. Good examples can be found in Zipp & Smith (1979), Leighley & Nagler (1992), Oppenhuis (1995), Franklin (1996), Franklin, van der Eijk & Oppenhuis (1996), Burbank (1997), van Egmond, de Graaf & van der Eijk (1998), Anderson (2000), and Anduiza (2002).

16 As in Almond & Verba (1989: chapter 5), Barnes & Kaase (1979: 43), Asher, Richardson & Weisberg (1984: 15 ff.), Kaase (1989: 25–6), or Conway (1991: chapter 5).

17 Van Sickle & Dalton (2005) include contextual factors to explain protest action, but their indicators are probably too crude to be considered real indicators of the political context: Freedom House scores on levels of democracy.

18 Koopmans (1996) makes a similar claim based on empirical analyses of participation and protest in several European countries.

19 On the interaction between contextual opportunities and individual characteristics, see Leighley (1995 and 2001) and Anduiza (2002).

20 Another way of conceptualising opportunities for participation is to see them as being more circumstantial in nature. Rosenau (1974) and Beck & Jennings (1979) discuss the varied opportunities granted by the emergence of new issues or new political conflicts and how these may affect different social groups to a greater or lesser extent.

21 In addition, fluctuations in circumstance affect different political organisations differently, depending on the type of selective incentives they offer. Groups which offer intangible selective benefits (supportive or expressive) are more vulnerable to economic and ideological changes because, these being 'luxury' goods, the demand for them is very elastic to changes in price, revenue and tastes (Hansen 1985).

22 Walker (1991: 78) presents very interesting data on the evolution of patronage in the creation of different interest groups in the United States. Of more relevance to the argument presented here is the evolution of citizen groups: between 1960 and 1983 they have seen contributions from foundations quadruple and aid from private companies and the government almost double in relation to the support received by organisations created in the period from 1836–1929. See other discussions of the various trends and consequences of public and private funding of movement organisations in Jenkins (1998), Jenkins & Halcli (1999), Brulle & Jenkins (2005), Minkoff & Agnone (2006).

23 See, for example, Snow, Zurcher & Ekland-Olson (1980), Morris (1984), Kriesi & van Praag (1987), Klandermans (1989), and McAdam & Fernández (1990).

24 See, for example, Kitschelt (1986), Kriesi (1989) and Tarrow (1994). The concept of POS and its application in this study is discussed in greater detail in Chapter six.

25 Chapter six presents in detail the definition of each of these aspects, as well as their empirical operationalisation. For the moment a summarising reference to some of the most relevant hypotheses will suffice.

26 This is a common claim in the research on social movements. See, for example, Kitschelt (1986), Koopmans & Rucht (1995), and Rucht (1996).

27 The model shown in Figure 1.1. focuses on the hypothesised links between the 'explanatory' factors and political membership and attempts to provide the possible micro-mechanisms between the former and the latter through the main elements of the rational calculus of collective action. Research on social psychology shows that, indeed, these elements are interconnected but this is of no primary importance to this study. In fact, micro-mechanisms are only spelled for analytical and theoretical purposes, as they will not be subject to empirical testing in the remaining parts of the book due to the lack of data on these elements of rational decision-making.

28 When referring here to private citizens only bureaucrats and other agents of public administration who influence public decisions due to their position within the bureaucratic or governmental apparatus are excluded. However, this definition is not intended to exclude, as Huntington & Nelson (1976: 5) or Verba, Nie and their colleagues (1971, 1972 and 1978) do, the activities of political party leaders, candidates or interest group professionals, thereby distinguishing between professional politicians and participants. To use the same example offered by Huntington & Nelson (1976: 5) in rejecting the distinction between voluntary participation and mobilised participation – 'it would not make sense to say that a soldier who is conscripted does not participate in war while a voluntary soldier does' – it does not seem very reasonable to consider that the general leading the soldiers is not participating in the war simply because he is a military professional. Therefore, professionals should be included in the concept of political participation. This is purely a conceptual debate, as the type of information available for this study, which comes mainly from national surveys, does not allow us to distinguish between political professionals and 'common' citizens.

29 The concept of organisation is, clearly, broader than that of association and covers a larger number of objects. One definition of organisation is, for example, that offered by Stinchcombe (1965: 142): 'a set of stable social relations deliberately created, with the explicit intention of continuously accomplishing some specific goals or purposes. These goals or purposes are generally functions performed for some larger structure.'

30 A discussion of the definition of the third sector and its relationship to concepts such as civil society and the non-for-profit sector can be found in Salamon et al. (1999: chapter one and Appendix A). It is important to stress that these terms are not employed here because they refer to a broader object of study. This study is only concerned with associations and, more specifically, political associations.

31 Curiously, Lane (1965: 75) anticipates the debate on social capital over thirty years and states: 'Clearly, there are marked differences between a bowling club and a political club and these differences will undoubtedly be associated with the effect of the organisation upon (1) the political process and (2) the political interests and motives of the individual members.'

32 I use the terms political associations and organisations interchangeably; and the latter does not include the state (although it is sometimes considered a political organisation) or other governmental bodies.

33 van Deth (1997) also distinguishes between political and social organisations by looking at their main objectives and, later, to the results of a factor analysis (van Deth & Kreuter 1998), but without relating his classification to a definition of political participation.

34 In another piece, Knoke (1982: 173) refers to 'social influence associations' and he equates them with organisations oriented towards political objectives. He defines them as organisations which: 'have as a major objective the changing or preserving of societal conditions, for which they must usually influence decision makers in other institutions (legislatures, government agencies and executives, courts, etc.) to apply *their* authority and resources to implement the policies and programs preferred by the associations.'

35 However, it is important to stress that what is commonly included under the label of interest groups also comes under the term political associations employed throughout this study. The problem is that, as Baumgartner and Leech (1998: chapter two) point out, the terminology may vary substantially with respect to what is included in the category of interest groups. In fact, one of the problems highlighted by these scholars is the terminological confusion in this subfield. Some researchers limit the consideration of interest groups to formal associations and organisations which defend public or private interests, while others include all types of organised interests, thereby including corporations, institutions, cities, etc. Whatever the interpretation, this study is not strictly concerned with interest groups as a whole, rather with the subset of organisations which is generally included in this category: political associations.

36 This is the option favoured by Verba, Schlozman & Brady (1995: 59).

37 The alternative employed by Verba, Nie & Kim (1978: 100).

38 See, for example, Dekker, Koopmans & van den Broek (1997), Wessels (1997), and van Deth & Kreuter (1998).

39 Dalton, Küchler & Bürklin (1990).

40 Pizzorno (1981).

41 Rucht (1990) and Kitschelt (1990).

42 Offe (1988), and Dalton, Küchler & Bürklin (1990).

43 This does not necessarily mean that they do not engage in institutional politics, rather, when they do, they are not representing a certain constituency but act as some sort of advisor or monitor of the policies and decisions adopted.

44 Kriesi also considers movement-supportive organisations (media, churches, shops, etc.) and movement associations (self-help groups, and clubs), but these are distinct from both SMOs and traditional political organisations in that they do not generally engage actively in mobilising collective action.

45 A reflection on the concept of membership can also be found in Baumgartner & Leech (1998: 30–3).

chapter two | analysing political membership in western democracies

INTRODUCTION

The aim of this chapter is to provide a general overview of the main issues involved in the comparative analysis of political membership in western democracies. For this purpose, firstly, the crucial aspects of case selection, measurement and data sources in the analysis of political membership are discussed. This is followed by a somewhat detailed description of the general patterns of associational involvement in western democracies, which contributes to the framing of the analysis of engagement in political organisations. This distinction between different types of voluntary associations brings up the crucial debate concerning the various strategies that can be employed for classifying organisations into political and non-political associations. Finally, the chapter provides a thorough description of the main focus of attention in this study: political membership. Through the analysis of a wide array of cross-national and longitudinal survey data, the chapter will illustrate the notable differences in levels of political membership in western democracies and their stability over time.

THE COMPARATIVE ANALYSIS OF POLITICAL MEMBERSHIP: CASES, MEASUREMENT AND DATA

This study intentionally restricts its focus to western democracies, more specifically to those that were consolidated as such in the 1980s.[1] The main aim is, thus, to approximate a comparative research design of *most similar systems*. These countries have been economically, politically and culturally interdependent throughout the twentieth century and have, therefore, been exposed to similar economic, political and social processes. Western nations have in common similar forms of political organisation, primarily in terms of sharing democratic forms of government and of respecting, to a similar degree, citizens' effective political rights. They are also similar in a crucial aspect for political participation: their levels of economic development. As van Sickle & Dalton (2005) show, the degree of economic and democratic development is a decisive factor not just for explaining cross-national variations in levels of political participation but also for detecting individual-level sources of those variations, and for understanding the real meaning of the same forms of political action across countries. Contrarily, including too dissimilar cases in the analysis tends to confound rather than to clarify the underlying patterns of political participation, their meaning and their explanations.

We are therefore dealing with a group of countries which are 'most similar' in terms of the basic conditions of possibility that allow individuals to join political associations. Furthermore, one of the main goals of this study is to analyse the role of a certain set of macro-political factors – political opportunity structures and political mobilisation – and, for this purpose, it is important that the differences between countries are limited, to a large extent, to differences related to these factors. It would not make much sense to focus on these aspects if we were to study countries that were extremely different in terms of their levels of social, economic or political development.[2] Undoubtedly, social, economic and cultural differences do exist between western democracies but these are relatively small when compared to those existing between these countries and, for example, Latin American, Asian or African countries.

Restricting the study to western democracies is, therefore, intended to ensure the real equivalence of cases, of the meaning of the behaviour under study, and to keep some fundamental variables under control.[3] Additionally, extending the scope of the study beyond western democracies would pose serious problems of equivalence of measurement instruments. The use of survey data in less developed societies or in sharply different cultural settings not only introduces serious problems of equivalence in the translation of many concepts; it also introduces serious doubts about the equivalent reliability of the data-collection process. In this line, Dogan (1994: 41) discusses how research in comparative politics has repeatedly shown that low levels of development are related to lower levels of reliability for all types of data. Surely, survey data are not exempt from these limitations, if only because of the tremendous difficulties in obtaining representative samples in contexts that are socially and geographically adverse.

Clearly, restricting the design to western democracies imposes the same restrictions on our conclusions. This study will, therefore, make no attempt to generalise beyond the group of countries included in it.

Measuring membership with survey data
Comparative research on all forms of associational membership faces a series of methodological problems, the solutions for which can never be fully satisfactory. A first problem is the very definition of membership. As discussed in Chapter one, membership of an association can be determined in two different ways: setting an external objective criterion or using individuals' self-definition of membership of a given organisation. Thus, we might define someone as a member if the individual is formally registered with the organisation or participates regularly in the activities of the group.[4] An alternative is to ask citizens directly about their organisational memberships.[5] Neither option is without problems. External definitions

are likely to underestimate levels of membership, insofar as many organisations do not keep formal registration procedures such as fees, membership forms, etc. On the other hand, were we to attempt to define membership by participation in the activities of the organisation, we would face a double problem with the measurement of such activities and the selection of the groups, given that many of them do not require their members to participate in the activities promoted by the association.[6]

Defining membership through subjective reports presents other problems that are no less significant. Subjective definitions are, by necessity, varied and divergent, and individuals who have the same relationship to an association may define themselves differently: for many people the payment of a fee to an association does not establish a membership linkage but only one of economic contribution; for others, this link makes them feel they are members of the organisation. In addition, opting for the subjective definition of the respondent entails adopting a more flexible criterion as regards the type of behaviour considered; and the heterogeneity of modes of membership will therefore be greater, as well as unknown. In other words, if the researcher does not define externally which behaviour qualifies as membership, and it is rather the subjects who decide whether they are or not to be considered members, the level and type of activism that goes with this membership will tend to vary more. And, unless we explicitly ask which activities this membership entails, the extent of this variation will also be unknown.

Consequently, as analysts, the choice is between relying on self-definitions of associational membership and, thus, grouping potentially heterogeneous behaviours; and restricting the definition of membership to specific observable behaviours while ensuring a greater homogeneity of the action under scrutiny.

In this study, however, the former option was chosen: self-definitions of membership are used as the sole criterion. This choice is linked to the use of surveys as the source for obtaining membership data. There are, in fact, few alternative sources. A fairly unrealistic option[7] would be to try to produce a broad census of people registered with groups and associations but, again, we would encounter the problem that many organisations do not keep formal registers (not to mention in time-series form) of their membership figures. Moreover, even if this was viable, it would not necessarily be more reliable than the use of surveys. Many associations artificially inflate the number of members they have, because claimed membership size can be a critical resource (Knoke 1990b: 6).

Notes to Table 2.1

GSS = General Social Survey; ANES = American National Election Study; ACPS = American Citizen Participation Study; WVS = World Values Survey; EVS = European Values Survey; EB = Eurobarometer; CID = Citizenship, Involvement and Democracy Project Common Core.

[a] The questionnaire does not specify whether it is formal or informal discussions.

[b] There is a general question about involvement in volunteer work, but none related to specific groups and associations.

[c] Wording slightly different for EVS and WVS studies with potential implications on interpretation of results ('spend time with people in clubs and voluntary associations' versus 'spend time socially with people at sports clubs or voluntary or service organization'.

[d] Only asked for charities and human rights groups.

Source: Own elaboration from the original questionnaires.

Table 2.1: The measurement of associational involvement in American and cross-national surveys: dimensions included in the questionnaires

Items included	GSS 1974–94	ANES 1985 Pilot	ANES 1996	ANES 2000	ACPS 1990	WVS 1981	WVS 1990–93	WVS 1995–97	EVS-WVS 1999–00	EB 1983–98	CID 1998–01	ESS 2002–03	EB 62.2 2004	CID-US 2005
Explicit list of groups (number)	Yes (16)	Yes (10)	Yes (22)	Probes (7)	Yes (20)	Yes (10)	Yes (16)	Yes (9)	Yes (15)	Yes (9/12)	Yes (28)	Yes (12)	Yes (14)	Yes (18)
Membership/belonging	Yes	Yes	Yes	Yes	Yes	Yes	Yes	Yes	Yes	Yes	Yes	Yes	Yes	Yes
Voluntary time/work for a group	1987 only	Yes	No	No [b]	Only for 3 types	Yes	Yes	No	Yes (only work)	No	Yes	Yes	Yes (with voluntary)	Yes
Active member (self-assessment)	1987 only	Yes	No	No	Yes	No	No	Yes	No	Asked in 1983	Yes	Yes	Yes (with activism)	Yes
Money donations/ contributions to group	1987 only	Yes	No	No	Yes	No	No	No	No	No	Yes	Yes	Yes	Yes
Multiple memberships within group categories (maximum)	No	Yes	Yes (4)	Yes	Yes	No	No	No	No	No	No	No	No	No
Name of groups (maximum)	No	Yes	No	No	Yes (1)	No	No	No	No	No	No	No	No	No
Groups take stands on public issues/try influence governmental action	No	Yes	Yes	Yes	Yes	No	No	No	No	No	No	No	No	No
Leadership role	1987 only	No	No	No	Yes	No	No	No	No	No	Yes	Yes	Yes	Yes
Attend group meetings	1987 only	Yes	Yes	No	Yes	No	No	No	No	No	Yes	Yes	No	Yes
Reasons for membership	1987 only	No	No	No	Yes	No	Yes	No	No	No	No	No	No	No
Formal political discussions within group	No	No	Yes [a]	No	Yes	No	Yes	No	No	No	No	No	No	No
Informal political discussions within group	No	No	Yes [a]	No	Yes	No	No	No	No	No	No	No	No	No
Group provides services for non-members	No	No	No	No	Yes	No	No	No	No	No	Yes	No	No	No
Frequency of time spent in organisations	No	No	No	Yes (hours)	No	No	No	No	Yes [c]	Only in 50.1 [d]	No	No	No	No

Throughout this volume, political membership will, thus, be measured by distinguishing between respondents who claim to be members of political organisations and those who do not.[8] And the only source for this information about memberships will be international social surveys.

Yet, despite the importance of studying associational membership for recent debates on social capital, surveys specifically designed to measure the various aspects of citizens' social and political participation have not incorporated reliable indicators of associational membership until very recently.[9] In fact, most of the available indicators aimed at measuring participation in associations are not very different to those designed by Verba & Nie (1972) over thirty years ago. Table 2.1 shows how associational participation has been operationalised in the main surveys in the United States and the cross-national surveys of the last two decades.[10]

As we can see, American surveys have experimented more with different formulations of membership items, whilst including more varied question sets. The Eurobarometers (EBs) and World Values Surveys (WVS) generally do little more than ask about membership of a list of associational categories (Table 2.2). Broad views of associational membership have been infrequent, in part also due to the fact that the complexities introduced by the detailed analysis of these behaviours cannot usually be afforded by general socio-political surveys that do not specifically focus on citizen participation. Most surveys that include questions related to participation in organisations have as their main purpose the study of electoral behaviour or public opinion in general. Thus, the collection of information on citizens' social and political participation in these surveys is merely instrumental, as potential correlates of their main object of analysis (voting, attitudes, etc.).

Two of the few exceptions are the survey designed by Verba and his colleagues (the American Citizen Participation Study), and the survey of the project Citizenship, Involvement and Democracy (CID) conducted in Europe in 2000–1, and later in the United Sates in 2005. Both, and in particular the latter, study various dimensions of associational involvement, without restricting the focus to membership alone. But, usually, cross-national surveys provide us with limited information on the multiple dimensions of associational engagement. And, almost invariably, they do not address the issue of the geographical scope of associations, thus obscuring the distinction between local and national memberships.

As well as forcing us to restrict our analyses almost exclusively to membership, the use of surveys in a comparative study of associational membership introduces further difficulties. We need to find international surveys that applied the same questionnaire in a significant number of countries and which included items on membership of different sorts of associations. For western democracies, this

Notes to Table 2.2

[a] A distinction is made between "Social or religious organisations involved in charitable activities" and "Religious or parish organisations not involved in charitable activities".

[b] They appear in two separate associational categories: "Sports clubs and associations" and "Hobby or special interest clubs".

Source: Own elaboration from the original questionnaires.

Table 2.2: List of groups available in each survey or series of surveys

Groups listed for membership	WVS 1981–82	EB 19 1983	EB 28 1987	EB 34 1990	WVS 1990–93	WVS 1995–97	EB 47.2 1997	EB 49 1998	EB 50.1 1998	EVSWVS 1999-00	CID 2001–2002	ESS 2002–2003	EB 62.2 2004	CID-US 2005
Political parties	X	X	X	X	X	X	X	X	X	X	X	X	X	X
Trade unions	X	X	X	X	X	X	With parties	X	With parties	X	X	X	X	X
Professional associations	X	With trade unions	With trade unions	With trade unions	X	X	With trade unions	With trade unions	With parties			With business	X	With business
Community groups	X	X	X		X	X			X	X	X	With other	With other	With other
Environmental	X	X	X	X	X	X	X	X	X	X	X	With other	With other	With other
Women/feminist groups				X	X				X	X	X	With other	With other	With other
Third World/human rights	X	X	X	X		X	X	X	X	X	X	With other	X	With other
Peace movement					X				X	X	X	With other	With other	With other
Consumer groups		X	X	X		X	X	X	X	X	X	With other	With other	With other
Animal rights				X			With environ.	With environ.	With environ.	With environ.	X	With environ.	With environ.	With other
Welfare/charity groups	X	X	X	X	X	X	X	X	X[a]	X	X	With other	X	X
Religious or church groups	X	X	X	X	X	X	X	X	X[a]	X	X	X	X	X
Education, arts, music, cultural	X	X	X	X	X	X	X	X	X	X	X	With other	X	X
Youth organisations/children	X	X	X	X	X		X	X	X	X	X	With other	X	With other
Sports or leisure groups/hobby	X	X	X	X	X	X	X[b]	X[b]	X[b]	X	X	X	X	X
Health care groups					X	X			X	X	X	With other	X	With other
Other groups		X	X	X	X	X	X	X	X	X	X	X	X	X

has only happened in the cases of some EBs (only in six surveys from 1983, 1987, 1990, 1997, 1998 and 2004),[11] of the WVS co-ordinated by Inglehart (1981–82, 19903, 1995–7, 2000, 2005–6), the European Values Survey (EVS) of 1999, the CID survey conducted in seven west European countries between 2001 and 2002 and in the European Social Survey (ESS) of 2002–3.[12]

Secondly, it is important to ensure that we are accurately measuring the phenomenon that interests us: membership. To do this, it is essential that the list of organisations be as complete as possible.[13] Despite the fact that most surveys include a category for 'other associations', respondents are more likely to remember their associational affiliations when presented with a complete list of organisations. As we can see from Table 2.2, various types of groups are systematically included in all available surveys (political parties, unions, environmental organisations, charities, religious and educational/cultural groups), while some others are only included in a few. The more complete surveys – in terms of the list of organisations presented to interviewees – are those included in the CID project,[14] the 1990 WVS and the 1999–2000 EVS/WVS.

For longitudinal studies it is necessary that the organisations listed and the countries studied in each survey remain the same. This last condition is only partially fulfilled, however. Neither the EBs nor the WVS provide the same list of groups in each survey, nor are all the countries included in the same surveys. In Table 2.3 we see that only a group of eight European countries (West Germany, Belgium, Denmark, France, Great Britain, the Netherlands, Ireland and Italy) appears in almost every available survey. The rest, up to 20 countries, are present in at least two. In this respect the 1990–1 and 1999–2000 WVS/EVS also stand out as the most complete surveys, as they include 18 of the 20 western countries included in this study.

These limitations restrict the possibilities for comparison. Nevertheless, data can sometimes be combined to make the most of the available information. Hence, this book will present data from multiple surveys. Sections that describe the phenomenon of political membership will include data from several of the available surveys. However, chapters that present and develop the analytical model will focus on the most complete survey that was available when this study was conducted: the 1990–3 WVS.[15]

In summary, the inclusion of a large number of countries in the analysis of political membership for comparative purposes should improve the quality of the results and the conclusions that can be derived from them. Yet, we will still have to proceed with caution when drawing certain type of conclusions, as the data sources are far from perfect.

ASSOCIATIONAL MEMBERSHIP IN WESTERN DEMOCRACIES

The study of participation in associations in Europe and other western democracies has stimulated a growing interest in the various social sciences, particularly

Table 2.3: Countries included in each cross-national survey

Countries	WVS 1981–82	EB19 1983	EB28 1987	EB34 1990	WVS 1990–93	WVS 1995–97	EB47.2 1997	EB49 1998	EB50.1 1998	EVS/WVS 1999–00	CID 2001–02	ESS 2002–03	EB 62.2 2004
Austria					X		X	X	X	X		X	X
Belgium	X	X	X	X	X		X	X	X			X	X
Canada	X				X								
Denmark	X	X	X	X	X		X	X	X	X		X	X
Finland	X				X	X	X	X	X	X		X	X
France	X	X	X	X	X		X	X	X	X	X	X	X
Great Britain	X	X	X	X	X		X	X	X	X	X	X	X
Greece		X	X	X	X		X	X	X	X		X	X
Iceland	X				X					X			
Ireland	X	X	X	X	X	X	X	X	X		X	X	X
Italy	X	X	X				X	X	X		X	X	X
Luxembourg		X	X	X		X	X	X	X			X	X
Netherlands	X	X	X	X	X		X	X	X	X	X	X	X
Norway	X				X	X					X	X	X
Portugal			X	X	X		X	X	X	X	X	X	X
Spain	X		X	X	X	X	X	X	X	X	X	X	X
Sweden	X				X	X	X	X	X	X	X	X	X
Switzerland					X	X				X	X	X	
United States	X				X	X	X	X	X	X	X*	X*	
West Germany	X	X	X	X	X		X	X	X	X	X	X	X

* The CID-US survey replicates both the original European CID and the ESS questionnaires.

Source: Own elaboration from the original questionnaires.

encouraged by the diffusion of the concept of social capital and its supposed versatility when promoting virtuous social and political dynamics. Nonetheless, the great majority of published documents that analyse the phenomenon of associational membership do so by focusing on specific countries (mainly the United States) and there are relatively few cases where a clearly comparative approach has been adopted.[16]

In the remaining pages of this section we will offer a general and fundamentally descriptive overview of the phenomenon of associational membership in western democracies. Primarily, we will examine the large variation in the levels of associational membership in different countries and its evolution since the 1980s. This will allow us to situate the more specific phenomenon of political membership within the broader context of associational membership in western societies.

How many citizens are involved in associations? Which associations do they join? How has associational membership evolved in western democracies? Although imperfect, the available international surveys allow us to grasp, at least partially, cross-national patterns and longitudinal trends.

Graph 2.1 shows the evolution in the general levels of associational membership in 18 western countries from 1981 to 2004.[17] A first clear pattern that emerges from Graph 2.1 is the large cross-national variations in membership levels, with oscillations between 90 per cent in Iceland in 1990 and 19 per cent in Spain in 1987.[18] While in some countries a large majority of adult citizens belong to associations, in others this is only true of a minority. Moreover, there is no uniform pattern in the evolution of membership over time. Growth trends are visible in Belgium, Canada, the Netherlands, Denmark, Sweden and, particularly, in Finland. The Scandinavian countries and the Netherlands consistently show higher percentages of associational membership. We find the opposite pattern in South European countries (Italy, France, Portugal, Greece and Spain). In between we find mainly countries such as Germany, Belgium, Great Britain and Ireland.

Graph 2.2 portrays the evolution of the average number of associational domains citizens join, once they decide to join one.[19] As we see, cross-national variations remain significant. In some democracies, citizens not only have a greater tendency to join groups and associations but they also join several. The cases of the Scandinavian countries and the Netherlands are the most extreme but there is also a significant level of multiple membership in North American countries. By contrast, in central and South European countries the vast majority of citizens who are members of associations only belong to one, as the average rarely approaches two.

The longitudinal patterns are also interesting. It is not possible to discern whether a clear increase or decrease in general levels of membership has taken place between 1980 and 2004 in western democracies; it seems clear, however, that multiple membership has indeed increased in most countries. This is true for all countries, to a greater or lesser extent. Even in South European countries, multiple membership has increased.[20] In addition, we see that, far from decreasing, cross-

Graph 2.1: The evolution of associational membership in western countries

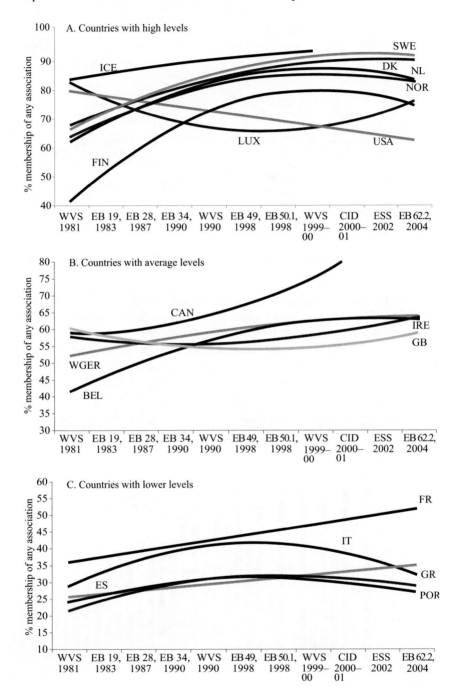

Graph 2.2: The evolution of the number of associational categories citizens belong to

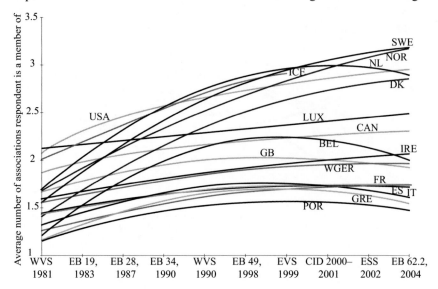

national differences in the breadth of citizens' associational participation have in fact increased. Even though multiple memberships are common to all countries, they are more so in nations with higher levels of associational involvement.

Turning our attention to a substantially more active form of membership – unpaid volunteering – gives some additional nuances to our view of associational membership in western democracies (Graph 2.3). In the early 1990s, citizens in

Graph 2.3: Membership and voluntary work in associations, WVS 1990–93

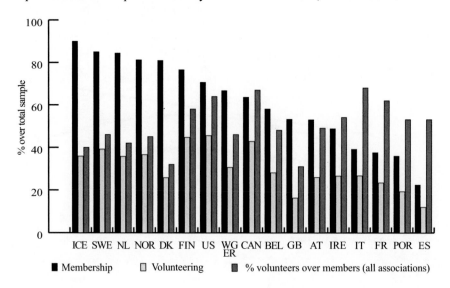

Graph 2.4: Forms of associational involvement in Europe, ESS 2002–2003 and US-CID 2005

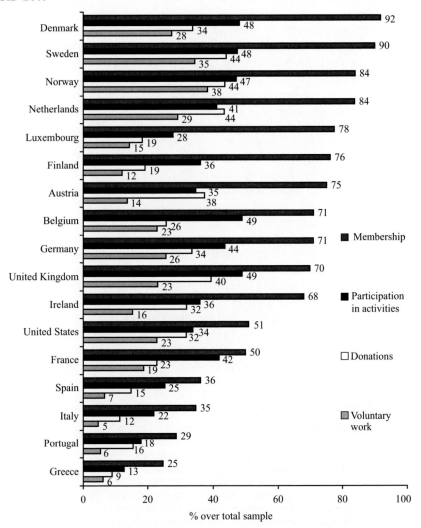

North America, together with the Finns, were more ready to devote time to the associations they joined. Interestingly enough, the high levels of membership in the Netherlands and the Scandinavian countries were not transformed into equivalent proportions of active engagement. Furthermore, although South European countries still display the lowest percentages of volunteering, they do not differ excessively from many other countries in this regard. Moreover, if we consider the percentage of activists or volunteers as a proportion of those belonging to any association, we find that, in South European countries, over half the members engage actively in the associations they join. This is particularly true in Italy, where the proportion of activists or volunteers is among the highest of all western nations, with almost 70 per cent of members volunteering their time and work.

The patterns in cross-national variations for active forms of associational involvement are even clearer when we analyse data from the first round of the European Social Survey (ESS), conducted between 2002 and 2003 in 16 Western European countries and in 2005 in the United States.[21] Graph 2.4 shows the distribution of four forms of associational involvement in each of these countries.

As we can see, cross-national differences for simple membership are similar in magnitude to those we find for active forms of associational engagement. Membership oscillates between 92 per cent for Denmark and 25 per cent for Greece – almost four times more members in the former – while participation in activities fluctuates between 49 per cent in Belgium and the United Kingdom and 13 per cent in Greece (again almost four times more in the former than in the latter). However, the cross-national gap widens a bit more for unpaid voluntary work, which varies between 38 per cent for Norwegians and 5 per cent for Italians – a ratio of 7.

What these figures are, nevertheless, concealing is the fact that, in Southern Europe, citizens who join associations are much more likely to become actively engaged. If we compare the proportion of active members[22] across all countries (Graph 2.5), we find that the distribution changes significantly. Scandinavian countries are no longer heading the rankings and southern countries are no longer at the bottom.

Hence, citizens in western democracies seem to face different incentives and constraints to join associations than to become actively involved in them once they decide to join. In this line, Dekker & van den Broek (1998) distinguished between three worlds of civil society[23] that are very descriptive of the associational reality

Graph 2.5: Percentage of active memberships, ESS 2002–2003 and US-CID 2005

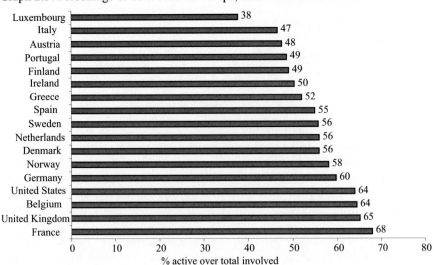

% active over total involved

of western democracies: the *parochial*, characterised by low levels of membership but a high proportion of activists and typical of Southern Europe;[24] the *active*, with medium to high levels of membership and very high levels of activism, characteristic of Northern America; and the *broad*, with very high levels of membership but medium levels of volunteering, more typical of Scandinavian countries and the Netherlands. A large number of countries are to be found in between these three 'ideal' types (Germany, Belgium, Great Britain, Austria, Switzerland, etc.).

In summary, an overview of the patterns and trends of associational involvement clearly shows significant and consistent cross-national variations. Scandinavian and Dutch citizens stand out for their eagerness to join all sorts of associations and to join several of them; while South Europeans are quite reluctant to do so. However, associations in countries such as France or Spain can rely on their members becoming actively engaged in their activities to a greater extent than organisations in countries with higher levels of membership.

HOW TO CLASSIFY ASSOCIATIONS? POLITICAL VERSUS NON-POLITICAL MEMBERSHIP

Many scholars have drawn distinctions between political and social or non-political organisations.[25] In general terms, these classifications are based on the theoretical or empirical assumption that not all groups are equivalent or, more precisely, that membership and participation in them have differing causes and consequences. For example, various studies indicate that participation in associations with markedly political goals is more likely to be conducive to other forms of political participation than membership in non-political associations.[26]

The consequences of different types of membership have also been debated in the literature on social capital. Putnam (1993, 1995a and b, and 2000), for example, argues that the creation of social capital is a spillover effect of engagement in non-political associations (bowling leagues, scouts, bird-watching groups, etc.), while other scholars (for example, Boix & Posner 1996, and Hardin 2000) consider that associations that pursue public goods are more capable of promoting habits of co-operation. Thus, public-interest organisations should be more useful for the production of public goods such as institutional efficiency or the proper functioning of democracies.

Hence, this study is based on the distinction between political and non-political organisations, with the aim of focusing specifically on membership of political organisations as a distinct form of political participation. In this regard, our distinction relies on a theoretically driven definition and draws on the work of various scholars who have made similar typological choices.[27] Thus, political organisations or associations are defined as *those formally organised groups that seek collective goods (whether pure public goods or another type of collective goods) and which have as their main goal to influence political decision-making processes, either by trying to influence the selection of governmental personnel or their activities, to include issues on the agenda, or to change the values and preferences which guide the decision-making process.* Therefore, 'social' or non-political associations and organisations are, by this definition, either those that pursue private goods (sports associations, religious associations, many youth associations, etc.) or those which, while still pursuing public goods, do not 'primarily' aim at influencing the political arena (health-care associations, artistic/cultural associations, etc.).

Beyond the general definition, however, a more complicated aspect is to classify associations as political and non-political when confronted with a list in a survey questionnaire. As Verba, Schlozman & Brady (1995: 58–9) point out, 'technical' decisions on how to measure what is political have important substantial consequences. The *American Citizen Participation Survey* (ACPS), designed by these scholars, allows us to explore further the implications of our 'technical' decisions when distinguishing between political and non-political associations. This survey asked respondents if they believed that the groups and associations they joined took public stands – either nationally or locally – and this was asked for all the associations in which respondents were involved. When respondents participated in or contributed economically to more than one association in a specific category (for example, more than one sports association), their responses were related to the association that they deemed to be more important in terms of their participation or contribution. With this question format it is possible to explore the consequences of alternative definitions and operationalisations of membership in political organisations.

One option is to classify as political associations all those for which at least 50 per cent of respondents claimed the ones they joined took public stances.[28] In other words, if 50 per cent of the respondents who are members, for example, of women's organisations consider that their association adopts political stances, we will classify all women's organisations as political associations. A second possibility is to limit our consideration of a political member to only those respondents who consider that their own association adopts a political stance. In this way, only if an interviewee says that the women's organisation she is a member of adopts a political stance will we consider that this person is a member of a 'political association'. Finally, the survey allows us to also define political associations using a purely theoretical and *a priori* definition, as the one provided in previous pages. Hence, we can compare the results for the theoretical definition with those obtained with a more 'empirical' definition, based on respondents' feedback about the political nature of the organisations they join.

Undoubtedly, when respondents have not been asked any question about the political or public behaviour of their associations – as is the case in all cross-national surveys – this latter option is the only alternative we have to distinguish between political and non-political organisations.[29] Therefore, it is of great relevance for the validity of this study to analyse the possible implications for our results of employing pre-defined theoretical definitions.

Graph 2.6 shows the percentage of members of political associations in the

United States (ACPS data) when we employ each of the three alternative operational classifications of political organisations.[30] The Graph illustrates the significant differences that exist in the estimation of the percentage of political members depending on the definition we adopt: from 14 per cent of the adult population if we use the *a priori* (more restrictive) theoretical definition, up to 53 per cent if we use the evaluations of the interviewees themselves as a criterion. Therefore, using the theoretical and *a priori* definition of political associations is a conservative option: we underestimate, rather than overestimate, the proportion of people who are exposed to political stimuli in the associations they join.

Furthermore, to what extent does one or another definition of political associations relate to the real political behaviour of its members? We would expect that the more restrictive the definition is, the more homogenous the behaviour of the individuals grouped. We would also expect citizens who recognise that they are politically involved in some sense (because their associations take political stances) to be, at least, more politically aware. We can grasp some of these implications with respondents' answers to the frequency with which they engage in political discussions. Initially, we would expect respondents grouped according to the 'theoretical' definition, as well as those who claim that their association adopts political stances, to discuss politics often. The results shown in Graph 2.7 partially contradict these expectations.

While individuals who are members of associations that fall under the 'theoretical' type of political organisations show a substantially greater tendency to discuss politics on a daily basis, respondents who join associations that adopt political stances do not discuss politics more often than other Americans. In this sense, when the data allow us to choose between producing classifications based on a

Graph 2.6: Political membership: the effects of question wording and of the definition of political associations, ACPS 1990

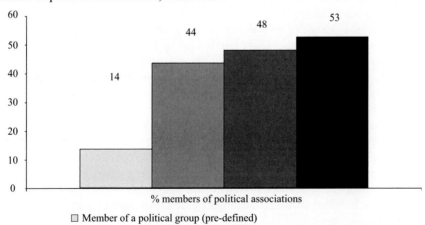

% members of political associations

☐ Member of a political group (pre-defined)
■ Member of a group which R considers to take stands on public issues
■ Member of a group 50% of Rs considered to take stands on public issues
■ Member of a group 50% of valid Rs considered to take stands on public issues

Graph 2.7: Political membership and frequent political discussion: the effects of the definition of political associations

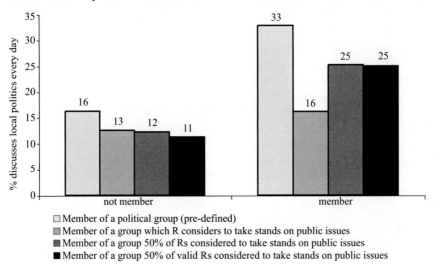

□ Member of a political group (pre-defined)
▨ Member of a group which R considers to take stands on public issues
▦ Member of a group 50% of Rs considered to take stands on public issues
■ Member of a group 50% of valid Rs considered to take stands on public issues

theoretical definition of what is political and those which are informed by the perceptions of the respondents, it seems more appropriate to adopt the definition used by Verba, Schlozman & Brady (1995) and aggregate these perceptions as a basis for classification. It is reasonable to assume that individual perceptions about the political nature or engagement of associations are more subject to error than the aggregation of these. Clearly, when the questionnaire does not allow us to take into account citizens' perceptions, we will have to content ourselves with theoretically informed and *a priori* definitions. Fortunately, our results seem to confirm that this option is not inferior from the point of view of measuring more or less homogeneous behaviours.

Additional evidence of the validity of the operationalisation of political membership used throughout this study is provided by the survey of a representative sample of Spanish citizens included in the international project Citizenship, Involvement and Democracy (CID).[31] This survey also investigated the political nature of associations, and included two questions on (a) the occurrence of political conversations or discussions at the meetings or activities of the association and (b) the association's adoption of a stance on issues of public or political interest.[32] The results shown below and derived from this study are even more relevant than those already presented from the ACPS survey, since the items on associations were designed by a European research team and are, thus, more relevant to the European context. Moreover, many of the associations listed are very similar to the ones included in the large majority of cross-national surveys analysed throughout this study.

Table 2.4 displays the list of associational categories included in the Spanish questionnaire for the CID project, and marks in each column which of them are

Table 2.4: Possible definitions of political membership, CID-Spain 2002

Associational categories	Member of a pre-defined political association	Member of a category 50% of Rs say politics is discussed	Member of a category 50% of Rs say adopts public stances
Sports clubs or outdoor activities clubs			
Youth associations		X	X
Environmental organisations	X	X	X
Associations for animal rights/ protection	X		
Peace organisations	X	X	X
Humanitarian aid or human-rights organisations	X		X
Charity or social-welfare organisations			X
Associations for medical patients, specific illnesses or addictions			
Associations for disabled persons			
Pensioners' or retired persons' organisations			
Political parties	X	X	X
Trade unions	X	X	X
Farmers' organisations	X		X
Business or employers' organisations	X	X	X
Investment clubs			
Professional organisations	X	X	X
Consumer associations	X		X
Parents' associations			
Cultural, musical, dancing or theatre societies			
Other hobby clubs/societies			
Automobile organisations			
Residents', housing or neighbourhood associations	X		
Immigrants' organisations	X	X	
Religious or church organisations			
Women's organisations	X		
Associations for war, victims, veterans, or ex-servicemen			
Associations for victims of terrorism	X	X	X
Other clubs or associations			

Source: Own elaboration from data in study no. 2450 of CIS. The crosses signal the categories included under each definition of political associations.

grouped under the label of 'political associations', according to each of the operational definitions set out in previous paragraphs.[33] As we can see, the most important divergences between the three classifications stem from only three kinds of association. On the one hand, the *a priori* theoretical definition of political associations

Table 2.5: Comparison of five indicators of political membership, CID-Spain 2002

Member of a political association (theoretically pre-defined)	Member of an association where politics is discussed	Member of an association that takes public stands	Member of an association 50% of Rs say politics is discussed in meetings	Member of an association 50% of Rs say it takes public stands
[1]	[2]	[3]	[4]	[5]
[2] 0.361				
[3] 0.395	0.567			
[4] 0.683	0.366	0.379		
[5] 0.716	0.372	0.410	0.801	1

Source: Study no. 2450 of CIS. Own elaboration. All correlation coefficients are significant at the 0.001 level (bilateral).

excludes youth organisations, whereas respondents' perceptions seem to indicate that these associations in Spain are quite politicised. Over half of those who participate in their activities claim that politics is discussed at meetings and activities and that the association adopts political positions. In two other cases the complete opposite is true. Although the theoretical definition of political associations leads us to include neighbourhood associations and women's organisations, the results seem to indicate that most of these associations are not as highly politicised in Spain as we could expect.[34]

To what extent are these operational definitions of political membership equivalent? Table 2.5 presents the results of a bivariate correlation analysis between the five possible indicators. As we see, the indicator for political membership employed throughout this study, which is based on an *a priori* theoretical definition of what a political association is, seems to pass this simple validity test. Our definition revolves around (i) the pursuit of collective goods, and (ii) attempting to affect political decision-making. In this regard, the high correlation with participants' own perception of the political nature of associations (indicators 4 and 5)[35] serves to validate it sufficiently for further analyses.

Unfortunately, as we already pointed out in Table 2.2, not all associations are listed in all cross-national surveys; thus, it is useful to specify which associations are included under the category of 'political' organisations in each of them (Table 2.6). As we saw, some surveys are more complete than others in the range of associations they cover, and they differ, in particular, in the coverage of organisations related to new social movements (NSMs).[36]

Unions and professional associations are, to many readers, less obvious examples of 'political' organisations. Many scholars would argue that these are economic, rather than political, associations, and that citizens join them to obtain private goods (services, social benefits, labour protection, etc.). Several studies have shown that Scandinavian unions, in particular, are organisations with little political activity; fundamentally, they are providers of welfare services.[37] However, if

Table 2.6: Political organisations included in each survey

	WVS 1981	EB 19, 1983	EB 28, 1987	EB 34, 1990	WVS 1991	EB 49, 1998	EVS 1999	CID 2001	ESS 2002	EB 62.2, 2004
Consumers' associations		X	X	X		X		X		X
Human-rights organisations	X	X	X	X	X	X	X	X	X	X
Professional, business or farmers' organisations	X	*	*	*	X	*	X	X	X	X
Local community action / neighbourhood groups	X				X		X	X		
Women's groups		X			X		X	X		
Animal-rights groups					X		+	X	+	+
Peace organisations					X		X	X	+	
Environmental organisations	X	X	X	X	X	X	X	X	X	X
Political parties	X	X	X	X	X	X	X	X	X	X
Trade unions	X	X	X	X	X	X	X	X	X	X
Defence of elderly rights										X
Defence of interests of patients / disabled										X
Interest groups for specific causes										X

Source: Own elaboration. * With trade unions. + With environmental organisations.

we stick to the definition of 'political' organisations employed throughout this study, there can be little doubt in this respect: trade unions, as well as professional, and business organisations (i) fundamentally pursue collective goods, and (ii) have as one of their main objectives the influencing of political decision-making.[38]

In addition to the Spanish data referred to on previous pages, other studies corroborate the clear political dimension of these organisations in other countries.[39] And Walker adds to this with his conclusion:

If one holds the view that citizen-sector groups pursue public goods while profit-sector groups pursue private goods, that view is simply wrong. Groups of both types typically advance public policies with consequences that go well beyond their memberships. (Walker 1991: 93)

Furthermore, Wilson's classical work (1995 [1974]) also includes unions and business organisations amongst the political organisations that are the main object of his analysis. Thus, there seems to be enough evidence to support the choice made in this study to consider these organisations 'political' in this sense.

POLITICAL MEMBERSHIP: PATTERNS AND TRENDS

For the remaining part of the volume, this study is only concerned with political membership and we shall therefore move on to describe in greater detail the evolution of membership of political organisations. Graph 2.8 presents the different longitudinal trends of political membership in western democracies and portrays the substantial cross-national variation in levels of political membership. Whereas in some countries political membership has remained at stable levels – especially in South European countries – in others a clearly decreasing (Luxembourg, Great Britain and Germany) or increasing (the Scandinavian countries, Belgium and the Netherlands) trend is evident. Moreover, except for the Scandinavian nations, levels of political membership do not usually reach 50 per cent of the population.

High levels of political membership in Scandinavia are, however, not solely due to the high rates of union membership typical of these countries. As we can see in Graph 2.9, even if we exclude unions from the set of political associations, Scandinavian citizens are, with the Dutch and North Americans, those who join political associations most frequently. Although the variation between countries is noticeably reduced when we exclude union organisations, this is not the case when we compare ratios of political membership across countries. Hence, when we include unions, the country with the greatest percentage of members of political associations (Iceland) has proportionally four times more than the country with the lowest percentage (Spain); but when we exclude unions, the country with the highest levels (the Netherlands) has 6.5 times more political members than Spain.

More importantly, cross-national differences in levels of political membership, far from decreasing, seem to increase with time. As an illustration, the results of

Graph 2.8: Trends in political membership in western democracies, 1981–2004

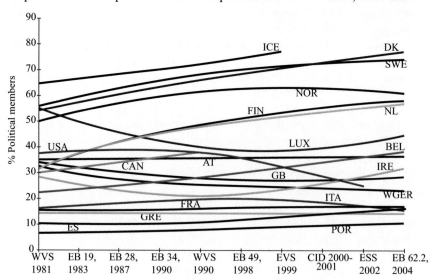

Graph 2.9: Levels of political membership with and without trade unions, WVS 1990 and EVS 1999

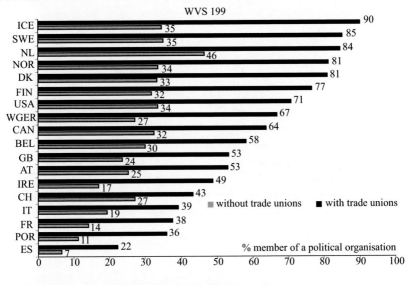

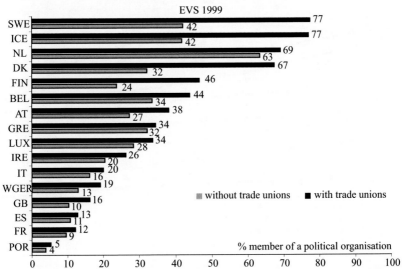

the 1999 European Values Survey indicate that this gap is now much greater: Scandinavian citizens are more than 15 times more likely to join a political organisation than the Portuguese, whether we include unions or not.

Consequently, a first set of conclusions we can draw from these descriptive analyses are that (i) political membership varies significantly across western democracies; (ii) these variations have been sustained – and may even have increased – over the last decade; and (iii) this is not primarily due to the different

Graph 2.10: Trends in party membership, 1981–2004

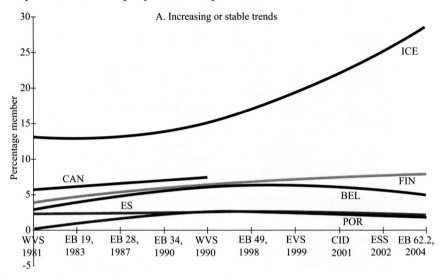

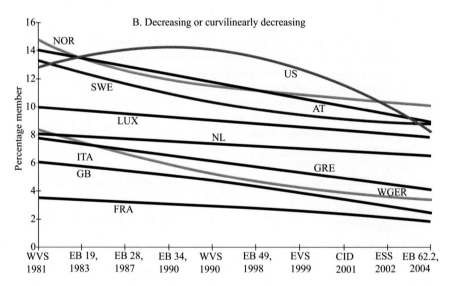

patterns of union membership in Scandinavian countries.

It is, nevertheless, interesting to monitor these patterns and trends for specific categories of political organisations. As already detailed in Table 2.2, the list of groups included in each survey varies significantly and one of the most obvious consequences of this is the lack of continuous time-series data. Figures are available in more than three surveys only for the following political organisations: parties, unions, environmental groups, human rights groups and consumer organisations.

Graph 2.11: Trends in union membership, 1981–2004

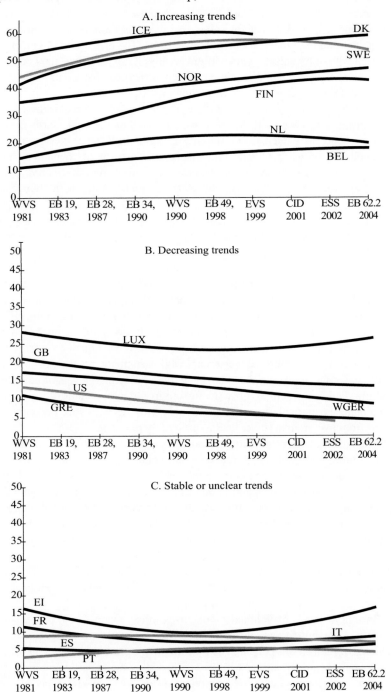

The evolution in the membership of these specific forms of political groups can be seen in Graphs 2.10 to 2.12.[40] Differences across countries in levels of membership are much larger for some organisations (unions and environmental groups, for example) than for others (consumers). The proportion of citizens who join each type of organisation also differs greatly: it ranges between 60 per cent of union membership in some Scandinavian countries to a bare 1 or 2 per cent of members of consumer groups in most countries.

Secondly, trends also vary depending on the type of group considered. Trade union membership seems to have grown in Scandinavian and North European countries, whereas a decrease or stability is common in other western nations.[41] The evolution of party membership displays diverse trends depending on the country, as we already know to be the case from other sources (Selle & Svasand 1991, Katz, Mair *et al.* 1992, Widfeldt 1995, Dalton & Wattenberg 2000, Mair & van Biezen 2001); but declining trends tend to prevail.[42] Human rights groups and environmental organisations, by contrast, have enjoyed growing public support in most countries and, with few exceptions, membership of consumer groups has remained relatively stable.

In general, when we scrutinise specific types of political organisations we find that countries with higher overall levels of political membership are consistently on the high range for all types of political organisations. For example, Scandinavian countries combine exceptionally high rates of overall political membership with large percentages of party members, trade-union members and members of new social movement organisations (NSMOs). Equally, Dutch citizens stand out as being among the westerners who participate most in all 'new' types of political associations but they also have moderately high levels of union membership. The spectacular growth in environmental memberships in the Netherlands is particularly striking; in only two decades this percentage has tripled from just around 10 per cent to around 30 per cent.

When we focus on cross-national and cross-organisational variations at a given point in time, we can see that Scandinavian countries are fundamentally exceptional in what regards trade union membership (Table 2.7).[43] Although they also show high levels of membership in other political organisations, they only depart substantially from such countries as the Netherlands, the United States and Switzerland in unionisation. Political parties have a greater following in some Scandinavian countries, in Austria and in the United States.[44] And environmental organisations reach very high proportions in the Netherlands but also have sizeable memberships in Sweden, Denmark and Switzerland. What seems to be indisputable is that South European countries have the lowest levels of political membership, regardless of what groups we focus on.

Turning to levels of voluntary work in political groups – the percentages of activists – we notice that differences across countries decrease considerably (Table 2.8). First of all, percentages of voluntary work are very low in all countries. Scandinavian unions are still among those that incite participation the most; however, even in these countries, activism levels are very low, especially when

Graph 2.12: Trends in membership of other political organisations 1981–2004

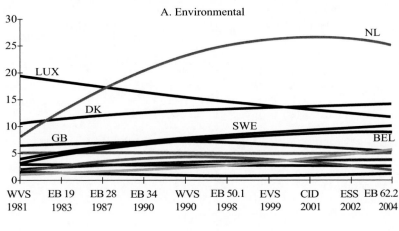

A. Environmental

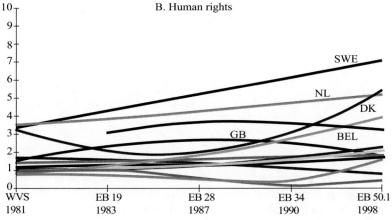

B. Human rights

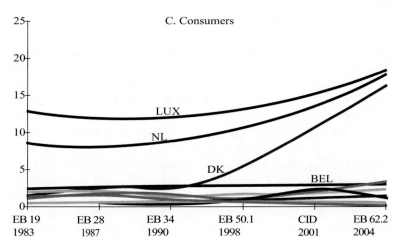

C. Consumers

Table 2.7: Political membership disaggregated, WVS 1990–93

	Trade unions	Political parties	Profess-ional associa-tions	Commu-nity action groups	Environ-mental	Human rights/3rd World	Women's groups	Peace move-ment	Animal rights groups
Iceland	60	15	15	2	5	3	7	1	2
Sweden	58	10	12	2	11	9	3	3	7
Denmark	49	6	12	5	12	3	2	2	4
Norway	42	14	16	3	4	5	3	1	2
Finland	36	14	15	3	5	6	3	2	1
Netherlands	19	10	13	5	24	13	6	3	12
Austria	19	12	6	2	3	2	4	1	4
Belgium	16	6	6	5	8	6	9	2	8
W. Germany	15	7	9	2	4	2	6	2	5
Great Britain	14	6	11	3	6	2	5	1	2
Canada	12	7	16	5	7	5	7	2	3
Ireland	9	4	5	3	2	2	5	1	1
United States	8	14	14	5	8	2	8	2	5
Italy	7	6	6	2	5	2	0	1	2
Switzerland	6	9	13	3	10	-	-	-	-
France	5	3	5	3	2	3	1	0.5	2
Portugal	5	5	4	2	1	1	0	0.5	1
Spain	3	1	3	1	1	1	1	1	1

The figures are the percentages of members over the total sample. Countries are ranked in descending order of the percentage of trade union members.

compared to their huge levels of trade-union membership. Secondly, when levels of activism are considered, North Americans are neck-to-neck with Scandinavian citizens in their preparedness to contribute their time to political organisations. Finally, South European countries are no longer invariably at the bottom of the ranking; many of them show levels of activism that are similar to those of northern nations.

Hence, 'traditional' political organisations – political parties, unions and professional organisations – are still prevalent in most western nations as vehicles of political engagement. Only environmental organisations attract a sizeable proportion of western citizens – and only in a limited number of countries – whilst other political groups related to the new social movements (NSMs) have a very limited following. Consequently, it is also interesting to explore the distinction between 'traditional' and 'new' political organisations. If 'new' political groups provide a different kind of linkage with citizens, and depart from the traditional representative dynamic of political action, it is likely that the factors that motivate citizens being attracted to them will differ from those attached to 'traditional' political memberships.

The results presented in Graph 2.13 show that, in nearly all western nations, traditional political memberships exceed memberships of 'new' political organisations by a ratio of 2 to 1. For every two people who join a party, a union or a professional association, only one joins an organisation related to NSMs. These differences are

Table 2.8: Voluntary work/activism in political organisations, WVS 1990–93

	Trade unions	Political parties	Professional associations	Community action groups	Environmental	Human rights/ 3rd World	Women's groups	Peace movement	Animal rights groups	All political organisations
Finland	8	7	3	2	3	7	3	1	1	20
Canada	4	4	4	3	3	5	4	2	1	18
Sweden	6	4	1	3	2	3	2	1	1	16
United States	2	5	3	1	3	5	4	1	2	16
Norway	6	4	1	1	1	3	1	0	0	13
Iceland	3	4	1	0	2	3	3	0	0	13
Belgium	2	1	3	3	3	2	3	1	2	13
Italy	2	4	2	1	2	1	0	1	1	12
Austria	2	3	1	1	1	1	2	0	1	11
W. Germany	2	3	1	1	1	2	3	1	2	11
Netherlands	1	3	2	3	3	2	2	1	1	11
France	2	2	3	1	1	3	1	0.5	1	10
Denmark	3	2	2	1	1	3	0.5	0	0	9
Ireland	1	2	3	1	1	1	2	0	0	9
Portugal	1	3	1	1	1	1	0	0	1	7
Great Britain	1	2	1	1	2	2	0	0	0	6
Spain	1	1	1	1	1	1	0	0.5	1	5
Switzerland	-	-	-	-	-	-	-	-	-	-

The figures are the percentages of volunteers/activists over the total sample. Countries are ranked in descending order of the percentage of activism of all political organisations.

even larger in Scandinavian countries and are small only in Belgium and the Netherlands. Furthermore, although in some countries the predominance of traditional political memberships has been fading away during the 1990s – as indicated by ratios closer to 1 for 1999 – this is by no means a general pattern. In most countries the relative proportions of membership of traditional and new political organisations have remained relatively stable between the early and late 1990s.

Another interesting aspect is the extent to which there is an overlap between traditional and new political memberships. To what extent do citizens join different types of political organisations simultaneously? The research on social movements has repeatedly shown that – even if they sometimes confront traditional politics and politicians – NSMs are closely linked in many ways to traditional political organisations, especially parties and unions (see Kriesi & van Praag 1987 and Schmitt 1989). The results displayed in Graph 2.14 support this conclusion to a great extent, and particularly for the Netherlands, where the vast majority of citizens who join political organisations are members of NSMOs and often also of traditional political groups as well.

Generally, countries with high levels of overall political membership show a great degree of overlap between 'traditional' and 'new' memberships (the Benelux, North American and Scandinavian countries), but this is not always the

Graph 2.13: Percentages of traditional and new political membership (VWS 1990–93) and comparison of traditional to new membership ratios (WVS 1990–93 with EVS 1999)

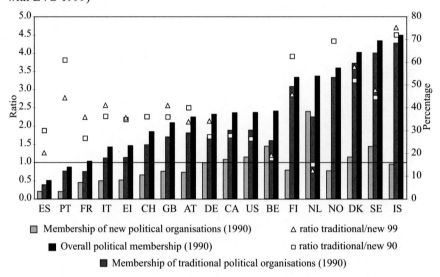

case. And there seem to be two opposing patterns of political membership: one in which 'new' political organisations prevail (in the Netherlands and Belgium) and another in which 'traditional' political actors reign (the Scandinavian countries). In a large number of countries, though, citizens tend to join exclusively traditional political groups; but a relevant proportion are (also) involved with new political organisations. Furthermore, this distribution across types of political membership has been rather stable over the last decade.

In summary, membership of political organisations has remained fairly stable throughout recent decades. There are no clear signs of increasing engagement – not even spurred by the consolidation of NSMs – but there is no evidence of general crisis or decline either. Scandinavian and North European countries invariably show the highest levels of political membership, partly due to extensive unionisation but also partly due to the great following that NSMOs have had in these nations.

Moreover, cross-national variations in political membership have also remained stable or might even have increased. And, when we look at the 'market share' of traditional and new political organisations, there are no clear signs of an overwhelming or generalised crisis in the capacity of traditional political organisations to attract members; nor can we find a spectacular or general growth in the attraction of 'new' politics. Even with all the talk about new styles of doing politics or about the crisis of traditional politics, citizens' organised engagement in the political arena is first and foremost channelled through traditional political organisations. In this regard, the Dutch pattern is the exception rather than the norm.

Graph 2.14. Degree of overlap of traditional and new political memberships, WVS 1990–93 and EVS 1999

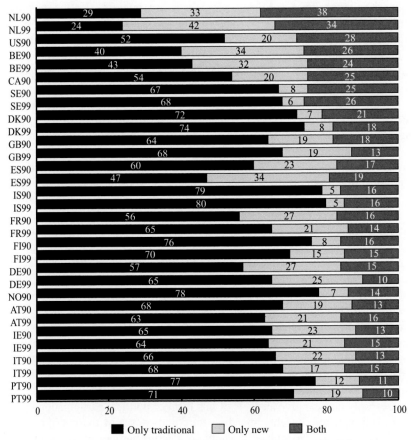

The percentages are computed only for the subsample of respondents who belong to any political organisation

DISCUSSION

From the descriptive cross-national analysis presented in this chapter, three distinctive patterns of engagement in associations in western democracies have emerged. The first pattern, typical of Northern American countries and some central European countries, is characterised by relatively high to moderate levels of membership and activism; a second pattern, typical of Scandinavian and North European countries, with extensive but fundamentally passive memberships; and a third pattern, characteristic of South European countries, with a marginal number of members but with very intense levels of activism. As we have seen, these distinctions are equally useful when we focus on the study of political membership.

Hence, patterns of political membership are in many ways similar to general patterns of associational membership. However, a number of particularities in citizens' organisational political engagement are evident. On the one hand, although Scandinavian countries are among the ones with larger numbers of political members, the following of political organisations is more moderate when trade unions are disregarded. And, in turn, the Netherlands and Northern American countries show patterns of political membership that are less dependent on unionisation.

On the other hand, engagement in political organisations is, to a much greater extent, a matter of passive involvement. Volunteering and other forms of active engagement are very common for most forms of associational engagement and in many western countries around half of those involved in an association are also actively participating in its activities; this is generally not the case for involvement in political organisations. Rarely do more than a third of those involved in political associations have an active engagement in their associations' daily activities or volunteer their time for them. Furthermore, active participation in political organisations is more frequent in nations with low levels of political membership. For example, in France, Italy and Spain, around half the citizens who join political organisations are also actively contributing to their causes; in sharp contrast, less than a quarter of Scandinavian and Dutch political members are also political activists. Thus, engagement in political organisations is, fundamentally, about passive membership and support. And it is, precisely, because these are relatively effortless contributions that the vast cross-national variations in political membership become all the more interesting and puzzling. Why are South European citizens so unlikely to join political organisations – even if they will generally not be expected to devote their time to the associations – and why are Scandinavian, Dutch and Northern American citizens so inclined to join them?

A broadly comparative analysis of this form of political participation is apt to offer many valuable insights into the nature and causes of these striking cross-national variations. Undoubtedly, studying a large number of cases limits the opportunities for detailed and in-depth analysis of the specific particularities of each nation. But, in exchange, we will gain in our capacity to provide general conclusions that will apply to a large number of western democracies. Moreover, relying on survey sources – rather than official figures or statistics – has the advantage of allowing multilevel analyses that can simultaneously take into account both individual- and contextual-level factors.

This is, indeed, the goal of the remaining chapters in this book. Chapter three will study in some detail the individual-level factors that are related to joining political organisations. As we will see, citizens' socio-economic attributes, values and attitudes are wholly insufficient to provide an adequate account of the magnitude of the cross-national variations in political membership that exist across western democracies.

NOTES

1 This excludes all the current democracies in central and eastern Europe, as well as in Africa, Asia and Latin America. Other OECD countries that could have been included are excluded, either due to insufficient data (e.g. Australia) or to limitations in the equivalence of cultural, social and political institutions (e.g. Japan and Turkey).

2 To find out that cross-national variations in levels of political membership are related to levels of democratisation would be fairly trivial.

3 A very interesting collection of studies on the problem of equivalence in comparative research can be found in van Deth (1998).

4 Consequently, Knoke (1990b: 6) defines a member as any individual who has, at least formally, the right to choose leaders and, at least indirectly through these leaders, to express opinions about the association's decisions.

5 A third possibility would be to combine the two approaches. Verba, Schlozman & Brady (1995: 58–68) consider that anyone who claims to be a member or contributes economically to the association should be defined as a 'member'.

6 Nowadays, numerous public interest groups only request economic contributions to their cause and do not organise activities or provide channels for active participation. On other occasions, even when organisations conduct activities in which members may participate, the main role of members is to contribute financially to the association. This phenomenon is known as 'chequebook participation' (Jordan & Maloney 1997).

7 This is especially the case in a comparative study.

8 McPherson (1981) finds it more appropriate to use the total number of memberships or affiliations. However, there are good conceptual and methodological reasons not to do so in this study. First, differences across countries are large regardless of whether we use dichotomous or count variables; but there is a greater cross-national variation when we use the former type of variable. Secondly, using the total number of memberships would be problematic conceptually, as surveys do not usually provide information on the number of associations as such but rather only on the number of associational categories of which the respondent is a member. Hence, count variables would underestimate the real number of associational memberships and, even worse, might introduce different biases in underestimation across countries. A dichotomous measurement of membership introduces fewer biases in the analyses.

9 As we shall see later in this chapter, a notable exception to this general rule is the survey designed by the European Science Foundation network, *Citizenship, Involvement and Democracy* (CID) coordinated by Jan W. van Deth. Further discussions on how to measure associational involvement can be found in Verba, Schlozman & Brady (1995: 59–62, 91–3 and 542–3), in Putnam (2000: 58–62 and Appendix I), van Deth (2003) and Morales and Geurts (2007).

10 A few American surveys are included for reference because it is in the United States where the research on associational behaviour and political participation has developed most. A more exhaustive review of these surveys can be found in Smith (1990). Most of the surveys used in this study have been obtained from the ICPSR database at the University of Michigan. The original data collectors, the ICPSR and other institutions who contributed economically to their compilation and distribution, are not liable for my interpretation of these data. Complete references to the studies used can be found in Appendix 1.

11 All EBs up to number 67.3 in 2007 have been consulted. EB 56.1 in 2001 only asks about membership of sports or leisure associations, charity or voluntary associations and political parties. EB 66.3 in 2006 includes a wide list of associations but only asks for active involvement or volunteering.

12 The US-CID survey of 2005, despite its name, replicates the European Social Survey battery for associational involvement rather than the original European CID survey.

13 Numerous studies exist to confirm the fundamental relevance of the overall setup of the list of organisations included in the questionnaires designed to study associational membership (Almond & Verba 1989 [1963]: 246, Baumgartner & Walker 1988, Smith 1990, Baumgartner & Walker 1990, Verba, Schlozman & Brady 1995, Putnam 2000). Nevertheless, problems of measurement go beyond the mere number of associations included (see Morales 2002).

14 Unfortunately, the 2002–3 ESS considerably reduced the original list of associations taken from the CID project.

15 The full dataset of the 1999–2000 EVS/WVS only became publicly available in 2005–6, after the core analyses of this study had already been completed.

16 There are few more than the following: Curtis (1971), Almond & Verba (1989 [1963], chapter 10), Wuthnow (1991), Curtis, Grabb & Baer (1992), Gaskin and Smith (1995), Dekker & van den Broek (1998 and 2005), Seligson (1999), Schofer & Fourcade-Gourinchas (2001), Bowler, Donovan & Hanneman (2003), and Morales & Geurts (2007). Howard's book (2003) focuses only on Eastern Europe.

17 To facilitate the view of the trends, countries have been divided into three groups according to levels of membership: between 60 and 90 per cent, between 40 and 60 per cent and those with levels below 50 per cent.

18 All graphs show the estimated trends so as to facilitate the view of longitudinal patterns, beyond the random fluctuations across surveys.

19 The reader should always keep in mind that the cross-national surveys employed in this study never ask for the number of associations strictly speaking, and we only have information about the various categories or domains (sports, religious, educational, etc.) of the associations they engage in. Figures in Graph 2.2 are for the subset of respondents who are members of at least one organisation.

20 Other analyses, not shown here, indicate that this increasing trend is stable regardless of the number of associational categories included in each survey.

21 The 2002–3 ESS was also conducted in three post-communist countries and Israel but these nations are not included among the cases analysed in this book.

22 Active members are those who participate in activities or do voluntary work in any association.

23 Although I am not convinced by the re-adoption of the term 'civil society' due to problems with its definition, the distinction they make between the three associational worlds seems interesting for subsequent research.

24 Probably, 'marginal activism' would be a better term for the same concept.

25 See, for example, Almond & Verba (1963), Lane (1965), Verba & Nie (1972), Verba, Nie & Kim (1978), Verba, Schlozman & Brady (1995), Wilson (1995 [1974]), van Deth (1997), Wessels (1997), van Deth & Kreuter (1998), and Warren (2001).

26 See, for example, Jacoby (1965), Babchuk & Edwards (1965), Verba & Nie (1972), Rogers, Barb & Bultena (1975), Pollock (1982), Opp (1989), Knoke (1990b). This is not to say that

apolitical organisations will never act as agents of political socialisation (see Erickson & Nosanchuk 1990).

27 See, for example, Almond & Verba (1963), Verba & Nie (1972, chapter 11), Pollock (1982), Verba, Schlozman & Brady (1995) and Leighley (1996). In Morales (2004: 94–9) the rationale for preferring theoretical typologies over empirical taxonomies is discussed.

28 Here two slightly different possibilities were available: to consider all respondents involved or to limit the analysis to respondents who gave valid answers to the question on public stands alone. With the former option, the following groups were classified as political: veterans' groups, senior people organisations, women's organisations, trade unions, professional organisations, political issue groups, and parties and candidates groups. If the latter was selected, to this list we could add nationality/ethnic groups, civic non-partisan organisations, liberal/conservative groups and neighbourhood organisations. The results for both options are shown.

29 In Morales (2004) the reader can find a thorough discussion of the problems involved in using dimensional techniques for making this distinction.

30 The 'theoretical' classification of political associations includes the following categories: organisations active on a particular political issue, non-partisan or civic organisations interested in the political life of a community or the nation, organisations that support general liberal or conservative causes and organisations active in supporting candidates in elections. This classification of groups as 'political' is based on Stolle & Rochon's (1998) distinctions, among which the following categories of organisations are included: political clubs, political parties, international-affairs clubs, peace, environmental, and temperance organisations, third-world and human-rights groups.

31 This survey was conducted by the Spanish Centre for Sociological Research (CIS), under contract with the project's research team, based at the Universidad Autónoma de Madrid, led by Professor José Ramón Montero, and funded by the Spanish Ministry of Science (SEC 2000-0758-C02). The author was a member of this research team and wishes to acknowledge the principal investigator and funders.

32 Unfortunately, an error in the routing during the process of questionnaire editing resulted in these two questions being asked only to respondents who had participated in an association's activities, and were not asked, as planned, of all respondents involved in any association – whether members, participants, financial contributors or volunteers. Another significant difference – although this time intentional – between the Spanish questionnaire and the one used for the ACPS is that this item was not asked for each of the associational categories in which the respondent was involved. To shorten this part of the questionnaire, the question was formulated in such a way that anyone who participated in more than one association responded according to the association they considered most relevant. The only real expected consequence of this formulation is that it reduces the number of cases each evaluation is based on; but there is no reason to expect that aggregate distributions would differ had it been formulated as in the ACPS.

33 Definitions based on respondents' perception of the association's engagement in political issues are not included as, in this case, the survey did not enquire about this aspect for all the associations the respondent joined (in the case of multiple memberships) but only for the one the respondent regarded as most important.

34 These two cases are, in fact, on the limits of what we would consider political associations,

as only 30 per cent of those who participate in the activities organised by neighbourhood associations claim that politics is discussed; for women's associations this figure is 24 per cent. Nevertheless, 40 per cent and 48 per cent respectively consider that their associations do adopt a political stance.

35 Indicator number 5 is equivalent to the one used by Verba, Schlozman & Brady to distinguish between political and non-political associations.

36 For the 2002–3 ESS, neither consumer nor women's associations are included because they are bunched in the same item with organisations that cannot be considered political: with automobile organisations for the former, and with clubs for the young, retired/elderly, and friendly societies for the latter. These groupings have resulted in a very unfortunate loss of information for the type of analyses we are interested in.

37 See an example of this argument in Lind (1996).

38 Sceptics should be reminded that Olson (1965 and 1982) specifically refers to unions, professional associations and business or industrial associations when addressing the problem of collective action – that is, the pursuit of collective goods – and the problem of a demand overload in advanced societies.

39 See Knoke (1990b: 80–1) for an analysis relevant to the United States. Moreover, recent data from six European countries collected for the international CID project and analysed by Lelieveldt & Caiani (2007) confirmed that associations of economic interests (unions, professional associations and business owners' associations) generally demonstrate a greater frequency than average in their contact with politicians and political authorities. For their part, using the same database, Lelieveldt, Astudillo Ruiz & Stevenson (2007) show that economic interest groups are fundamentally devoted to representative activities (representation of interests and lobbying).

40 It is in these graphs that we can best appreciate the problem of estimation with both the EBs and the WVS. As we can see, the 1990 EB and the 1990–93 WVS provide different percentages for the same moment in time and, in some cases, the difference in estimation is substantial and systematic. A more detailed analysis of these limitations of international surveys can be found in Morales (2002).

41 The trends unveiled by these survey data are, generally, consistent with those obtained with membership figures provided by unions. See Ebbinghaus & Visser (2000). Some differences – sometimes in the opposing direction – are however, apparent for the following countries: France, Ireland, Italy, Luxembourg, Spain and Denmark.

42 Again, some differences in the trend are evident for Belgium, Greece and, especially, Finland.

43 Only the 1990–93 WVS data are shown here, as this survey includes the most complete list of political organisations for the greatest number of countries, in addition to being the survey used, for the same reason, in the multivariate analyses of the forthcoming chapters. As with any cross-sectional survey, estimation errors are likely but – given the longitudinal trends – these seem to affect all political organisations similarly and do not substantially alter the ranking of countries.

44 It should be pointed out that, given that the questionnaires use the English term 'belong' to refer to membership, Americans must have interpreted this question from an affective viewpoint as regards political parties; the European concept of party membership cannot be translated to the American case.

chapter three | joining political organisations: the role of resources and attitudes

INTRODUCTION

Who joins political associations in western democracies? What individual attributes account for the fact that some citizens join political organisations while other refrain from doing so? Are social inequalities and the uneven distribution of socio-economic resources the reason why we find wide cross-national variations in political membership? Or are political orientations and a nation's political culture more relevant? In summary, can we understand patterns of political membership in western democracies just by looking at their citizens?

This chapter addresses these and related questions in several steps. The first section briefly summarises the various mechanisms that connect socio-economic resources and political attitudes to political participation. Then it proceeds to describe how education, age, gender, occupation, and some other aspects related to an individual's socio-economic status (SES) relates to membership of political associations in western nations. The second section focuses on the important cross-national variations that we find in how resources and attitudes have an impact on political membership. As we will see, we find substantial evidence that the same attributes do not contribute equally in all countries to explaining why citizens join political organisations. In other words, we find clear hints that resources are context-specific and that inequalities in education, occupation or income are not necessarily similarly determinant across space. The final section employs multilevel modelling to show that individual attributes alone are insufficient to account for the notable cross-national variations in political membership. Regardless of their socio-economic resources and their political attitudes, citizens in certain countries – notably South European countries – are systematically less likely to join political associations. Thus, neither relatively higher levels of economic development and educational attainment in Scandinavian and other North European countries, nor the existence of more widespread feelings of political alienation and inefficacy in South European countries can adequately explain the differentials in engagement in political organisations across western democracies.

WHO JOINS POLITICAL ASSOCIATIONS? THE IMPACT OF RESOURCES, SOCIAL BACKGROUND AND ORIENTATIONS

From a host of studies of political participation we know that social inequalities in participation persist (Verba & Nie 1972, Verba, Nie & Kim 1978, Barnes & Kaase 1979, Jennings & van Deth 1989, Kaase 1989, Parry, Moyser & Day 1992, Verba, Schlozman & Brady 1995, Teorell, Sum & Tobiasen 2007). Some socio-economic resources, such as education, income, or age, are systematically related to various forms of political participation. Equally, possessing certain attitudes and orientations, such as an interest in politics, or feelings of political efficacy, is invariably related to participatory behaviours. And past research has shown that who it is that intervenes in decision-making processes might have a substantial impact on the decisions that are finally made, because participants and non-participants usually do not share the same preferences.[1]

Thus, social inequalities are very frequently transformed into political inequalities, and these into policy decisions and representation. Individual attributes – such as one's age, gender or ethnic background – can become powerful determinants of political behaviour. Yet, the underlying mechanisms of how and when certain individual socio-demographic attributes transform into political resources are not always self-evident.

Some scholars have argued that people who are better-off will use their social and economic power to promote their own personal or group interests (Pizzorno 1966, Milbrath & Goel 1977: 86 ff., Parry, Moyser & Day 1992: 64 ff.). Thus, socio-economic resources foster political participation because they determine citizens' social and economic interests. Citizens who are better off participate more because they have more interests to defend. Those who can benefit more will be more inclined to engage in politics. The other version of this approach relates resources to the cost component of collective action (O'Brien 1974 and 1975). The greater costs of participation for the less well off, who have to assure their own survival and cannot dedicate time and effort to leisure-related activities, deter them from political action.

Both arguments are problematic. For one, the relationship between resources and participation is not always unidirectional. Sometimes, the individuals with the most resources refrain from participating in public affairs and leave 'politics' to the middle classes.[2] And, frequently, less-well-off citizens have organised in political parties and trade unions precisely to reduce social inequalities and to reduce the costs of collective action. Besides, less resourceful groups have as many reasons to engage in political action as the most privileged ones: so much have the latter to lose as the former to win.

An alternative set of mechanisms link SES and political participation via the intermediation of civic attitudes and orientations (Almond & Verba 1989 [1963], Verba & Nie 1972, Huntington & Nelson 1976, Verba, Nie & Kim 1978). Resources are related to specific social norms that determine how individuals are politically socialised. People with more privileged backgrounds develop positive civic attitudes and orientations, while individuals socialised in less advantaged environments are not exposed to this kind of stimulus. Thus, socio-economic resources are transformed into political inequalities insofar as they determine the generation of certain attitudes and orientations. In this sense, the non-univocal relationship between SES and participation is due to the fact that political attitudes play an intervening role.

A later development of this argument stresses the connection between SES, life-experiences and the acquisition of resources for participation (Brady, Verba & Schlozman 1995, Verba, Schlozman & Brady 1993 and 1995, Verba, Burns & Schlozman 1997, Schlozman, Burns & Verba 1999). Thus, the SES defines the location of individuals in a network of social relationships and resources that determine their ability to obtain the relevant information and skills to participate in public affairs. Education, gender, age and income constrain, to a great extent, the type of life-experiences individuals confront. In turn, these life-experiences are linked to the development of certain skills that foster or hinder participation in politics. In short, SES is relevant because it provides the resources that are transformed into skills that can be successfully used in the public sphere.

Finally, other scholars have argued that socio-economic resources have an impact on participation primarily, through the intermediation of mobilisation processes (Booth & Babchuk 1969, Klandermans & Oegema 1987, Knoke 1990a, Rosenstone & Hansen 1993, Leighley 1995). The SES affects opportunities for participation because not all social groups are equally exposed to political mobilisation. People with higher education and income are more frequently the target of intentional mobilisation by groups and organisations. The latter expect higher rates of success among citizens with greater resources and, additionally, these citizens usually possess more of the resources and skills that will make a difference for the organisations' causes (Booth & Babchuk 1969: 179).[3] On the other hand, informal contacts and the greater reach of the social networks of the better off multiply their participatory chances (Verba & Nie 1972: 133). People with greater resources not only participate more but their social environment – they tend to live in richer neighbourhoods – also multiplies their inclination to participate (Huckfeldt 1979, Giles & Dantico 1982, Leighley 1990).

Individual social inequalities are, thus, reinforced by the social context where people live. Resourceful individuals are even more integrated into the public sphere when they live in richer neighbourhoods.[4] Social pressure acts as a potent drive to engage in politics: when an individual is surrounded by (other) persons of a high SES, participation is seen as a social obligation imposed by informal social norms to which one must conform (Huckfeldt 1986: 149–50).

Thus, various mechanisms operate to make SES, skills, and orientations powerful sources of participatory inequalities. In the remaining parts of this section we will explore how they are indeed linked to political membership in western democracies.

Socio-economic resources: education and income

Of all socio-demographic attributes, education and income are the most frequently valuable in encouraging political action. Education fosters citizens' participation because it lowers the cognitive costs of participation and provides information useful for political action. Although formal education does not necessarily supply individuals with information on the institutional workings of contemporary democracy, it affects the way citizens process political information and the way they make political decisions (Sniderman, Brody & Tetlock 1991, Popkin 1991). Additionally, people with higher educational attainment tend to interact more with other people of higher education, thus exposing them to greater political stimulation and information (Berelson, Lazarsfeld & McPhee 1954).

Table 3.1 shows the connection between political membership and levels of education.[5] In most western countries, education is positively and linearly related to political membership. And, in some countries, people with higher education are up to five or even seven times more likely to join political organisations than individuals with little or no formal education. Educational inequalities in political membership tend to be smaller in Scandinavian countries and larger in South European and

Table 3.1: Educational level and political membership, 1990–93 and 1998

Country	WVS 1990–93				EB 49 1998			
	Primary or less	Some secondary education	Higher or university degree	Ratio higher/ lower	Primary or less	Some secondary education	Higher or university degree	Ratio higher/ lower
Switzerland*	8	30	42	5.1				
United States	13	31	56	4.2				
Spain	5	8	19	3.8	7	18	37	5.3
Italy	15	34	50	3.2	12	17	27	2.3
Ireland	14	26	44	3.1	9	16	29	3.4
France	10	15	30	2.9	18	16	19	1.0
G. Britain	24	34	59	2.4	18	30	54	2.9
Canada	24	32	52	2.2				
Portugal	12	17	24	2.0	4	22	26	7.0
Belgium	28	40	50	1.8	11	21	37	3.4
Denmark	42	67	72	1.7	50	62	69	1.4
Germany	32	39	53	1.7	17	23	48	2.8
Norway	46	54	65	1.4				
Netherlands	44	52	64	1.4	34	50	59	1.7
Iceland	66	71	76	1.2				
Finland	49	44	61	1.2	35	46	62	1.8
Sweden	66	69	72	1.1	54	66	74	1.4
Austria	43	34	40	0.9	28	30	51	1.8
Greece					8	8	13	1.6
Luxembourg					46	38	56	1.2

Note: The figures are percentages of membership of any political organisation. Countries are ranked in descending order of educational inequalities (ratio) for 1990–93. * The data for Switzerland are not fully equivalent to the rest because some political organisations were not included in the questionnaire.

Graph 3.1: Income and political membership, WVS 1990–93

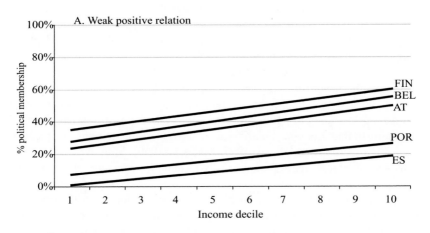

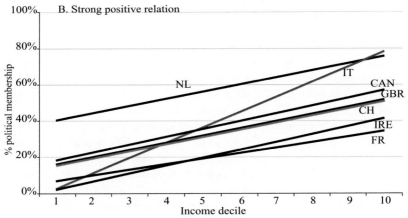

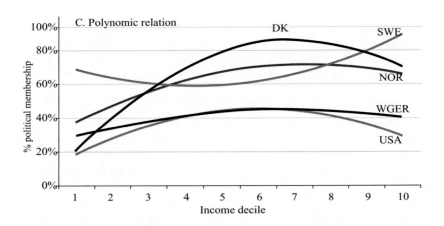

Anglo-Saxon countries. Furthermore, participatory inequalities related to educational resources are relatively stable in most countries.[6]

Income is also a crucial resource for some forms of political action. Individuals with higher incomes are more able to afford the time and money required to participate in public affairs. In the specific case of political membership, higher income is likely to foster organisational involvement in multiple ways. Individuals with higher earnings can contribute to a greater number of organisations to defend their interests and preferences. Some scholars have pointed to the mushrooming of political organisations that devote a substantial part of their efforts to find economic contributors and patrons and promote 'chequebook' participation (Jordan & Maloney 1997, Maloney 1999). Moreover, people with greater economic resources can more easily form new associations to defend their causes.

In general, we would expect a positive and linear relation between income and political membership but the transformation of income inequalities into participatory inequalities may vary substantially across countries, depending on the degree of mobilisation of the less advantaged groups by left-wing parties and class-based trade unions (Rokkan & Campbell 1960, Verba, Nie & Kim 1978).

Graph 3.1 confirms that, in most western nations, the relationship between income and political membership is, in fact, positive and linear.[7] The strength of this association varies across cases. While in such countries as Italy and Ireland participatory inequalities are clearly linked to income levels, in other nations – Austria, Finland, or Spain – income is less determining for political membership.

Yet in some other countries the relationship between income and political membership is curvilinear, such that membership increases with income up to a certain point – generally around the central deciles – and then decreases, although not to the same low level found among lower-income individuals. In West Germany, this relationship is almost non-significant; in the case of Sweden, the relationship is precisely the opposite, with people of higher and lower incomes being more likely to join political organisations than citizens with middle incomes.

The results for the Scandinavian countries are somewhat surprising, since economic inequalities seem to have more of an impact than we would expect, given the strength of social-democratic parties and unions. Additionally, these results seem to be stable, when the 1998 data are checked. Hence, in most western nations, income is a relatively important driver of political membership.

Other SES factors: social class, age, and gender
However, resources are surely not the only socio-demographic attributes linked to unequal opportunities for participation. Other SES factors, as determined by social class, age, gender, and family situation, condition citizens' political participation.

Certain social classes are more likely to organise to defend their interests. For example, manual workers have a long-standing tradition of union membership, while the traditional middle classes and business-owners have promoted professional associations and business organisations. In the opposite case, the social and

Table 3.2: Political membership and social class, EB 49 (1998)

	Inactive	Manual workers and supervisors	Non-manual routine	New middle classes	Traditional middle classes and small business owners	Total	Ratio higher/ lower value
Portugal	3	6	24	39	18	11	13.8
Spain	7	12	26	52	19	16	7.3
Ireland	8	13	15	41	26	15	5.1
Belgium	13	24	29	49	26	23	3.7
Great Britain	16	21	38	55	27	30	3.5
Greece	5	10	8	16	11	9	3.3
Italy	10	19	23	28	28	17	2.7
Finland	28	50	67	67	54	50	2.3
Austria	21	33	32	46	45	32	2.2
France	13	19	13	25	10	17	2.2
W. Germany	20	28	20	41	32	26	2
Sweden	45	75	76	86	69	67	1.9
Netherlands	37	49	53	59	71	49	1.9
Denmark	43	74	73	78	62	65	1.8
Luxembourg	38	43	50	58	42	44	1.5

Note: The figures are percentages of membership of any political organisation. Countries are ranked in descending order of class inequalities (ratio).

professional context of non-manual routine workers and of labour-market outsiders has not contributed to their political organising. And we know that the new middle classes have a greater tendency to participate in politics, especially when employed in the public sector.[8]

Table 3.2 shows the relation between social class and political membership in fifteen European countries in 1998.[9] From the results we can tell that, indeed, the new middle classes have a greater tendency to organise themselves politically, while the non-working population is much more reluctant to join political associations. These patterns are common to most West European countries. In all countries, manual workers and supervisors show intermediate levels of political membership that, in many cases, are close to the national average.

Nevertheless, social class is not equally relevant to political membership across the board. In some countries, social class is a clear source of significant participatory inequalities – especially in South European and Anglo-Saxon countries – while in others, class gaps, although still noticeable, are much smaller.[10]

However, these results might be influenced by the type of political organisations listed in the EB 49 questionnaire.[11] The inclusion of trade unions and professional associations may exert strong leverage over the results, as the working environment of some of the class groups is more conducive to unionisation. Table 3.3 shows the relation between social class and political membership when trade unions and professional associations are excluded.

Indeed, class patterns change substantially. Individuals who are not employed

Table 3.3: Social class and political membership, without trade unions and professional associations, EB 49 (1998)

	Inactive	Manual workers and supervisors	Non-manual routine	New middle classes	Traditional middle classes and small business owners	Total	Ratio higher/ lower value
Portugal	2	1	9	13	8	4	14.7
Spain	6	8	19	34	11	11	5.3
Ireland	7	5	6	19	20	9	4.1
Great Britain	14	7	16	29	24	15	4.0
Belgium	9	9	17	33	20	14	3.7
Greece	4	5	5	12	7	5	3.3
Italy	8	7	14	14	17	11	2.4
Finland	16	10	16	21	23	16	2.4
Netherlands	29	34	39	49	63	38	2.2
France	11	13	7	14	13	11	2.0
Austria	18	24	21	29	32	23	1.8
W. Germany	15	14	13	22	21	15	1.7
Denmark	27	26	35	41	37	32	1.6
Luxembourg	28	34	33	42	40	33	1.5
Sweden	36	36	38	53	39	39	1.5

Note: The figures are percentages of membership of any political organisation. Countries are ranked in descending order of class inequalities (ratio).

are no longer always the least engaged in political organisations and they frequently share the lowest percentages of membership with manual workers and supervisors. On the other hand, although the new middle classes continue to have a much greater tendency to join political groups, the traditional middle classes show similar percentages in several countries. But in general terms, it does not seem that the exclusion of trade unions and professional associations has any significant impact on the degree of inequality that social class introduces to political membership, given that the relative differences between the least and most participative classes remain practically unaltered. Overall, the most advantaged social classes are systematically more inclined to join political organisations, even though unionisation somewhat mitigates the gap for manual workers in many countries

Thus, we see that income and occupational inequalities have a substantial impact on political membership. But, what about other SES factors? We will now turn our attention to age, gender and family situation.

Age is a usual suspect for explaining various forms of political engagement. The relation between age and political participation varies importantly, depending on the type of participation and the country we consider (Dalton 1996: 55 ff.). Frequently, this relationship is curvilinear, in such a way that middle-aged persons are the most active, and the youngest or the oldest are the least. This pattern was considered, for a long time, the most common and was usually linked to life-cycle determinants (Verba & Nie 1972: chapter 9, Verba, Nie & Kim 1978). However, when focusing on less conventional or more confrontational forms of political action, this relationship turns out to be linear and negative (Dalton 1996: 78 ff.). Scholars argue that, in general terms, older people participate more in politics because age provides the skills and knowledge relevant for participation. On the other hand, middle-aged individuals take over social and family responsibilities that generate more reasons to be concerned about public affairs.

Further to this, in many cases, it might be difficult to establish if the effect attributed to age is strictly related to the life-cycle or if it is masking generational effects (Barnes & Kaase 1979: 524, Jennings 1987, Dalton 1996: 81). In fact, some scholars have argued that age as such has no effect on political participation and that any impact is to be attributed to either cohorts (or generations), or to the period (Brady & Elms 1999). However, we can only determine this with good longitudinal data (Mason & Fienberg 1985).

With the available data we can only explore the relation between political membership and age and we cannot evaluate hypotheses on generational effects. Graph 3.2 shows the association between age and political membership for the 18 Western countries included in the 1990–93 WVS.[12] In most countries the relation is curvilinear, such that the highest levels are to be found among adults aged 40 to 60 – the exceptions being Spain and Portugal, where age seems to bear little relation to political membership. In some countries – the Netherlands, the United States and Switzerland – it is the youngest that join political organisations the least; whereas, in other democracies, political membership sharply decreases with age – as in several Scandinavian countries, Italy and Ireland.

Age patterns change when we distinguish between types of political membership.[13] While traditional political membership shows the common curvilinear

Graph 3.2: Age and political membership, WVS 1990–93

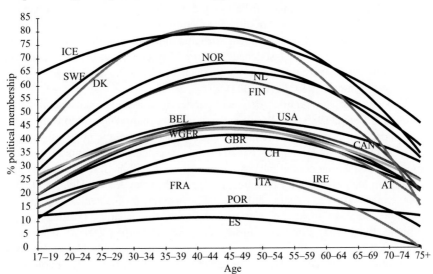

pattern, this is not the case for membership of new political organisations. In some countries – Spain and France, for example – it is the youngest citizens who most frequently join organisations linked to NSMs; while in others – Italy, the United States, Norway, Switzerland and Austria – the highest participation is found among adults aged 26 to 35; finally, in some countries the elderly are the most likely to join new political organisations. In summary, for 'new' political organisations, there is no common curvilinear or linear relationship between age and membership for all western countries and its impact is context-dependent.

Therefore, the life-cycle hypothesis put forward by Verba & Nie (1972) for political participation does not seem to hold for political membership. It is difficult to sustain this hypothesis, given the various patterns of age-effects that we detect for different types of political membership. Thus it is more likely that some sort of generational effects are in place or, at least, we would have to relate age-effects to the development of different issue interests more than with different participatory abilities or strictly life-cycle aspects.

Gender is also frequently related to substantial participatory inequalities. Being a woman can, in many cases, become a social barrier to participating in public affairs, which have traditionally been regarded as a 'man's thing'.[14] The existence of a notable gender gap in political participation was first studied with regard to electoral participation (Duverger 1955). Later on, Verba, Nie & Kim (1978) highlighted the substantial and constant gender gap present in political participation in seven countries (Austria, India, Japan, the Netherlands, Nigeria, the United States and Yugoslavia), the magnitude of which varied both from country to country and between political activities. These scholars attributed such differences to a certain phenomenon of inhibition, '[women] care [about politics] but are held back by rules or norms or lack of opportunity' (254). The existence of this phenomenon was confirmed by evidence for a different interaction between educational levels, organisational affiliation and psychological political involvement with political activity. Several studies have confirmed the existence of important gender gaps in non-electoral political participation, although these seem to have decreased noticeably in the last decades (Parry, Moyser & Day: 143 ff., Gundelach 1995, Topf 1995b, Verba, Burns & Schlozman 1997, Burns, Schlozman & Verba 2001: 69 ff., Inglehart & Norris 2003).

Focusing on the relation between gender and associational membership, Almond & Verba (1989 [1963]: 248) attributed cross-national variations mostly to the gender gap. For Britain, the gender gap in associational membership was still persistent in 1989 and the gap between men and women was of around 8 per cent, and of around 21 per cent in the case of unionisation, although it was almost non-existent in the case of party membership (Parry, Moyser & Day 1992: 150). The 2000 Citizen Audit in Britain confirms the persistence of this gender gap in associational membership at the start of the twenty-first century (Pattie, Seyd & Whiteley 2004: 104). Similarly, Burns, Schlozman & Verba (2001: 79 ff.) analyse with great detail the gender gap in political membership in the United States in 1990. While 53 per cent of American men are involved (are members or contribute

Table 3.4: Gender and political membership, WVS 1990–93

Country	Overall political membership			Member of traditional political organisations only			Member of new political organisations only			Member of traditional and new political organisations			N
	women	men	ratio m/w	women	men	ratio m/w	women	men	ratio m/w	women	men	ratio m/w	
Finland	53	54	1.0	37	44	1.2	5	3	0.6	10	7	0.7	588
Iceland	70	73	1.0	49	64	1.3	5	2	0.3	16	8	0.5	702
Sweden	68	71	1.0	41	52	1.3	8	4	0.4	19	15	0.8	1029
Belgium	38	39	1.0	10	21	2.0	18	8	0.4	10	11	1.1	2794
Canada	36	40	1.1	15	27	1.8	11	5	0.4	10	9	0.9	1731
Ireland	23	24	1.1	11	20	1.9	8	3	0.3	4	2	0.4	1000
Netherlands	51	57	1.1	9	23	2.6	24	10	0.4	18	23	1.3	1018
Norway	53	62	1.2	39	51	1.3	6	3	0.5	8	8	1.0	1239
Denmark	60	69	1.2	41	51	1.3	6	4	0.7	14	14	1.0	1026
Great Britain	30	37	1.2	14	29	2.2	9	3	0.3	7	5	0.6	1484
United States	35	41	1.2	12	27	2.3	11	5	0.4	12	9	0.7	1965
France	13	20	1.5	6	13	2.0	5	4	0.8	2	4	1.9	1002
Austria	30	45	1.5	16	38	2.4	10	2	0.2	4	6	1.3	1460
W. Germany	30	45	1.5	11	34	3.2	14	6	0.4	5	6	1.1	2102
Switzerland*	22	39	1.8	11	28	2.5	6	5	0.9	4	5	1.3	1358
Portugal	9	19	2.0	7	14	1.9	1	2	2.1	1	2	2.9	1184
Italy	15	30	2.0	9	21	2.4	4	6	1.5	2	4	1.9	2018
Spain	5	11	2.1	3	7	2.7	2	2	1.0	1	2	3.0	2636

* The data for Switzerland are not exactly equivalent to the rest because some political organisations were not included in the questionnaire. Countries are ranked in ascending order of gender inequalities (ratio) for overall political membership.

with money) with some sort of political organisation, only 44 per cent of women do so. Even among those who are involved in associations, women show less of an inclination to be members of or contribute money to those organisations that take political stands (57 per cent versus 64 per cent of men). Additionally, men join a greater number of political organisations than women do.[15]

Table 3.4 illustrates the relation between gender and political membership in the 18 western countries included in the 1990–93 WVS. This table shows both the gender gap with respect to general political membership and with regard to specific types of political organisations.

In most countries, the gap in political membership is small. Greater gender differences are prevalent in Central and South European countries, where men are up to two times more likely to join a political organisation than women. The gender gap is larger and more widespread for membership of traditional political groups. In this case we see that Scandinavian countries – with small gender differences – clearly depart from the more general pattern of men being between two and three times more likely than women to join these organisations.

Interestingly, we find the opposite results when we focus on membership of new political organisations. Women are much more likely to join these organisations and this pattern is common to all countries, outside Southern Europe. Nevertheless, these differences are not as large as the gap between men and women for traditional political organisations. Finally, when we look at simultaneous membership of both traditional and new political groups, we see that gender differences vary substantially across countries: in some, it is women that show a greater propensity to join both types of groups as in several Scandinavian and Anglo-Saxon countries, whereas in other countries it is men who behave more in this way. The 1998 EB 49 data confirm these same patterns almost a decade later. Thus, the gender gap in political membership continues to be sizeable in many European nations.

Closely related to the gender gap is the individual's family situation. Generally, participation scholars have claimed that being married and having children increases the likelihood of participating in politics, because it contributes to greater social integration and embeddedness and because it increases the stake in public affairs (Booth & Babchuk 1969). However, other scholars have argued that both marital status and child-rearing have different effects on men and women. *A priori*, it is reasonable to expect that married women with children will have more difficulties in participating in politics, as they tend to bear the major domestic and childcare burdens. Nevertheless, the available empirical evidence does not provide clear support for these conclusions.

Parry, Moyser & Day (1992: 148 ff.) show that marriage limits British women's political participation to a great extent, as they tend to participate less than married men, whereas single women tend to participate more than single men. But, on the other hand, they show that, in the British case, child-rearing has multiple and contradicting effects on gender inequalities, depending on marital status and working situation. For example, married women with children and a job participate much less than men in the same situation, but they participate more than men when they do not have a job. In turn, single mothers are more active in politics than single fathers, regardless of their working situation.

For the American case, Burns, Schlozman & Verba (2001: 221 ff., 307 ff.) show that marital status and child-rearing have no significant effects on the levels of associational membership of American men and women, nor do they have a different impact depending on gender. Hence, surprisingly enough, marital status and child-rearing seem to have no substantial effect on gender inequalities in political participation, although they might have an indirect effect through differential labour-market integration. According to these results, the fact that women have less free-time available – due to family obligations – does not seem to be a crucial factor in political inequalities in the United States.

Table 3.5 presents the relation, first, between marital status and political membership, and second, between child-rearing and political membership. In general terms, having a partner or being married increases the likelihood of joining a political organisation in most European countries, with the exception of Southern

Table 3.5: Marital status, number of children and political membership, EB 49 (1998)

Country	Ratio political membership with couple/no couple			Percentage of political membership for women			Percentage of political membership for men		
	Total	Women	Men	0 children	1-2	3 or +	0 children	1-2	3 or +
Portugal	0.8	0.6**	1.1	8	12	6	13	13	0
Spain	1.0	0.7**	1.2	12	16	0	20	219	40
Greece	1.2	0.5**	1.8**	4	5	4	13	15	17
Denmark	1.2**	1.2**	1.1**	56	72	79**	67	73	69
Sweden	1.2**	1.2**	1.2**	61	78	58**	67	71	85
Austria	1.3**	1.2*	1.5**	27	27	23	35	45	67*
Finland	1.4	1.3	1.6**	45	66	62**	42	67	39**
Belgium	1.4**	1.4**	1.4**	16	23	30	27	33	6
Germany	1.4**	1.3**	1.5**	17	19	28	32	44	14*
Ireland	1.4**	1.2	1.7**	10	12	9	16	25	24
Italy	1.5**	1.2	1.6**	12	13	11	22	27	67*
Netherlands	1.5**	1.6**	1.4	43	51	48	54	55	56
France	1.6**	1.5**	1.5**	12	15	18	21	26	17
Great Britain	1.6**	1.3**	2.0**	29	20	9**	33	38	55*
Luxembourg	1.8**	1.6**	2.0**	35	44	39	53	45	29

Note: For ratios, statistically significant differences between respondents living and not living in couples are marked. In the case of the two sets of columns for the number of children, the asterisks indicate whether the relation between the number of children and political membership is statistically significant as indicated by the F statistic of the analysis of variance. * Statistically significant difference for $p<0.05$. ** Statistically significant difference for $p<0.01$.

Europe and Finland, where marital status is not significantly related to political membership. It is precisely in these same South European countries that marital status has a different impact for men and women.[16] In Spain, Greece and Portugal, married women or women in partnerships join political organisations less than single women. However, in these same countries, married men are more inclined to be members of political groups than singletons. Hence, in most South European countries, being part of a couple causes women to refrain from public affairs while promoting male engagement. These patterns remain very much the same when we distinguish between traditional and new political membership.

With regard to child-rearing, our results would indicate that, in most European nations, it does not have any consequence for political membership for either men or women. There are, nevertheless, some interesting exceptions. In Scandinavian countries, women with more children are more likely to join political organisations – although in Sweden this pattern does not extend to those with three or more children. In the opposite case, British women drastically retreat from political organisations when they have children, while British men show just the opposite behaviour. Hence, child-rearing in Britain does clearly seem to discourage women from participating and has the inverse effect for men.

Yet, in general terms, our results support Burns, Schlozman & Verba's (2001) conclusions for the American case, as the common belief that family obligations put women in a politically disadvantaged position does not seem to hold. Women with children are, generally, no less likely to join political organisations than women without children. If at all, raising children is linked to higher levels of political membership for both men and women.

Social embeddedness and integration: community size and religious practices
As we have seen, in most West European countries, having a family is an integrative force that fosters political membership rather than distracting from it. However, other aspects of citizens' lifestyles are also thought to have an integrative function that promotes political participation. We will now explore the impact of the size of the community individuals live in, as well as of their religious practices.

The size of the community in which citizens live and its empirical connection to participation has been subject to debate for many decades (Dahl & Tufte 1973, Verba, Nie & Kim 1978, Mabileau, Moyser, Parry & Quantin 1989, Parry, Moyser & Day 1992, Baglioni, Denters, Morales & Vetter 2007).

Contradictory claims have been advanced about the link between community size and political participation or associational membership.[17] On the one hand, it is argued that smaller communities foster individuals' participation because information costs are lower, social networks are closer, social pressure to conform increases, the possibility to have an impact on the final result of political action is greater, and the feeling of belonging and commitment to the community tends to be greater (Dahl & Tufte 1973: 13–14, 42).[18]

In contrast, a number of scholars have argued that larger communities induce greater participation and political membership. This is what Verba, Nie & Kim (1978: chapter 13) termed the 'mobilization' hypothesis. Cities contribute to the emergence of a greater number of more varied interests and groups, since the diversity of beliefs, values, goals, and social characteristics of their inhabitants is greater. Moreover, greater social and political diversity is an incentive to participation because there is more conflict and less pressure towards conformity (Dahl & Tufte 1973: 13–14, 97–8, 108). Subcultural heterogeneity, therefore, produces a wider range of participation opportunities. Besides, the greater development of mass media in big cities means that these participatory opportunities will get more publicity and that public affairs will generally be more frequently the subject of information (Oliver 2001: 41).

Some scholars think urbanisation also favours political membership because it reduces recruitment costs for organisations, while increasing the ability of members to communicate with each other and with the association leaders (Kau & Rubin 1979). Finally, urban areas can also foster citizen participation due to their socio-economic composition, as their citizenry is generally better educated and wealthier.

Both sets of hypotheses seem reasonable and plausible. Thus, these possibly opposing effects could very well have as a consequence that we would not find a common and general pattern, or even no association whatsoever, between community size and participation. As Oliver (2001: 22) points out, it is not sufficiently clear which would be the real mechanism working out the connection between

Graph 3.3: Size of the community and political membership, WVS 1990–93

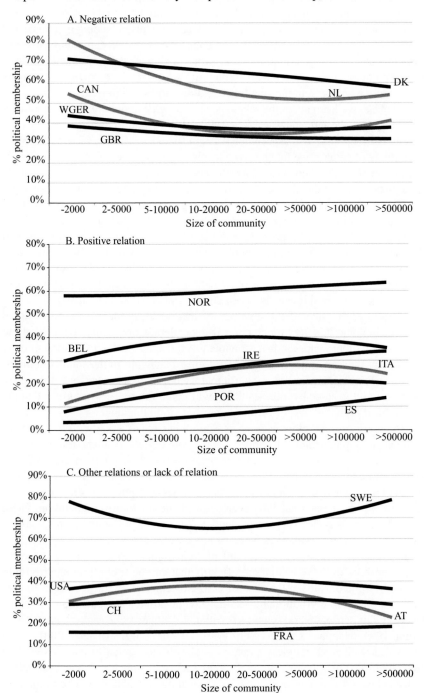

community size and political participation. And he concludes that this relation is a complex one: some forms of political participation are favoured by a smaller sized of the community (for example, contacting local officials, attending meetings, and community activity), while for others the connection between community size and participation is contingent on the type of urban setting we consider. Hence, associational participation increases with community size in the large metropolitan areas but decreases with size in the small metropolitan areas and in rural areas.[19]

What can we learn about the relationship between community size and political membership in Western countries? The 1990–93 WVS allows us to explore the connection between these two aspects for Western societies.[20] Graph 3.3 shows the different types of patterns we find between levels of political membership and community size in 16 Western countries.[21] The bivariate analyses seem to confirm what we have just discussed: the size of the community can impinge on political participation in various directions and in complex ways. We cannot even claim that in all cases, not even in most countries, living in big cities is related to a lower likelihood of joining political organisations. In some countries – the Netherlands, Canada and Denmark – people in smaller communities are more inclined to join political organisations. However, in Norway, Ireland and Spain big-city dwellers join political organisations the most. In several other nations political membership is most frequent in medium-sized towns (between 20,000 and 100,000 inhabitants).[22]

Therefore, the size of the community has no clear-cut impact on political membership, and it is very much context-dependent. Community size is likely to interact with other factors. It is reasonable to expect that social integration into the community will not foster individuals' political behaviour in the smaller communities where social norms are not participatory but quite the reverse. Yet, here we can only point to some hypotheses that might guide future research, given that the data at hand do not allow for further exploring along this line.

Religiousness and religious practices are often cited as a major driving force of political participation and behaviour.[23] People who frequently attend religious services or who participate in the activities organised by their religious congregation may be more inclined to participate in public affairs, for various reasons. Frequent contact with people with whom they share values and practices generates social networks where mutual trust will develop, thus fostering future co-operation. These networks, as well as the institutional characteristics of the religious centres,[24] favour the mobilisation of parishioners when causes emerge that require it.

In addition, religious practice and participation in church-related activities may contribute to the development of skills that can be usefully transferred into the public sphere. And, in the case of ethnic or cultural minorities it can importantly help to create group identities that favour political mobilisation (Peterson 1992). In this sense, several scholars (Wuthnow 1994 & 1999, Jackson et al. 1995, Smidt 1999, Halman & Pettersson 1999, de Hart 2001, Uslaner 2001) have claimed that citizens' religious practice is closely connected to their associative behaviours. More specifically, everything seems to indicate that church-attendance is linked to greater levels of associational membership in a good number of

Graph 3.4: Religious practice and political membership, WVS 1990–93

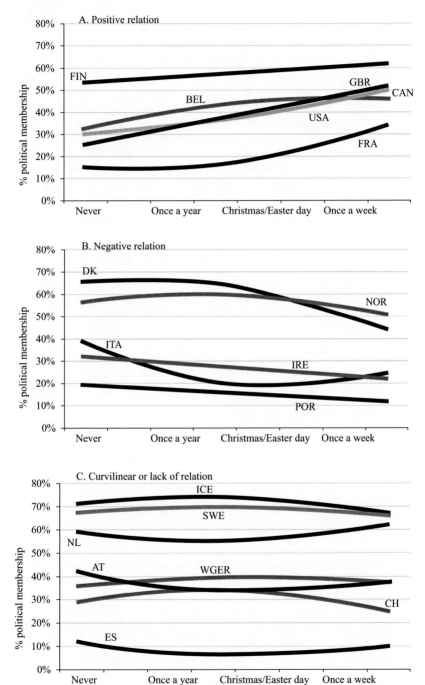

countries, although not necessarily in all (see Halman & Pettersson 1999).

Is there any connection between political membership and the religious practices of citizens? Does religious integration foster individuals' political participation through organisations? In the following pages I will measure religious integration with the frequency of church attendance, as well as by membership of religious or church associations. Church attendance is in itself a good indicator of religious integration, as it manifests the extent to which the individual has developed a religious identity that is dependent on an institutional system (Bréchon 1999). Religious associational membership provides further information on the degree of commitment to such an identity, as well as on the social networks the individuals have access to due to their religious practices.

Graph 3.4 illustrates the several forms that the relation between church attendance and political membership adopts. These results confirm the claims of other scholars (especially, Bréchon 1999 and Halman & Pettersson 1999) about the importance of national contexts. Thus, of the 18 western countries considered here, in six of them (Belgium, Canada, the United States, Finland, France and Great Britain) frequent church-attendance is linked to higher levels of political membership, in five nations (Denmark, Ireland, Italy, Norway and Portugal) to less political membership, and in the rest the association is more complex (curvi-

Table 3.6: Religious and political memberships, WVS 1990–93

Country	All political organisations	Only traditional	Only new	Both traditional and new
Iceland	1.3*	1.3*	0.7	1.7*
Norway	1.1	0.9	1.1	2.2*
Sweden	1.1	1.0	1.4	1.2
Finland	1.1	1.0	0.9	2.0
Denmark	1.1	0.8	1.9	1.8
Great Britain	2.1*	1.2	3.1*	6.3*
United States	2.0*	2.2*	1.5*	2.1*
Canada	1.9*	1.4*	2.3*	2.9*
W. Germany	1.6*	1.3*	1.9*	2.5*
Switzerland	1.6*	1.4	1.0	3.8*
Netherlands	1.3*	1.2	0.8	1.9*
Spain	4.0*	2.7*	4.8*	9.3*
France	3.5*	2.9*	2.8	7.6*
Ireland	2.5*	1.4	5.1*	6.2*
Belgium	2.2*	1.2	2.4*	3.9*
Portugal	2.1*	1.7*	7.7*	0.6
Italy	2.0*	1.8*	2.8*	2.1
Austria	1.8*	1.5*	2.8*	2.4*

Note: The figures are the ratios between the average percentage of political membership among members of religious associations and that of non-members. The asterisk indicates significant ratios for p<0.05. The dotted lines separate groups of countries that are mainly Protestant, religiously mixed, and mainly Catholic. Within each of these groups, countries are ranked in descending order of the gap (ratio) in political membership between members and non-members of religious associations.

linear) or there is no such connection. And these results do not attest to any clear pattern based on denomination.

Yet, the results in Graph 3.4 mask substantial variations that emerge when we analyse separately the effects of church attendance on traditional political membership and new political membership (results not shown). Religious practice has, for the most part, negative effects on traditional political membership and positive effects on new political membership.[25]

However, religious practice is not the only means of religious integration. The information on the religious and church-related associational memberships of respondents allows us to explore the connection between religious social networks and political mobilisation. Table 3.6 shows that, in most western countries, religious membership fosters political membership, with the exception of Scandinavian countries – which are mostly Protestant. In general terms, whenever religious associational membership is relevant, it is connected both to traditional and new political organisations. And we do not find substantially different patterns between religiously mixed and Catholic societies.

Hence, whereas church-attendance shows mixed patterns of connection with political membership and is very much context-dependent, membership of religious organisations is more clearly linked to membership. This suggests that the structural component of social interaction within religious institutions might be more important than faith-related aspects.[26]

Civic and political orientations

While SES and social integration are clearly relevant for political membership, various studies have shown that the impact of these structural factors is very frequently mediated by civic and political orientations (Rokkan & Campbell 1960, Verba & Nie 1972, Milbrath & Goel 1977, Verba, Nie & Kim 1978, Parry, Moyser & Day 1992, Verba, Schlozman & Brady 1995). In the next pages we will, thus, explore the bivariate relation between civic and political orientations, and political membership. We will focus on variables that measure the psychological involvement of citizens with politics in its three dimensions: affective (interest, efficacy, and importance attributed to politics), cognitive (political information and knowledge), and behavioural (political discussions). And we will also analyse the relation between political membership and social trust, value structures (materialist versus postmaterialist) and attitudes toward social change (reformism versus conservatism).

Sigel & Hoskin (1981, chapter 2) have elaborated on the concept of political involvement. They argued that the latent variable is tridimensional and includes affective, cognitive and behavioural elements. Here we will disregard those behavioural aspects that are forms of political participation. Consequently, an interest in politics, the importance attributed to politics and individuals' political efficacy all point to the affective dimension; news consumption and subjective perception of one's own political informedness[27] will serve to measure the cognitive elements; finally, the frequency of political discussions, as well as attempting to persuade other citizens on political matters, will help us tap the behavioural dimensions that do not overlap with political participation.

Psychological involvement in politics can, thus, be conceived of as an attitudinal prerequisite for political membership. Even if, frequently, citizens join political organisations for other reasons, or due to the effectiveness of recruitment processes, it is reasonable to expect that whoever joins an organisation with political aims will show greater psychological involvement with public affairs.

Table 3.7 shows that, indeed, the affective dimension of psychological involvement with politics is closely related to political membership. However, it is the degree of interest in politics that better discriminates among those who do and do not join political organisations. In some countries, the importance attributed to politics, as well as internal political efficacy, is not related to this form of political participation.

Therefore, having feelings of political powerlessness does not prevent citizens in Belgium, Canada, Sweden and Iceland from joining political groups, while having no interest in politics acts as a potent disincentive to join them. On the other hand, these attitudes have more of an impact in those countries (especially, South European ones) where both the levels of political membership and political

Table 3.7: Political membership and the affective dimension of political involvement

| Country | WVS 1990–93 | | | EB 49 (1998) | |
	Interest	Importance	Efficacy	Interest	Importance
Spain	3.8*	2.6*	2.1*	7.2*	3.3*
Italy	3.2*	2.8*	2.7*	7.4*	3.9*
Portugal	2.9*	2.3*	2.4*	24.7*	3.8*
Ireland	2.2*	1.6*	2.4*	7.4*	3.1*
Switzerland	2.2*	1.4*	---		
France	2.0*	2.3*	2.2*	6.8*	5.0*
United States	1.9*	1.5*	1.8*		
Great Britain	1.8*	1.9*	2.3*	6.2*	5.2*
Netherlands	1.8*	1.5*	1.3*	3.1*	2.1*
Austria	1.8*	1.4*	0.7*	5.4*	3.0*
W. Germany	1.7*	1.6*	1.4*	8.6*	8.8*
Belgium	1.7*	1.6*	1.3	4.3*	3.2*
Canada	1.7*	1.4*	1.2		
Norway	1.4*	1.1*	1.3*		
Sweden	1.2*	1.2*	1.1	1.6*	1.4*
Finland	1.2*	1.4*	1.6*	1.9*	1.5*
Denmark	1.1*	1.0	1.2*	1.8*	1.9*
Iceland	1.1*	1.1	0.9		
Greece				5.8*	1.8
Luxembourg				9.8*	7.4*

Note: The figures are the ratios between the average percentage of political membership for the highest and lowest categories of political involvement. Asterisks signal ratios statistically significant for $p<0.05$. Countries are ranked in descending order of the ratio for interest in politics.

involvement are lower, in such a way that political membership is mostly limited to those individuals with a strong interest in politics.

The results are similar when we analyse the relation between the cognitive dimension of political involvement and political membership (Table 3.8). As in the case of interest in politics, it is the more general indicator of subjective evaluation of one's own level of political informedness that has a greater impact on political membership. In all European countries, individuals who feel they are not informed about politics show less of an inclination to join political organisations. The gap between the most and the least informed is really substantial in Southern Europe and in some Central European countries, while it is much smaller in Scandinavian countries.

Attentiveness to current affairs through the radio and the newspapers is much less relevant for political membership. And, in any case, other analyses (not shown here) demonstrate that subjective perceptions of informedness are much more strongly related to real levels of information than news attentiveness is.

Table 3.9, lastly, analyses the bivariate relation between the behavioural dimension of political involvement and political membership. As we see, in most countries, political membership is connected to behavioural aspects of psychological involvement with politics. We are certainly not surprised about these results; however, it is worth noting that this is not the case in all countries since, in the Netherlands, Finland and Sweden, citizens who join political organisations are not always more inclined to discuss politics or to try to persuade their fellow citizens on political matters. Once again, the most striking gaps between the most and the

Table 3.8: Political membership and the cognitive dimension of political involvement, EB 49 (1998)

Country	Informedness (subjective evaluation)	News on the radio	News readership
Greece	40.2*	3.4*	1.7*
Portugal	30.5*	7.2*	2.3*
Ireland	10.0*	1.5	0.9
Luxembourg	10.0*	2.2*	6.2*
W. Germany	9.0*	2.2*	4.0*
Spain	8.4*	3.4*	1.6*
Italy	7.7*	3.5*	0.9
Austria	5.8*	1.0	1.0
Great Britain	5.0*	1.4	2.2*
Belgium	4.6*	2.2*	1.1
France	4.5*	2.9*	1.7*
Netherlands	2.5*	1.7*	1.5*
Finland	1.8*	1.7	1.2
Sweden	1.8*	1.3	1.3
Denmark	1.7*	2.7*	1.4

Note: The figures are the ratios between the average percentage of political membership for the highest and lowest categories of political involvement. Asterisks signal ratios statistically significant for $p<0.05$. Countries are ranked in descending order of the ratio for informedness.

Table 3.9: Political membership and the behavioural dimension of political involvement, EB 49 (1998)

Country	Discussion			Persuasion		
	Never	Frequently	Ratio	Never	Frequently	Ratio
Portugal	5	47	9.4*	3	23	8.7*
Spain	8	40	4.9*	9	22	2.6*
Greece	4	18	4.2*	4	20	5.3*
Ireland	8	30	3.9*	9	22	2.6*
Italy	9	34	3.8*	11	22	1.9*
France	9	34	3.8*	12	38	3.1*
W. Germany	13	45	3.6*	10	42	4.0*
Belgium	16	57	3.5*	14	40	2.9*
Great Britain	15	51	3.5*	20	46	2.3*
Austria	17	53	3.1*	18	53	2.9*
Luxembourg	28	62	2.2*	37	58	1.6*
Netherlands	35	66	1.9*	37	50	1.3
Denmark	44	71	1.6*	58	71	1.2*
Finland	40	55	1.4*	46	53	1.1
Sweden	59	75	1.3*	63	62	1.0

Note: The figures are the average percentages of political membership for the highest and lowest categories of political involvement. The ratios are calculated between these two percentages. Asterisks signal ratios statistically significant for $p<0.05$. Countries are ranked in descending order of the ratio for discussions.

least involved in politics are to be found in South European countries and the smallest differences in Scandinavia.

In short, the various dimensions of psychological involvement with politics seem to be closely related to political membership. Individuals with more positive orientations towards politics, who are more informed about politics and who discuss political issues more frequently are more likely to join a political organisation.[28]

Another civic orientation that has received great attention in studies of associational behaviour is social trust. Some scholars have claimed that trust in others – especially in strangers – is a basic orientation that enables social co-operation and collective action, thus being one of the main indicators of social capital (Putnam 1993, 1995a and b, 2000, van Deth 1997, Stolle & Lewis 2002). However, the relation between social trust and associational membership has not been clearly established and several studies have shown the absence of a substantial correlation between them at the individual level (Newton 1999 and 2001, Norris 2002), even when analysing panel data (Claibourn & Martin 2000). Regardless of this, some researchers still argue that participation in associations promotes social trust and vice versa, and that this connection between the two will be larger when the association pursues public goods (Boix & Posner 1996, Herreros 2004). Undoubtedly, all political organisations – as defined here – pursue public goods, so if this relationship holds we should detect it in our analyses.

Table 3.10 explores the bivariate association between social trust and political membership in its different types and compares it with membership of any

Table 3.10. Associational membership and social trust, WVS 1990–93

	Any association	Political associations	Only traditional political associations	Only new political associations	Both types of political associations
Netherlands	0.18*	0.13*	-0.07*	0.06	0.17*
Denmark	0.17*	0.10*	0.02	0.04	0.08*
Italy	0.15*	0.09*	0.04	0.03	0.09*
Great Britain	0.14*	0.17*	0.12*	0.02	0.12*
Belgium	0.14*	0.11*	-0.01	0.07*	0.11*
France	0.14*	0.10*	0.05	0.05	0.08*
Finland	0.13*	0.10*	0.01	0.08	0.10*
Austria	0.12*	0.13*	0.06*	0.05	0.11*
Switzerland	0.12*	0.11*	0.02	0.06	0.13*
Ireland	0.12*	0.05	0.03	0.02	0.04
Norway	0.11*	0.09*	0.04	0.04	0.06*
United States	0.09*	0.15*	0.08*	0.02	0.11*
Canada	0.09*	0.12*	0.08*	0.02	0.06*
W. Germany	0.09*	0.03	-0.01	0.04	0.03
Iceland	0.08*	0.04	-0.07	0.01	0.16*
Sweden	0.07*	0.11*	0.02	0.01	0.10*
Portugal	0.07*	0.03	0.00	-0.01	0.09*
Spain	0.03	0.05*	0.03	0.03	0.04

Note: The figures are Pearson product-moment correlation coefficients between each type of associational membership (0-1) and social trust (0-1). Asterisks signal coefficients statistically significant for $p<0.05$.

association. Although social trust and political membership are related, the magnitude of this association is not really overwhelming. In several countries the correlation coefficient is not even statistically different from zero and, in many others, we find a quite small correlation. Secondly, it seems that trust is mostly related to multiple political memberships; in other words, trusting citizens tend to join multiple political organisations – traditional and new – simultaneously. But even in these cases, the effects of trust are modest.

Attitudes toward social change – radical, reformist or conservative – as well as value priorities – as measured by Inglehart's (1990) scale – have also been put in connection with political participation. Individuals' values are linked to their preferences and priorities over public issues and thus they can exert influence on their participatory decisions. *A priori*, we would expect that people with more extreme ideological positions – either because they wish radical changes to take place or for their conservatism – will have more incentives to organise politically. As to value priorities, we would expect postmaterialist citizens to be more likely to join new political organisations and less likely to join traditional ones, and vice versa with regard to materialist citizens.

Table 3.11 indicates that in some countries ideological orientations are relevant to understanding associative behaviour but these orientations are not relevant in many others. On the other hand, we also see that citizens with the most extreme political opinions are not the ones who most frequently join political organisations.

Table 3.11: Political membership and attitudes toward social change, WVS 1990–93

	Radical	Reformist	Conservative	F-Statistic
Spain	23	8	6	14.94*
Italy	29	24	12	7.25*
Portugal	5	16	14	1.91
France	17	17	13	1.04
Great Britain	21	37	27	6.97*
United States	27	41	36	5.51*
Canada	42	41	28	6.51*
Ireland	19	24	23	0.24
W. Germany	35	41	35	3.94*
Austria	36	39	34	1.04
Belgium	47	41	39	0.84
Netherlands	52	57	48	3.16*
Denmark	40	67	63	2.90*
Norway	46	61	55	2.27
Iceland	59	73	65	2.39
Finland	53	56	45	1.02
Sweden	71	71	63	1.23

Note: The figures are percentages of political membership. Asterisks signal statistically significant relationships for $p<0.05$ (F-statistic, analysis of variance).

Thus, in countries such as Spain and Italy, people with more radical ideals are the most likely to join political groups; while in Great Britain, the United States, Germany, the Netherlands and Denmark political reformists do so to a greater extent.

But, contrary to what we expected, postmaterialist citizens are more likely to join all sorts of political organisations (Table 3.12). As a matter of fact, these citizens are more willing to join traditional political groups than new political organisations. Nevertheless, in many countries, value priorities do not really determine the type of organisation citizens will join as, in many cases, materialist and postmaterialist individuals are not differentially inclined to join traditional – or for that matter, 'new' – political organisations.

Summary of findings

A descriptive analysis of the relation between the various SES attributes and social integration of individuals and their political membership points to the existence of varied patterns of social inequalities with regard to this form of political participation in western countries. Educational resources introduce substantial inequalities in most countries but they are smaller in Scandinavia and stronger in Southern Europe and the Anglo-Saxon nations. Income inequalities are generally linearly transformed into participatory inequalities, although in some Scandinavian countries this relation is curvilinear. And social class is also an important source of participatory inequalities: the middle classes are better equipped to become politically mobilised than groups that are inactive in the labour market or manual workers. Class differences are also wider in Southern Europe and the Anglo-Saxon countries.

Yet, not all social inequalities originate in the economic sphere and many are

Table 3.12: Political membership and value priorities, WVS 1990–93

	Political organisations			Traditional political orgs.			New political orgs.		
	Material	Mixed	Postmat	Material	Mixed	Postmat	Material	Mixed	Postmat
France	7	15	29	5	10	13	1	3	10
G. Britain	35	31	43	24	20	23	6	6	8
Germany	30	36	45	16	22	23	12	9	12
Italy	11	20	36	8	14	21	2	4	9
Netherlands	41	52	62	21	15	16	12	18	20
Denmark	64	63	76	56	46	45	4	4	6
Belgium	26	38	53	12	14	22	9	15	12
Spain	5	8	14	3	5	8	1	2	3
Ireland	16	22	36	9	14	26	6	5	7
U. States	31	37	47	18	20	22	6	8	9
Canada	30	36	46	13	21	23	9	8	7
Norway	51	58	73	43	46	45	2	4	9
Sweden	63	69	77	46	49	40	3	5	7
Iceland	69	71	82	51	58	64	5	3	1
Finland	44	51	62	32	39	48	3	5	3
Switzerland	18	28	41	15	19	21	2	6	9
Portugal	13	13	25	12	10	15	1	1	4
Austria	21	35	46	15	24	29	3	7	10

Note: The figures are percentages of political membership.

connected to aspects such as age, gender, and family situation. Thus, younger citizens are less likely to join political organisations, although this pattern is not common to all types of political groups; and gender differences are larger in Southern and Central Europe and for traditional political organisations (parties, unions and professional associations), while family obligations are detrimental to participation almost exclusively for South European and British women.

On the other hand, aspects related to citizens' social integration are also of some importance. The size of the community in which individuals live is related to some extent to their associative behaviour. In some countries, living in smaller communities facilitates joining political organisations while in others, big-city dwellers are more inclined to join political groups. Likewise, religious integration is connected to political membership in complex ways, as church attendance is not univocally related to this form of political participation, while religious memberships seem to promote political membership.

Finally, in regards to civic and political orientations, having an interest in politics and feeling well informed about politics are the two main aspects that are most systematically related to political membership and they are also the ones that best discriminate between joiners and non-joiners. Social trust, ideological positions and value priorities – though related to political membership – have effects that are cross-nationally less consistent and, generally, weaker.

Hence, the evidence examined thus far suggests three tentative conclusions: (1) socio-economic inequalities in political membership are greater in Southern

Europe and Anglo-Saxon countries; (2) the mechanisms through which these differences in SES transform into participatory inequalities vary greatly across countries; and (3) other than an interest in politics, civic and political orientations are not major determinants of political membership.

Up to this point we have explored the relevance of socio-economic resources, social integration and civic and political orientations for explaining political membership. But to what extent can these sets of factors adequately account for the patterns of political membership in western democracies? In the next section, we put this model to the test; in order to determine the impact of resources, integration and orientations on citizens' political membership.

THE INDIVIDUAL DETERMINANTS OF POLITICAL MEMBERSHIP: RESOURCES, INTEGRATION AND ATTITUDES

The purpose of this section is to contrast the individual-level model of SES, social integration and political orientations and check its validity for explaining political membership in western democracies. For this purpose, multivariate logistic binary and multinomial regression analyses are performed for each of the 17 western countries, in order to analyse the impact of these sets of factors, first, on general political membership, and, second, on the different types of political membership. This modelling strategy allows us to evaluate how well the model adapts to each country.

Table 3.13 shows the results of 17 binary logistic regression analyses for each western country included in the 1990–93 WVS.[29] The dependent variable adopts a value of 1 when the individual is a member of any political organisation and a value of 0 otherwise. The model includes all the variables explored on preceding pages and that are available in this survey.[30] This is, thus, a quite complete model of individual-level factors related to political membership. The model is described by the following equation:

$$Ln \left(\frac{P_i}{1 - P_i} \right) = ß_0 = \sum ß_k \, x_{ik} \, , \, i = 1,\ldots, n; \, k = 1, \ldots, k \quad \text{(Equation 3.1)}$$

where $P_i = Pr(y_i = 1)$, and Y is the dependent variable previously defined,
x_{ik} = are the characteristics of individual i, and
$ß_k$ = are the regression coefficients associated to variable k.

Notes to Table 3.13: All coefficients indicate the change (increase or decrease) in the logit of the odds ratio (p/1-p) of the dependent variable (member of any political organisation = 1, not member = 0) when the independent variable increases its value in one unit. Given that all ordinal and scale variables (with the only exception of age) have been recoded such that the minimum value is expressed by an 0 and the highest value by a 1, coefficients can be interpreted as the impact each variable has on the dependent variable when it changes from its minimum to its maximum value. Only coefficients significant at p<0.10 are shown. Coefficients significant at p<0.05 are underlined, and at p<0.01 in bold. The sign --- means that this variable was not included in the final model (see note 30). The probability of the Chi-square of the Hosmer and Lemeshow goodness-of-fit test is shown: values lower than a 0.05 indicate a bad fit of the model to the data. N.a. = variable not available in the sample.

Table 3.13: Political membership in 17 western countries (WVS 1990–93): multivariate binary logistic regressions

	WGE	AT	BEL	CAN	DK	ES	USA	FIN	FRA	GBR	NL	IRE	ICE	ITA	NOR	POR	SWE
Education	0.40	---	---	1.81	1.13	1.45	2.44	---	1.75	1.74	1.49	1.60	---	1.01	0.96	0.58	---
Income	---	2.84	---	---	6.02	---	---	---	---	---	3.60	n.a.	n.a.	---	---	---	---
Income (squared)	---	-2.19	---	---	-4.54	---	---	---	---	---	-2.94	n.a.	n.a.	---	---	---	---
Work situation (ref=+30h)																	
Works <30 hours	---	-0.46	---	---	-0.91	---	---	---	---	-0.72	---	---	---	---	---	---	---
Inactive	-0.47	-1.00	---	-0.92	-1.99	---	---	---	---	-1.14	-0.42	-1.04	-0.51	-0.51	-1.33	-1.00	-1.35
Unemployed	---	---	---	-0.85	---	---	-0.51	---	---	-0.95	---	-1.55	-0.82	-1.31	---	-0.91	-1.51
Age	---	0.02	0.07	0.06	0.07	0.20	---	0.20	0.19	0.08	0.10	0.12	0.10	0.10	0.11	---	0.11
Age (squared)	---	---	-0.00	-0.00	-0.00	-0.00	---	-0.00	-0.00	-0.00	-0.00	-0.00	-0.00	-0.00	-0.00	---	-0.00
Woman (ref=man)	-0.45	---	0.36	---	---	---	---	---	---	---	---	---	-0.41	-0.41	---	-0.63	---
With couple (ref=no couple)	---	---	---	---	-0.67	---	---	---	---	---	---	---	---	---	---	---	---
Size of community	---	---	---	---	---	---	-0.41	---	---	---	---	---	---	---	---	---	---
Church attendance	---	---	---	0.48	---	0.84	-0.58	n.a.	-0.41	---	---	-0.88	n.a.	-0.64	-0.54	0.48	0.57
Religious assoc. member	---	1.10	1.68	1.02	---	1.78	1.18	---	1.81	1.14	---	1.45	1.10	1.36	1.82	1.82	1.82
Interest in politics	---	0.74	0.74	0.59	---	0.87	0.60	0.38	---	0.64	0.75	0.79	0.35	1.18	0.47	1.07	0.52
Political efficacy	---	---	---	---	---	0.47	0.38	0.73	1.00	0.72	0.89	---	---	---	---	---	---
Social trust	---	0.35	---	---	---	0.43	---	0.36	0.49	0.49	0.36	n.a.	n.a.	0.47	-0.50	0.61	---
Value scale (ref=material.)																	
Mixed	0.39	---	0.36	---	---	0.51	---	---	0.71	---	---	---	---	0.38	0.38	0.97	---
Postmaterialist	0.82	0.82	0.87	---	---	0.85	---	---	1.41	---	---	0.75	---	0.75	0.77	---	---
Attitude social change (ref= conservative)																	
Radical	0.21	---	---	1.07	---	0.89	0.45	---	---	---	---	---	---	0.68	---	---	---
Reformist	---	---	---	0.54	---	---	---	---	---	-0.35	---	---	---	0.66	---	-0.41	---
Intercept	-0.96	-2.74	-2.72	-4.36	-2.27	-8.88	-3.09	-5.42	-8.61	-4.31	-5.48	-4.50	-4.89	-3.00	-2.50	-2.50	-1.06
Cox and Snell's R2	0.082	0.139	0.136	0.160	0.294	0.110	0.163	0.098	0.136	0.191	0.185	0.173	0.085	0.201	0.130	0.130	0.108
Nagelkerke's R2	0.111	0.189	0.184	0.217	0.410	0.232	0.219	0.131	0.227	0.263	0.249	0.259	0.122	0.301	0.176	0.222	0.155
Hosmer –Lemeshow test	0.688	0.068	0.030	0.279	0.813	0.459	0.941	0.360	0.444	0.095	0.086	0.446	0.939	0.128	0.746	0.121	0.416
Number of cases	1834	1158	2504	1493	834	1886	1398	535	848	1250	676	967	700	1634	1056	948	924

The results in Table 3.13 suggest that it is not very useful to use a single common model of individual-level factors to understand political membership in western countries. Although some common patterns emerge, several countries present their own specific traits and, for these, the proposed model is not well suited – especially in Belgium, Austria, the Netherlands and Great Britain. For this very reason, evaluating the relative importance of the three sets of individual factors considered in this model – resources, social integration, and attitudes – is somewhat simplistic because it varies across western nations. For example, in Belgium and Finland, socio-economic resources are not a fundamental source of inequality in political membership. Likewise, in Denmark, and to a similar degree in Iceland and Sweden, civic and political orientations do not help us much to understand who joins political organisations.

Nonetheless, we can indeed extract some common patterns. In the great majority of countries, education is a fundamental resource when joining political associations. As for other forms of political participation, more educated individuals are more likely to organise politically. Similarly, in most societies, age shows a negative curvilinear relation (inverted-U shape) with political membership, such that the people in their middle-ages (30 to 60 years-old) join political organisations the most, while the youngest and the eldest do so to a lesser extent.

Integration into religious associations is also linked to political membership in nearly all countries; whereas church attendance does not, in general terms, bear much of a relation to political membership – and, when it does, its impact is negative. Finally, interest in politics is also strongly related to political membership in practically all western countries. Citizens who show a greater interest in public affairs are also the ones to join political groups more frequently.

Yet, other results contradict some of the hypotheses put forward in previous sections. For example, income inequalities seem to have little impact in most western countries. And, where income is a source of political inequality, this relation is not linear and it is middle-income citizens who join political organisations the most. Equally, these results provide little evidence of a relation between the size of the community and political participation. And, what is even more interesting, wherever it does, its impact can go in several directions. Thus, in Denmark, the United States and Norway dwellers in big cities are more reluctant to join political groups, whereas in Spain and Portugal these are precisely the ones to join the most. Finally, social trust seems hardly relevant to explain political membership in western democracies. Contrary to what much of the social capital scholarship suggests, social trust is not necessary to generate collective action. In most nations, trusting individuals are not more likely to join political groups, nor are mistrusting citizens less likely to do so. Undoubtedly, these results support scepticism about the role attributed to this civic orientation recently, or at least to its individualistic and generalised conceptualisation.[31]

Once again, we look in some detail at the distinction between 'traditional' and 'new' political organisations. To this end, we compare different types of political membership, employing multinomial logistic regression for each of our 17 western democracies. Multinomial logistic regression enables a comparison of the effects of each variable on multiple categories of a dependent variable (Agresti 1990).

We have, thus, divided respondents into four categories: (1) individuals who are not members of any political organisation; (2) members of traditional political groups only; (3) members of new political groups only; and (4) members of both traditional and new political organisations. The distribution into each of the categories is presented in Table 3.14.

The multinomial logistic model is described by the following equation:[32]

$$\text{Ln} \left(\frac{P_{ir}}{P_{il}} \right) = \beta_{0r} + \sum \beta_{kr} \, x_{ik}, \quad i = 1, ..., n; \, k = 1, ..., K; \, r = 1, 2, 3, 4$$

(Equation 3.2)

where $P_{ir} = \text{Pr}(y_i = r)$, and Y is the previously defined variable,
x_{ik} = are the characteristics of individual i, and
β_{kr} = are the regression coefficients associated to variable k for category r, and
r = 1 is the reference category ('not a member of any political group').

The results of the multinomial models for the 17 countries are shown in Tables 3.15, 3.16 and 3.17.[33] A first glance through the three tables reveals that no variable is statistically significant in all countries for any of the contrasts with the

Table 3.14: The distribution of the dependent variable: types of political membership, WVS 1990–93

	Not a member	Traditional	New	Both	N of cases
Iceland	28	57	3	12	702
Sweden	31	46	5	18	1047
Denmark	36	46	5	13	1030
Norway	43	45	4	8	1239
Netherlands	46	16	18	20	1017
Finland	47	41	4	8	588
Canada	61	21	8	10	1730
United States	61	20	8	11	1836
Belgium	62	15	13	10	2792
W. Germany	63	21	10	6	2101
Austria	64	24	7	5	1460
Great Britain	67	21	6	6	1484
Ireland	77	15	5	3	1000
Italy	77	15	5	3	2010
France	83	9	5	3	1002
Portugal	86	11	2	1	1185
Spain	92	5	2	1	2637

Note: The figures are row percentages. Countries are ranked in descending order of political membership.

Table 3.15: Political membership in 17 western democracies. Multinomial logistic regressions (contrast: only traditional vs not member)

Variables	WGE	AT	BEL	CAN	DK	ES	USA	FIN	FRA	GBR	NL	IRE	ICE	ITA	NOR	POR	SWE
Education			**0.10**	**0.18**	**0.1**	**0.12**	**0.24**		**0.21**	**0.16**				**0.13**	<u>0.05</u>	<u>0.09</u>	
Income			0.07	**0.14**			**0.12**			**0.13**		**0.24**		**0.19**	**0.09**		0.05
Work situation (ref=works + 30h)																	
Works <30 h. or self-employed		**-0.84**		**-0.57**	**-1.04**		**-0.38**			**-0.61**		<u>-0.69</u>					**-1.85**
Inactive	**-1.24**	**-1.61**	**-0.50**	**-1.70**	**-2.69**	**-0.85**	**-0.68**	**-1.01**	**-1.07**	**-1.50**	**-0.70**	**-1.97**		**-1.53**	**-1.21**	**-1.31**	**-1.46**
Unemployed		<u>-1.98</u>		-0.59							-1.73			<u>-1.25</u>	-1.38		-2.3
Age	0.01	0.02		0.02			0.02		0.03	0.02		0.02	<u>-0.01</u>	<u>0.01</u>	0.02	0.03	0.01
Woman (ref = man)	**-0.92**	**-0.66**	**-0.45**	**-0.38**		<u>-0.46</u>	**-0.72**		<u>-0.61</u>	<u>-0.38</u>	<u>-0.84</u>		-0.33		-0.22	-0.53	-0.30
No couple (ref=with couple)		<u>-0.32</u>	**-0.55**		**-0.68**	<u>-0.51</u>			<u>-0.65</u>		-0.58						-0.53
Size of community			-0.10		<u>-0.09</u>	0.16				0.08					<u>-0.10</u>	<u>0.10</u>	
Church attendance				0.14			0.09		<u>0.14</u>								
Interest in politics (ref=none)																	
Very interested	**1.52**	**1.21**	**1.06**	**1.08**		**2.22**	**2.03**		0.77	**0.86**	**1.62**	**1.71**	<u>0.75</u>	**2.89**	**1.19**	**1.66**	
Somewhat interested	**0.96**	**0.87**	**0.68**	**0.85**		**1.39**	**1.78**		0.59	**0.74**	**1.14**	<u>0.76</u>	<u>0.56</u>	**1.55**	0.57	**1.19**	
Not very interested		0.50				0.68	**1.50**				<u>1.00</u>			0.64			
Political efficacy		-0.11							0.19	**0.16**	0.19		<u>-0.16</u>			0.17	
Social trust		0.27					<u>0.30</u>			**0.53**							
Value scale (ref= mixed)																	
Materialist		<u>-0.50</u>		-0.43	0.42					0.40							
Postmaterialist			<u>0.41</u>					0.40				0.57				0.48	
Attitude social change (ref=reformist)																	
Radical					-0.97	<u>0.81</u>											
Conservative		-0.41															
Intercept	**-1.69**	**-0.86**	**-1.66**	**-3.19**		**-5.16**	**-5.48**	**-1.84**	**-3.99**	**-4.85**	<u>-1.78</u>	**-4.51**	**1.56**	**-4.04**	**-1.74**	**-4.64**	
N of cases in the model	2101	1460	2792	1730	1030	2637	1836	588	1002	1484	1017	1000	702	2010	1239	1185	1047

Note: Only coefficients significant at p<0.10 are shown. Coefficients significant at p<0.05 are underlined, and at p<0.01 in bold. The sign --- means that this variable was not included in the final model (see note 30).

Table 3.16: Political membership in 17 western democracies. Multinomial logistic regressions (contrast: only new vs not member)

Variables	WGE	AT	BEL	CAN	DK	ES	USA	FIN	FRA	GBR	NL	IRE	ICE	ITA	NOR	POR	SWE
Education	**0.14**	<u>0.11</u>			**0.17**	0.14	**0.22**			<u>0.14</u>	**0.14**	**0.23**		0.14	**0.19**	<u>0.18</u>	---
Income	**-0.11**											<u>0.2</u>					---
Work situation (ref=works + 30h)																	
Works <30 h. or self-employed		0.67															
Inactive		<u>0.77</u>	0.54														
Unemployed			0.71		1.08		-1.23			0.96		0.82		0.93		-2.19	-1.50
Age							0.06			0.01				<u>-0.03</u>			
Woman (ref = man)	**0.65**	**1.28**	**0.77**	**0.59**			**0.88**			<u>0.73</u>	**1.14**	**1.11**				<u>0.80</u>	
No couple (ref=with couple)	-0.30				-1.24						-0.66						
Size of community	-0.11	<u>-0.17</u>		-0.16		0.27	-0.15										
Church attendance	0.10		0.10	0.18						0.17				0.11			
Interest in politics (ref=none)																	
Very interested	**1.09**	<u>0.75</u>	**1.17**	**1.04**						<u>0.92</u>	**1.50**	<u>1.08</u>	**2.31**	1.90		1.38	
Somewhat interested	0.65	0.57	<u>0.44</u>	1.02						<u>0.87</u>	0.77						
Not very interested	0.73		0.59	0.90							0.85						
Political efficacy								<u>0.37</u>	<u>0.29</u>								
Social trust	0.44		0.44					1.19									
Value scale (ref= mixed)																	
Materialist		<u>-1.11</u>	-0.57														
Postmaterialist		<u>0.50</u>				0.65			1.07	0.53					1.18		
Attitude social change (ref=reformist)																	
Radical	<u>0.43</u>					0.94											
Conservative	<u>-0.56</u>	<u>-0.77</u>		-0.53												0.86	
Intercept	**-2.09**	**-4.27**	**-2.61**	**-2.89**	**-3.69**	**-7.13**	**-4.43**	**-6.63**	<u>-3.76</u>	**-5.06**	**-3.96**	**-7.95**	<u>-4.17</u>	**-4.03**	**-5.38**	**-5.71**	<u>-2.27</u>
N of cases in the model	2101	1460	2792	1730	1030	2637	1836	588	1002	1484	1017	1000	702	2010	1239	1185	1047

Note: Only coefficients significant at p<0.10 are shown. Coefficients significant at p<0.05 are underlined, and at p<0.01 in bold. The sign --- means that this variable was not included in the final model (see note 30).

Table 3.17: Political membership in 17 western democracies. Multinomial logistic regressions (contrast: traditional and new vs not member)

Variables	WGE	AT	BEL	CAN	DK	ES	USA	FIN	FRA	GBR	NL	IRE	ICE	ITA	NOR	POR	SWE
Education	**0.16**			**0.23**	**0.25**	**0.28**	**0.26**	0.19		**0.26**	**0.16**			0.18	**0.19**		
Income		0.11		**0.16**			0.12	-0.20			**0.11**	0.19					
Work situation (ref=works + 30h)																	
Works <30 h. or self-employed					-1.02												
Inactive	**-0.83**	-0.92		-0.90	**-3.03**	-0.91	-0.60	**-1.16**		-1.10	-0.88	-1.18		-0.99	**-2.34**	-1.82	-0.86
Unemployed																	-1.73
Age	**0.02**			0.03	0.03	0.03	0.02	**0.04**	**0.04**	**0.04**	**0.05**	**0.04**			**0.04**	-0.05	**0.02**
Woman (ref = man)						-0.75	**0.61**	0.66		0.67	0.53	**1.74**	0.72				
No couple (ref=with couple)	-0.42		**-0.85**					-1.25	-0.84						**-1.65**		**-0.55**
Size of community				-0.09	-0.13	0.17								-0.26		0.39	
Church attendance	0.11		0.11	**0.18**						0.26			0.20	-0.23			
Interest in politics (ref=none)																	
Very interested	**1.39**	**2.11**	**1.98**	**1.15**	**1.16**	**1.87**	**2.68**		**2.88**	**1.79**	**1.95**	**3.77**	**2.47**	**3.21**	**19.9**	**3.62**	**2.28**
Somewhat interested		0.92	**0.98**	0.61	**1.45**		1.31		1.53	**1.42**	**1.22**	**2.05**	**2.13**	1.65	**18.6**		**1.33**
Not very interested			0.41		1.11		0.90					1.92	1.35		**17.8**		0.78
Political efficacy		**0.20**	0.13		0.13		0.13	**0.48**		**0.47**	**0.30**	**0.53**		0.28	**0.30**	0.64	
Social trust		**0.74**	**0.54**				**0.53**	0.92		0.66	**0.68**		**0.80**			1.54	
Value scale (ref= mixed)																	
Materialist																	
Postmaterialist	0.53		**0.75**	**0.82**	0.63	0.69		0.79	**1.17**	0.74					0.81		**1.00**
Attitude social change (ref=reformist)																	
Radical	0.94								1.48								
Conservative	-0.47				-0.63												
Intercept	**-3.56**	**-5.45**	**-2.35**	**-5.42**	**-4.38**	**-8.55**	**-7.44**	**-4.95**	**-7.01**	**-7.05**	**-6.34**	**-11.6**	-2.32	**-5.32**		**-6.59**	**-2.22**
N of cases in the model	2101	1460	2792	1730	1030	2637	1836	588	1002	1484	1017	1000	702	2010	1239	1185	1047

Note: Only coefficients significant at p<0.10 are shown. Coefficients significant at p<0.05 are underlined, and at p<0.01 in bold. The sign — means that this variable was not included in the final model (see note 30).

category of respondents with 'no political membership', although some of them are relevant in most nations – e.g. gender, age, education, working situation and interest in politics. Some of the variables show interesting patterns, especially across the different categories of the dependent variable. For example, women are less likely to join traditional political organisations in most of the countries but are more likely to join 'new' political groups and, in some countries, are also more likely to become members of both types of organisations. Similarly, the working situation shows a complex relation with the phenomenon of political membership. While being in any situation other than working for 30 hours a week or more decreases the likelihood of being a member of traditional political organisations, and of being a member of both traditional and new, in a number of countries, the opposite is true for membership of new political organisations. In some cases, being inactive in the labour market, or being unemployed, increases the likelihood of joining 'new' political organisations.

If we turn to consider political attitudes and values, we find that interest in politics is, by far, the most relevant cognitive factor. However, it has a greater impact on the probability of joining traditional groups and an even greater one on the likelihood of joining both types of groups, than it does for membership of new political organisations. It seems, then, that membership of new political organisations could be thought of as less politicised or, alternatively, that citizens involved in these types of associations are more alienated from what is usually thought of as 'politics'.

It is also interesting to note that social trust is generally not relevant in the explanation of most types of political membership. It has, however, more of an effect when considering simultaneous membership of traditional and new political groups. Given that this is the least populated category, its impact has to be considered limited in absolute terms.

With regard to values, we see that whether citizens are materialist, postmaterialist or a mixture of the two is not too important for joining political groups. However, it has more of an effect for the prediction of simultaneous membership in traditional and new organisations. In the case of multiple political memberships, being a postmaterialist citizen increases the likelihood of joining both types of groups in several western countries. In the few cases where it is statistically significant, the pattern of the effect of the value index is consistent with that expected: membership of traditional groups is associated to materialist values (except in France), whilst membership of new and of both types simultaneously is related to postmaterialism. Values are, however, rarely relevant in South European countries. The patterns of effects of other variables remain the same as in the general model of political membership discussed in Table 3.13.

In general terms, a conclusion we could derive from these results is that the individual determinants of membership of new political groups usually show a greater variation across countries than the other two types of membership (membership of traditional political groups, and membership of both traditional and new political organisations). Thus, it seems that the former type of behaviour is more heterogeneous cross-nationally than the latter. This means that it is not advisable to impose a single explanatory model of the individual-level determinants of new political membership for all western countries, while it seems more reasonable to propose a general model of traditional political membership.

In summary, as for other forms of political participation, political membership is unequally distributed across different social groups. Socio-economic resources help adequately to distinguish who will join political organisations and who is less likely to do so. However, although socio-economic resources are important, they are so to a different extent, depending on the type of political membership and the country. Membership of new political organisations is less related to socio-economic resources and more so to attitudinal aspects such as an interest in politics and value preferences.

THE EXPLANATORY LIMITS OF INDIVIDUAL-LEVEL MODELS

Learning about citizens' attributes, the resources they have at their disposal, their living conditions, their attitudes and orientations, as well as the social networks in which they are embedded, is certainly fundamental to gaining a better understanding of who joins political organisations and what might drive them to do so. Yet, as I will show in the remaining pages of this chapter, explanatory models of political participation and, specifically, of political membership that are limited to individual-level factors are critically incomplete if we also wish to explain cross-national differences.

So far, all the analyses have shown that the impact of resources, social integration, and orientations does vary across countries. However, single-level techniques do not let us ascertain whether cross-national differences in the levels of political membership are explained by these individual attributes. And, as we have discussed in Chapters one and two, cross-national variations are both one of the most interesting, and least analysed aspects in the field of participation.

Some scholars have claimed that differences in the levels of political participation in western nations are related to their citizens' characteristics (Almond & Verba 1989, Inglehart 1990, Dalton 1996, Inglehart 1997, Torcal & Montero 1999), whether socio-economic or attitudinal. It is plausible that, in some countries, citizens are more inclined to join political organisations because they are more educated, have more social or economic resources and free-time, because they trust their fellow citizens more or they are more interested in politics. In the past, cross-national variations in participation have been attributed to varying degrees of social and economic modernisation (see, for example, Roller & Wessels 1996, Wessels 1997): participation is more common wherever public and universal education is more developed and the levels of economic development and well-being are greater.

Although formulated differently, modernisation explanations are one form of compositional explanation, as they only make sense if the effects of modernisation are linked to citizens' characteristics. Thus, for example, if the extension of universal education is at the root of higher levels of participation in certain countries, this must be because greater proportions of their citizenry attain higher degrees. Hence, once we control for levels of education and other similar variables across nations, country variations should be explained away.

With multilevel models,[34] we can tell whether significant cross-national differences persist once we take into account respondents' social and attitudinal characteristics. We will estimate a single model for all countries, while also estimating the variation of each country around the general model and the variance coefficient of the higher-level units.[35] Consequently, if, after controlling for all individual-level variables, the country of residence were not relevant to determining an individual's likelihood of political membership, then the variance coefficient at the higher level (countries) will not be statistically significant. In the opposite case, we will have to conclude that cross-national differences in political membership persist once we take into account their citizens' social and attitudinal composition.

Table 3.18 shows the results of the multilevel analysis of political membership.[36] A step-wise procedure of the introduction of sets of variables allows evaluation of the relative reduction in unexplained variance.

Thus, the empty model only estimates the intercept and the variation across countries and is described by Equation 3.3. Models 1a to 1c estimate the intercept, the variation across countries in the average level of political membership, as well as the effect of the several individual-level variables (Equation 3.4). Model 1a only incorporates variables related to individuals' socio-economic resources; model 1b introduces also factors related to the respondent's social status and integration, while model 1c includes as well the most relevant attitudes and orientations. Lastly, model 2 incorporates, as a reference point, the estimation of the random slopes for certain individual-level variables that showed differential effects across countries in previous single-level analyses (Tables 3.13 to 3.17). In this latter model, all parameters estimated in model 1c are included but, in addition, we are able to estimate the variation across countries around the average coefficients of education, income, church attendance, size of community and gender (Equation 3.5).[37]

$$\text{Logit } (\pi_{ij}) = \gamma_0 + u_{0j} \qquad \text{(Equation 3.3)}$$
$$\text{Logit } (\pi_{ij}) = \gamma_0 + \sum \beta_h x_{hij} + u_{0j} \qquad \text{(Equation 3.4)}$$
$$\text{Logit } (\pi_{ij}) = \gamma_0 + \sum \gamma_h x_{hij} + u_{0j} + \sum u_{hj} x_{hij} \qquad \text{(Equation 3.5)}$$

where, i = individual i, for I = 1, 2, 3, ..., n;
j = country j, for J = 1, 2, 3, ..., N;
$\pi_{ij} = p_{ij}/1-p_{ij}$, and $p_{ij} = \text{prob}(y_{ij}=1)$, for y=1 (member of a political organisation);
γ = average parameters estimated at the country level (level 2)
β = parameters estimated at the individual level (level 1)
x = variables measured at the individual level (level 1)
u_j = parameters of the variation or error across countries associated to parameters γ

Table 3.18: The individual determinants of political membership: multilevel analyses

Variables	Model 0	Model 1a	Model 1b	Model 1c	Model 2
Fixed parameters (indiv. level)					
Intercept	-0.549	**-1.426**	**-2.131**	**-2.654**	**-2.647**
Education		**1.029**	**1.268**	**0.938**	**0.923**
Income		**1.410**	**1.188**	**1.148**	**1.349**
Income (squared)		**-0.549**	-0.405	<u>-0.466</u>	<u>-0.572</u>
Working situation (ref= +30h)					
Works <30 hours		**-0.174**	**-0.227**	**-0.257**	**-0.239**
Inactive		**-0.586**	**-0.674**	**-0.688**	**-0.661**
Unemployed		**-0.630**	**-0.577**	**-0.572**	**-0.521**
Age			**3.707**	**3.413**	**3.332**
Age (squared)			**-3.495**	**-3.146**	**-3.049**
Woman (ref=man)			**-0.205**	**-0.111**	n.s.
With couple (ref=without couple)			n.s.	0.079	n.s.
Size of community			**-0.171**	**-0.225**	**-0.254**
Church attendance			**-0.235**	**-0.187**	<u>-0.279</u>
Religious membership			**1.127**	**1.079**	**1.074**
Interest in politics				**0.559**	**0.566**
Political efficacy				**0.273**	**0.268**
Social trust				**0.130**	**0.124**
Value scale (ref=materialist)					
Mixed				<u>0.129</u>	**0.148**
Postmaterialist				**0.489**	**0.516**
Attitude social change (ref= conservative)					
Radical				<u>0.218</u>	**0.209**
Reformist				**0.149**	**0.148**
Random parameters (country lev.)					
uij ~ N (0, Ωu): Ωu	0.85	0.67	0.59	0.59	0.35-1.36†
u0ij [intercept] *	0.85 (0.92)	0.67 (0.82)	0.59 (0.77)	0.59 (0.77)	1.36 (1.16)
u1ij [education]					0.12 (0.34)
u2ij [income]					0.24 (0.49)
u3ij [church attendance]					0.13 (0.37)
u4ij [size of community]					0.17 (0.41)
u5ij [gender]					0.06 (0.24)
Intraclass correlation +	0.21	0.17	0.15	0.15	0.10-0.29†
R2 dichotomous§	0	0.09	0.16	0.19	0.20-0.16†
% unexplained level-2 variance	21	15	13	12	8-24†
Number of cases (number countries)	23,754 (15)	16,063 (15)	16,063 (15)	16,063 (15)	16,063 (15)

Source: Own elaboration from 1990–93 WVS data.
All coefficients indicate the change (increase or decrease) in the logit of the odds ratio (p/1-p) of the dependent variable (member of any political organisation = 1, not member = 0) when the independent variable increases its value in one unit. Given that all ordinal and scale variables (with the only exception of age) have been recoded such that the minimum value is expressed by an 0 and the highest value

The results shown in Table 3.18 lead to several conclusions.[38] On the one hand, we see that model 1, in its three variants, improves our capacity to account for individual-level variations in political membership at the same time that it substantially reduces the unexplained cross-national variations (from 21 per cent in model 0 to 12 per cent in model 1c).[39] This means that some of the differences we find in the levels of political membership of western democracies are due to the diverse social composition of their populations.

Thus, these three models take into account the 'compositional' effect, in line with Roller & Wessels' (1996) and Wessels' (1997) arguments about the impact of varying levels of socio-economic modernisation. Nevertheless, it is also important to underline that political attitudes and orientations contribute very little or nothing to explaining variation across countries, since the intra-class correlation, as well as the total country-level variation of models 1b and 1c are of the same magnitude, and the difference in the percentage of unexplained variation attributable to countries is equivalent for both models. Thus, while socio-economic factors (resources and social integration) are, to a great extent, at the source of the different levels of political membership we find in western democracies, political and civic attitudes and orientations are somewhat irrelevant in explaining variations across countries in this form of political participation. In other words, North European citizens are more likely to join political organisations because they have more resources available and because they are socially more integrated into their communities than their South European fellows but not because their political culture is more apt to participation in politics.

Furthermore, the major impact of traditional sources of inequality in politics – age, income and education – is especially relevant; as well as the clearly curvilinear effect of age (Graph 3.5) and the slightly curvilinear effect of income.

Finally, these results (model 2) confirm our previous finding that a single model of political membership is not well suited for all western countries. When we allow for random variation of the coefficients of some of the main variables related to resources and social integration, we see that the variation around these parameters is, indeed, substantial.[40] For this reason, it is of some interest to look at this model more in detail.

As we can see in the lower section of Table 3.18, the variance parameters of the random coefficients are such that, in the cases of church attendance, size of community and gender, the effect of these variables can be positive, negative or nonexistent, depending on the country.[41] These results confirm those obtained in

by a 1, coefficients can be interpreted as the impact each variable has on the dependent variable when it changes from its minimum to its maximum value. Only coefficients significant at $p<0.10$ are shown. Coefficients significant at $p<0.05$ are underlined, and at $p<0.01$ in bold.

* For variation parameters, coefficients represent the component expressed in variance terms, and in brackets in standard deviations.

+ Proportion of the total residual variance attributable to country variance.

§ R2 for multilevel binomial regressions (see the details of its calculation and interpretation in Snijders & Bosker 1999: 225–6).

† The first value corresponds to the computation with all random coefficients variables in their maximum value (1), and the second to the same calculation with the variables fixed at their minimum value (0).

Graph 3.5: Age and political membership: predicted probabilities (model 2)

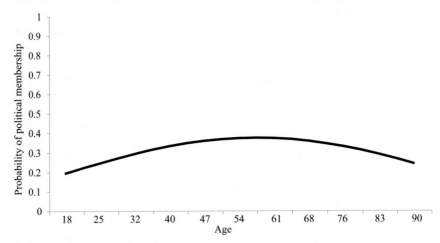

the preceding single-level analyses shown in Table 3.13, where the different effects of these factors on political membership were already apparent.

On the other hand, the correlations between the variances of these five variables and the intercept lead to other very interesting conclusions (see Table 3.19). Firstly, when inspecting the correlations with the intercept, we notice that the magnitude of the impact of income, church attendance and, especially, size of community and education increases as the size of the intercept coefficient decreases. In other words, those countries where citizens[42] join political organisations more are also the countries where these four factors introduce more political inequality.[43] Thus, other things being equal, a person with low levels of education

Graph 3.6: The varying impact of educational inequalities (model 2)

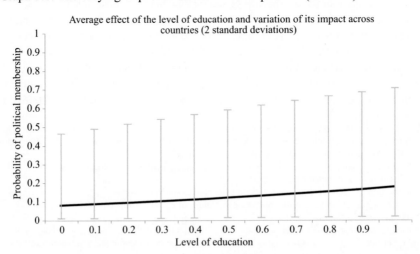

Average effect of the level of education and variation of its impact across countries (2 standard deviations)

Table 3.19: Variance correlations of individual-level variables (model 2 of random effects)

	Intercept	Education	Income	Church attendance	Size of community
Education	-0.798				
Income	-0.410	0.752			
Church attendance	-0.390	0.213	-0.237		
Size of community	-0.795	0.314	-0.015	0.167	
Gender	0.447	0.016	0.235	-0.219	-0.775

in Sweden is much more likely to join a political organisation than a person with those exact same attributes in Spain; however, that Swede is substantially less likely to join a political organisation than a highly educated fellow Swede, whereas the lowly educated Spaniard is almost as (un)likely to join any political group than a highly educated Spaniard. Graph 3.6 illustrates this varying impact of education, income, church attendance and size of the community with the example of the effect of education.

Finally, the strong correlation between the variance parameters of education and income indicates that the effect of both variables varies jointly across countries. Hence, in countries where education is a discriminating factor for political membership, so is family income and vice versa.

Therefore, models 1c and 2 in Table 3.18 are the best fit to understand the real impact the different individual-level factors have on political membership in western countries. Nonetheless, even such a complete individual-level model as this one does not contribute much to explaining the cross-national variations we initially detected. Consequently, it is necessary to consider systematically factors related to the social and political context in which citizens live.

CONCLUSIONS

This chapter has discussed the various mechanisms that link individual resources, SES and political orientations to political membership. The results have shown that the extent to which individuals' resources and social position are transformed into political inequalities substantially varies across western democracies. Education is a valuable resource in most countries but the impact of income and social class is restricted to a limited number of countries. Other aspects related to the SES of individuals also have a varying impact. For example, gender differences and family obligations are much more determining in Southern Europe than in other western countries. Likewise, citizens' social integration in their communities is not univocally linked to political membership. For example, the size of the community may foster or hinder political membership, while the effect of religious integration seems to be positive only through its structural component: membership of religious associations. Having an interest in politics is crucial for joining a political organisation in most nations, while other forms of psychological involvement with politics, social trust, and social values have a minimal effect. And, in this regard, the impact of the political culture of citizens is fairly limited, both within and across western democracies.

On the other hand, the analyses shown put into question the prominent role usually allotted to political attitudes and 'political culture'. In regards to membership of political organisations (with the exception of having an interest in politics), social values, civic attitudes and political orientations play a rather limited role in both accounting for within-country and cross-national variations in political membership. In contrast, socio-economic resources and SES stand out as comparatively much more relevant. And, in fact, their impact is notorious in most countries and interacts substantially with the context. As we have seen, and unlike common expectations, socio-economic resources are more discriminating in countries with higher levels of political membership. Thus, education and income introduce greater inequalities in organised political participation precisely in those places where citizens join political organisations the most.

Finally, our results suggest that, though important, the social and attitudinal characteristics of citizens are insufficient to adequately explain why some citizens join political organisations and others do not. And, especially, they do not help us much in understanding why are there such large differences in political membership across western nations.

Once we have shown that individual-level variables alone are insufficient to account for the large cross-national variations in political membership, the next chapters turn to consider the impact that contextual factors have on citizens' inclination to join political organisations in western democracies. In particular, we will focus on the extent to which the participation opportunities that political systems provide, as well as the patterns of political mobilisation by organisations, contribute to further our understanding of these vast differences in political membership among western citizens.

NOTES

1   See MacKuen, Stimson & Erikson (2003) for a suggestive analysis of the implication of different levels of public attentiveness to politics for the policy process.

2   See the interesting description that Huntington & Nelson (1976: 82) give of the Indian case and its deviation with respect to the common pattern of more educated individuals participating more in electoral politics (vote, electoral rallies and campaign contributions).

3   McPherson's (1981) analyses, using data from Booth & Babchuk, on the dynamic of voluntary associations' turnover, points to the possibility that social inequalities in membership are due to the lower rates of association-joining of the less well off and, to a lesser extent, to the higher rates of leaving them. Hence, people with more resources will get involved in a greater number of organisations during their whole life. McPherson points to the more than likely differential recruitment by organisations as the possible cause, and to the nature of the social networks into which different individuals are integrated.

4   However, the study by Oliver (1999) shows that the relationship between the more proxi-
    mate context and participation is more complicated than it may at first seem. His results
    show that, although the more privileged tend to participate more, it is the more socially het-
    erogeneous local communities that promote higher relative levels of participation.

5   Unfortunately, the items for education in the WVS and the EBs are more than problematic.
    Instead of asking for the highest degree attained, respondents were asked for their age when
    they finished full-time education. In addition, in the WVS, several countries employed a
    completely different item to gather information about education. The various item forms
    were recoded into a meaningful division between primary, secondary and university studies.

6   Educational differences have also been analysed for each type of political organisation ('tra-
    ditional' and 'new'). The results are not shown because they generally follow the same pat-
    tern. The only relevant exceptions are to be found in Belgium, where educational levels are
    irrelevant for membership of 'new' political organisations, and in Sweden and Austria, where
    the effect of education is the reverse for members of 'traditional' political organisations (high-
    er percentages among the less educated), clearly due to the impact of union membership.

7   The item on income was not included for Iceland. The graphs show the estimated trend lines.

8   Following Parry, Moyser & Day (1992) I have distinguished five groups to measure social
    class: manual and technical workers, traditional middle classes and owners, non-manual rou-
    tine workers, new middle classes, and inactive/non-working individuals. The latter category
    is not, strictly speaking, a social class but is, nonetheless, a relevant group for this study.

9   It has been impossible to use an equivalent variable with the 1990–93 WVS because the item
    that measures occupation is inadequate for class analysis. Besides, the variable on occupa-
    tion was different for three of the countries included in the analyses (Sweden, Iceland and
    Switzerland) and no information on the specificities of these country-specific variables was
    available in the documentation.

10 Results are very similar even when we distinguish 'new' and 'traditional' political organisa-
    tions. The only variation worth mentioning is that inactive groups are not always the less
    engaged in new political organisations, since non-manual workers are the least inclined to
    join NSMOs. This happens in half of the fifteen EU countries included (Denmark, Italy,
    France, Ireland, Luxembourg, Great Britain, Finland and Sweden).

11 Parties, trade unions and professional associations, human-rights organisations, environmen-
    tal groups, and consumers' organisations.

12 In Graph 3.2, age has been grouped in five years to avoid excessive variations due to the
    small number of cases for each single age. In any case, the results are the same when age is
    not aggregated in five-year groups. All lines are estimated polynomic trend-lines that adjust
    the average values for each five-year range.

13 Results not shown due to space limitations. They can be found in Morales (2004: Table 4.5).

14 Another social attribute that is also a barrier to participation similar to gender in many countries
    is race. However, given the limited extension of important racial differences in most European
    countries, I have opted not to include this variable in the empirical analyses that follow.

15 These scholars suggest that the gender gap in political membership is due to the different
    preferences of men and women when joining organisations and not so much due to a differ-
    ent perception of what is political and what is not. On the other hand, gender differences in
    participation are fundamentally related to the political arena, as women are equally as active

as men in the non-political domain.

16 In many cases, although percentage differences are large, they are not significant, due to the reduced number of cases in each category.

17 Dahl & Tufte (1973) present a magnificent summary of the main arguments that relate community size and democracy along the history of democratic theory.

18 Oliver (2001: 41) offers an additional hypothesis: big cities also hinder political participation due to the greater opportunity costs it entails. In big cities the opportunities and the range of choice of alternative activities is much greater than in smaller communities, where leisure supply is much more limited.

19 Oliver (1999 and 2001) also studies other issues related to the type of community and participation. For example, he analyses the effect of the degree of socio-economic segregation on local participation and he argues that the high levels of racial and class segregation introduced by the process of suburbanisation in the United States have as a main consequence the decrease in interest and in participation in local public affairs.

20 Unfortunately, the 1990–93 WVS data is problematic for some nations. There are no data on community size for Iceland and Finland; in Switzerland, the variable was coded differently; in the Netherlands and Canada, the sample did not include communities of the smallest size; and in Norway, Sweden and Austria the higher value groups several categories.

21 The graph shows the estimated polynomic trend.

22 When we check with the data of EB 49 (from 1998) the conclusion is similar: there is no single pattern. The results from EB 49 are not shown in this case because the variable on community size is not standardised for the 15 countries. An exploration of the CID dataset yields similar results: differing patterns across countries in the relation between political membership and size of community. For example, in the Netherlands and West Germany, political membership is higher in the smaller towns and rural areas; whereas in many other countries the pattern is the reverse or more complex. Likewise, the EB 62.2 of 2004 shows that in countries such as Austria, France and Spain political membership is substantially higher in bigger cities than in smaller communities, whereas again in the Netherlands the opposite is true, and in many other countries the relationship is unclear.

23 See extensive summaries of the literature relating religiousness and political behaviour in Norris & Inglehart (2004) and Norris (2002).

24 It is common to find the claim that religious denomination or congregation, in terms of the type of faith practised, has an independent effect on political participation. Thus, some scholars argue that Catholic, Orthodox, and Muslim faiths hinder the political participation of their followers, due to the moral values they proclaim and to the hierarchical structuring of their religious institutions (Putnam 1993). However, Djupe & Grant (2001) show that 'faith' as such has no impact on political participation and that – if anything – it is the level of political activism of different congregations and of their spiritual leaders that determines the degree of political involvement of parishioners. In addition, several pieces of research (Bréchon 1999, Halman & Pettersson 1999 and de Hart 2001) show that faith in itself has no relevant effect on associational membership. For this reason, I pay no special attention to denomination in the following pages.

25 Only in a few countries is the relationship between church attendance and political membership the same for both types of organisations (Spain, Ireland, Italy and Switzerland).

26 In Morales (2004: 208–10) more evidence in support of this claim can be found.

27 Questions on political information and media consumption are only available for EB 49 (1998), as the WVS 1990–93 does not include any item that measures the cognitive dimension of political involvement. EB 49 also includes an item on the subjective feeling of political knowledge but, unfortunately very few respondents answered positively and we exclude it from these analyses. In any case, the correlation between the subjective evaluations of informedness and of objective political knowledge is very high for all EU countries (between 0.6 and 0.8).

28 As we will see in following sections, the lack of indicators for these three dimensions in the 1990–93 WVS prevents us from performing multivariate analyses with all of them.

29 Switzerland was not included in the analyses because the Swiss questionnaire did not include several of the political associations that are used to compute the dependent variable, and thus the results would not be equivalent to those of other countries.

30 The specification of each of the 17 models has been done on a country basis and following a step-wise procedure. In a first step, all variables were included in the analyses, their coefficients were evaluated, and only those statistically significant for $p<0.10$ were retained. In a second step, the estimation was repeated with this more reduced set of variables. The results of the second, more parsimonious, model are the ones shown in Table 3.13.

31 Clearly, it is not the aim of this work to contrast the validity of social capital theories, nor of other forms of measuring trust. The item that is commonly included in questionnaires measures only individual generalised social trust.

32 The possibility that political membership, and especially some of its categories, had to be considered a 'rare event' (as defined by King & Zeng 1999) was taken into account. The methods and software described in King & Zeng (1999) have been used with this data, but the difference in the coefficients and the standard errors was negligible and, thus, they are not presented. We can, hence, conclude that none of the categories of this variable qualifies as a 'sufficiently rare' event. The model has been estimated with Stata 6 (© Stata Corporation). Since a great number of observations have item non-response problems, and to avoid the estimation bias that listwise deletion of incomplete observations entails, multiple imputation with the methods and software described in King *et al.* (1998) and Honaker *et al.* (1999) was performed.

33 The presentation of 17 multinomial models can never be easy. To facilitate visualisation of results, they are divided into three tables, one for each of the multinomial logistic equations. Thus, I prioritise country-wise comparisons at the expense of greater difficulty in comparing the results for the different categories of the dependent variables cross-sectionally. Moreover, these tables present the results of the models that only include those variables statistically significant at $p<0.10$ in a preliminary analysis for each country. The complete models are available upon request.

34 Multilevel models (also termed hierarchical or random-coefficients models) are designed for the analysis of data 'naturally' structured in several hierarchies or levels (for example, individuals within households and neighbourhoods or individuals within regions and countries), in such a way that we can consider variables related to the different levels of aggregation and adequately estimate their effects on variables measured at the lower level (see Hox 1995, Goldstein 1995, Kreft & de Leeuw 1998, Snijders & Bosker 1999). In this study, the two levels of interest are

the individual and the country of residence. However, in this chapter we will not consider country-level variables. This will be done in following chapters and especially in Chapter seven.

35 The model has the following general structure: Logit $(\pi_{ij}) = \gamma_0 + \sum \beta X_{ij} + u_{0j}$. Thus, level-2 error or variation (u_{0j}) is modelled, in our case for countries. Level-1 variation or error is in this case predetermined by $p_j(1-p_j)$. See Snijders & Bosker (1999: 213 ff.).

36 In all cases, *random intercepts* models have been estimated, such that we estimate the variation in the average value of political membership across countries. Additionally, as we will see in the next paragraphs, model 2 also estimates *random coefficients or slopes*. All models have been estimated with the software HLM 5 and the estimation has been done via *full-PQL* approximation. The results interpreted are those for the *non-linear logit-link unit-specific model*.

37 I have selected these variables following the results obtained in Table 3.13, which seemed to indicate the existence of different effects across countries.

38 The impossibility of estimating the parameters through Laplace approximation, due to the non-convergence of the algorithm, prevents me from presenting statistics on the goodness-of-fit of each model, which are generally based on the Deviation or the –2-log likelihood. The estimation via PQL, being a quasi-likelihood method, does not allow the computing of reliable statistics on the significance of the models. In any case, given the limited number of countries in the analyses, results should always be interpreted with caution.

39 This can be also seen in the decrease in the proportion of total variance that is attributable to countries (intraclass correlation), computed as $p = \dfrac{var\,(u_j)}{var\,(u_j) + \pi^2/3}$ following Snijders and Bosker (1999: 224).

40 Given the high number of parameters required to estimate the variance of random coefficients (variances plus correlations) the results are presented in two tables. The variances of coefficients are included in the lower section of Table 3.18, while the correlation of these coefficients with the intercept and among them is presented in Table 3.19. On the other hand, it is important to mention that the variation across countries in a random coefficients model depends on the values of the variables, whose effects randomly vary (Snijders & Bosker 1999: 105). For this reason I present two illustrative situations: one in which all variables adopt their minimum value (0) and the one in which they adopt the maximum value (1).

41 We know this when comparing each variation component expressed in standard deviations with the average coefficient of the respective variable.

42 We should remind the reader that all independent variables are expressed in a 0–1 range, where 0 represents the minimum value. Thus, the intercept reflects the likelihood of political membership for those individuals with lower education, lower income, lower age (15–16 years), etc., and with the values of the reference categories for categorical variables.

43 Anduiza (2002) found a similar pattern of variation of individual-level resources across European democracies for electoral abstention.

chapter four | the contextual determinants of political membership

INTRODUCTION

Individuals' resources, socio-economic status (SES) and political orientation are important because they provide (or fail to do so) the initial favourable dispositions to join political organisations. Having a university degree will not automatically assure political engagement and, in fact, the results presented in Chapter three show that, in a number of countries, university graduates refrain from joining political organisations. Equally, although having an interest in politics will foster political participation, many citizens who are highly interested in public affairs abstain from joining political organisations. What, then, triggers citizens to join political organisations? Resources, SES and attitudes are only the starting point and the social and political context and environment that surrounds the individual play a crucial role in the final outcome.

The social and political context determines the opportunities and the mobilisation cues that individuals receive. Without opportunities for organised collective action, and without mobilisation efforts by organisations, citizens interested in public affairs will face greater costs in joining political groups. Therefore, the structure of costs, benefits and incentives for collective action conditions citizens' inclination to join political organisations.

In this chapter, the various mechanisms that connect a variety of contextual aspects to citizens' political membership are discussed. Its main aim is to provide an over-arching framework that clarifies the ways in which different types of contextual influences drive (or fail to do so) citizens to join political organisations. First, we will present a brief discussion of how contexts and contextual influences are defined, as well as a reflection on the relevant contextual units for the study of political membership. The second section delineates the micro-mechanisms that connect macro- and meso-contexts with individual decisions to join political membership, in the light of debates about collective action. The third section describes the specific expectations and hypotheses that connect political opportunity structures – the macro-context – and the patterns and strategies of mobilisation – the meso-context – to varying levels of political membership across western democracies. Finally, the last section explores, unfortunately with limited survey data, the impact of micro-contexts – especially, the politicisation of family ties – on political membership in west European nations.

CITIZENS, CONTEXTS AND POLITICAL PARTICIPATION: WHICH CONTEXTS ARE RELEVANT?

It is hardly controversial to say that people behave differently depending on the time, space and environment in which they live. Yet, as Huckfeldt & Sprague (1993: 281) point out, surprisingly little attention is generally paid to the context or contexts of political action. Methodological individualism in the field of political behaviour has led, for many years, to a focus almost exclusively on individuals' attributes and on the social inequalities in participation. Thus, for decades, the study of political participation detached individuals from their contexts and, to a large extent, neglected the political dimension.

In contrast, contextual approaches to political behaviour start from the premise that individual political action is strongly conditioned by the environment. Hence, ignoring the context in which citizens act will usually entail a mis-specification of our models and a falling into the individual fallacy trap (Przeworski 1974, Brown 1991). Therefore, getting our models right will often require taking into account the possible effects that the context brings with it, incorporating contextual variables and studying the interaction between these and individuals' characteristics. And, while there may be a consensus around the relevance of the context for explaining individuals' political behaviour, the crucial issue is to determine which context is relevant, how and why.

As Przeworski emphasised (1974: 33ff.), a crucial part of contextual hypotheses or theories is the definition of the type of context relevant for the behaviour under scrutiny. What exactly do we mean by context and how is it defined?

Clearly, there are different types of context and contextual effects. Huckfeldt & Sprague (1993), following Przeworski & Teune (1970) and Eulau (1986), distinguished various types of contexts or environments and classified their different effects on individual behaviour. Thus, contexts may be defined by the level of aggregation of the population (neighbourhoods, municipalities, counties, provinces, regions, countries, etc.) or by their functions (place of residence, place of work or study, religious communities, etc.). Furthermore, we can distinguish between *environmental* effects, which are those produced by all external factors impinging on the individual (social and political institutions, social structure, physical environment, etc.), and *contextual* effects, which, according to Huckfeldt & Sprague (1993: 289), are the result of social interaction with the environment. Among the latter we should also include the aggregated individual properties that Przeworski & Teune (1970: 56) referred to.[1]

Given these definitions, a good part of the sociological literature on environmental or contextual effects on political behaviour has focused on the impact of the socio-economic environment and on social interaction (Przeworski 1974,

Huckfeldt 1979 and 1986, Giles & Dantico 1982, Huckfeldt & Sprague 1987, Huckfeldt, Plutzer & Sprague 1993, Kenny 1992, Pattie & Johnston 1999, Huckfeldt, Johnson & Sprague 2004, Zuckerman 2005). The attempt to move beyond the individualistic approach to social and political action has led to social groups and interaction being brought back into models of political behaviour.

As useful as the rediscovery of social embeddedness certainly is, we must stress that these are not the only relevant contexts and environments that impinge on citizens' political action. Too often, the socio-structural scholars seem to forget that citizens are not only surrounded by other individuals; they are also embedded in networks of organisations, institutions and rules of the game.

Institutions and political structures, consequently, provide the structure of incentives for individual action. What sometimes may seem minor aspects of the way political and social institutions work – such as the distance between polling stations and the quality of public transport mentioned by Hardin (1991: 371) – can have a fundamental impact on individuals' participation because they substantially affect the cost-benefit structure of collective action.

Another fundamental aspect of the definition of context is the choice of the level of the environment that is deemed relevant to determining individual behaviour (Przeworski 1974: 34 ff.). At what level of aggregation or function shall we measure the relevant interactions? In most cases, we will have a choice of levels of (territorial) aggregation: the neighbourhood, the local community, the region, or the country. Which of them is most relevant will very much depend on the specific research question, the approach, and the type of political behaviour we are interested in.

In general terms, if we are interested in the impact of social interactions, smaller levels of aggregation will be of most relevance – the neighbourhood or the local community. But when we are interested in studying the effect of wider macro or environmental factors, larger units will usually be a better choice. In this study, the nation is the most appropriate level of aggregation, because we are interested in explaining cross-national differences in political membership and because many of the relevant institutional and mobilisation factors are defined at this level of aggregation.

Certainly, the need to employ cross-national survey data also limits the possibilities for incorporating lower levels of aggregation into the analysis and microcontexts. Moreover, if the main differences in political membership are found at the national level of aggregation, it is reasonable to expect that they will be – to a great extent – linked to properties of the same level of aggregation.[2] And there is no logical or theoretical justification for assuming that, in all cases, the contexts closer to the individuals are the ones that will have a larger impact on their behaviour (Huckfeldt & Sprague 1993: 299).

Yet, even if the model of political membership presented in this study recognises the interdependence and social influence of individual political behaviour, and that it is quite likely that various environmental levels (local, regional, national) will interact in different ways to shape patterns of political membership, the type of cross-national data available do not allow systematic testing of the hypotheses that these levels of analysis might generate. We will need to content ourselves with some limited and partial analyses, which provide some hints on the likely effect of the family context on membership of political organisations.

THE MICRO-MECHANISMS OF CONTEXTUAL EFFECTS

More than two decades ago, Sprague (1982) emphasised the importance of providing a micro-theory consistent with contextual effects and analysis. Upon reflection, however, scholars have realised that the context does not necessarily affect, or affect in the same way, all types of political behaviour (see, for example, Huckfeldt, Plutzer & Sprague 1993). Indeed, in many cases, the context might be of little relevance – for example, for individual action devoid of social co-ordination – and in yet others we need to ensure that contextual effects are not simply tapping the residual element of models mis-specified at the individual level (Hauser 1974).

Chapter three has, precisely, shown that even a broad and complete individual-level model is insufficient to explain the differences in political membership across western democracies. Thus, there is sufficient empirical evidence to move beyond individual dispositions and attributes and systematically analyse the potential impact of various contextual factors. However, before doing so, we need to establish the links or causal micro-mechanisms that connect 'macro' structures and processes with 'micro' behaviour adequately. Because this study can only directly assess the impact of micro-contexts in the last section of this chapter, we need to provide plausible and reasonable mechanisms for the *macro* to *micro* transition (Coleman 1990).

Framing these macro to micro transitions in the logic of rational choice approaches has some advantages, as it helps to systematise relations and expectations. While critics of the rational choice approach have made many valid contributions to this debate, a careful consideration of the paradoxes that arise from the logic of collective action (Olson 1965) will contribute to structuring coherently our views on the sets of factors that are involved in individual decisions to participate in politics. One need not adhere fully to the rational choice perspective on political behaviour to value the insights that this approach brings to the empirical study of participation.[3]

In this regard, while rationalist models face serious difficulties in giving an account of the motivations that lead citizens to act collectively and of the benefits or incentives that they seek in organisations, rational choice theories are especially useful for our understanding of the impact of the cost structure of participation. This is especially relevant for this study, given that, in Chapter three, we already showed that 'motivations' are insufficient to explain political membership and, especially, its cross-national variations. Having an interest in politics, a certain ideological leaning or post-materialist values is not sufficient to make many citizens in a number of western democracies join political organisations. And this means that we need to pay special attention to the various processes through which the wider political context may impinge on the calculus of joining.

A warning note is required, though. Even if the following pages summarise in a rather formal way some of the core arguments of the rational-choice approaches to collective action, formal modelling is neither deemed essential nor (probably) useful for the aims of this study. Neither does the presentation of the arguments that follow imply that the decision to join a political organisation is believed to obey an explicit and utilitarian calculation by individuals – not even in terms of a wide notion of utility that would include normative motivations. Like Rosenau (1973) and Huckfeldt (1986: 152–3), this study takes the view that a substantial part of citizens' political activity is much more a response to social experiences and to interaction with mobilising agents than the result of individual calculations on costs and benefits. Rosenau expressed this idea very clearly:

> Most citizens, in other words, are not autonomous actors who calculate what ought to be done in public affairs, devise a strategy for achieving it, estimate their own resources, and then pursue the course of action most likely to achieve their goals. Their instrumental behaviour is often suggested, if not solicited, by others [...]. Thus, to conceive of the practices of citizenship as being largely sustained by independent action toward the political arena initiated by individuals is to minimize the relational context in which citizens participate in public affairs. (Rosenau 1973: 96)

Hence, the underlying notion that is favoured here is that of *purposive individuals* who seek certain ends by their actions and, therefore, may give reasons for their behaviour, rather than that of *rational* individuals whose behaviour is oriented to maximise their utility (see Coleman 1990: 13–18).

Within these premises, there are a number of rational models of collective action that include varying elements in the individual calculus of the decision to participate. The simplest proposition is described in Equation 4.1, where AC is the decision to act collectively, p_i is the probability that the individual's contribution will lead to the achievement of the common good that is sought, B is the main benefit (the collective good) and C are the costs derived from the action.

$$AC_i = (p_i * B) - C_i \qquad \text{(Equation 4.1)}$$

The Olsonian version (1965) also includes the crucial element of private benefits or selective incentives (Si) – as is shown in Equation 4.2.

$$AC_i = (p_i * B) - C_i + S_i \qquad \text{(Equation 4.2)}$$

Consequently, selective incentives – whatever they may be – facilitate collective action because they have a direct impact on the benefits the individual will receive at the end of the process. In the case of organisational membership, even if the provision of selective incentives may be relevant to determining the individual propensity to join political organisations, there is no reason to believe that this provision of selective incentives will systematically vary across western countries. Generally, most organisations that seek public or collective goods need to decide whether to provide selective incentives and the decision is very likely to be independent of the socio-political context in which the organisation acts.

Later developments of the models of collective action have introduced additional elements into the individual decision to co-operate. A first aspect is related to the efficacy, or effectiveness, of the group that acts jointly to provide the common good sought. Contrary to Whiteley's (1995) claims, incorporating some notion of the probability that the group will achieve the collective good – $p(B)$ in Equation 4.3 – is not equal to establishing a 'collective rationality' incompatible with rational-choice models. The effectiveness of the political organisation that requires the individual's contribution is, indeed, decisive for the common good to be provided at all and it is hardly rational to co-operate in a useless enterprise, especially if the individual has some previous information to evaluate its likely effectiveness. And Hansen (1985) showed that, indeed, individuals are more likely to join organisations after successful campaigns that resulted in the provision of the collective good. Yet, as Whiteley correctly argues, irrespective of the effectiveness of the group, a rational individual would not participate if her influence on the provision of the good was nil.[4] Therefore, the relation between one aspect and the other is adequately captured by a multiplicative expression.

A further element that has been included among the components that intervene in individual decisions to co-operate, and which is also linked to the effectiveness of the group, is the number of individuals who will also co-operate[5] – N in Equation 4.3. The link between this aspect and the individual decision to co-operate is not, however, completely clear.[6] Baron (1997: 321) considers that, for those individuals who include in their utilities the welfare of others, political action is more beneficial when others are not co-operating. Nonetheless, Baron recognises that, when the number of co-operators is excessively low, the probability of success of the action is also low. Hence, political action will be effective only when a substantial number of individuals are co-operating.

$$AC_i = [(p_i*B)\ p(B) + (aN - N2)] - C_i + S_i \qquad \text{(Equation 4.3)}$$

Where:
AC_i: the individual's decision to join the collective action
p_i: probability that the individual contribution will have an impact;
B: main benefit sought with action, or common/public good;
C_i: costs of acting;
S_i: private benefits or selective incentives;
$P(B)$: overall probability of the common good being provided;
N: number of individuals who co-operate;
a: constant value.

Yet Hardin (1991) argues that one of the fundamental aspects that distinguish the two main forms of collective action – *acting together*, or co-ordination, and *contributing* together, or co-operation – is their functional relation with the number of other persons that participate in the collective action. The relation between co-ordination and the number of participants shows increasing marginal returns and provides an incentive for collective action on the part of new participants, as it reduces the costs of repression derived from the same. The relation between co-operation and the number of participants has, on the contrary, a functional form of decreasing marginal returns: up to a certain level, the increase in the number of participants increases the resources available and the efficacy of the group and, therefore, the probabilities of obtaining the collective good; but, after a certain point, a larger number of participants makes individual contribution more and more irrelevant, reducing the chance of joining the group (Hardin 1991: 366–7). Given this relationship, the structure of incentives to co-operate is, according to Hardin, always that of no co-operation, irrespective of the number of other individuals who already co-operate.

However, Oliver (1984) shows empirical results that seem to contradict this conclusion. In her study on activism in neighbourhood groups, she illustrates situations where the relation between the number of co-operators and the decision to act is negative: her respondents said they contributed actively to obtain the common good because 'nobody else would do it'. Actually, this finding is not necessarily incompatible with the formulations of Baron and Hardin, if we take into account the 'magnitude' of the common good. In other words, if the good that is sought does not demand a large quantity of resources and can be provided by the co-operation of a few active persons, the relationship that Oliver finds may be perfectly compatible with other versions of the relationship between the number of participants and the decision to act.

In the general situation, the typical relationship between both aspects may be expressed in a parabolic expression such as that of Equation 4.3 although, as Oliver indicates, there may be interactions with other elements that change the functional form. Hence, when the number of participants is low, its increase will heighten the likelihood of joining the group but, beyond a certain threshold of participants, the likelihood decreases. But, eventually, the number of participants is likely to have an impact on the decision to co-operate with a political organisation, be it because of its impact on the expected benefits of the action or because it alters the impact of individual action.[7]

As a result, after a review of the different approaches to the paradox of collective action, we can distinguish four main elements that intervene in an individual's decision to join a political organisation and which may vary depending on specific environmental characteristics:[8] (a) the expected impact of the individual contribution, (b) the expected benefits of participation, (c) the costs derived from action, and (d) the estimated probability that other individuals will co-operate.[9] How does the broader political context affect each of these elements?

Figure 4.1: A variant of the analytical model

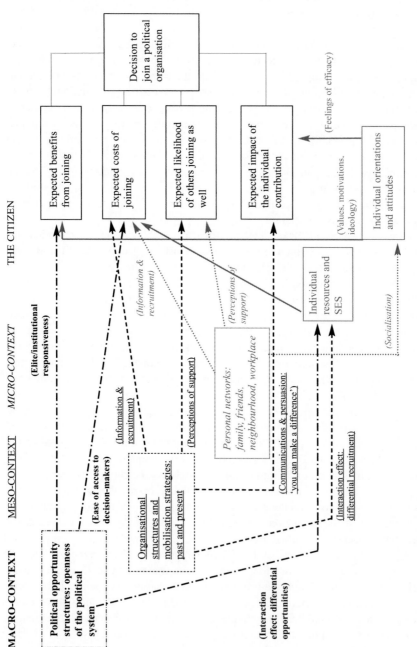

Font and line patterns identify the various levels of analysis for each set of factors: individual, micro-contextual, meso- and macro-contextual.

The political context and expected benefits from joining political organisations
Figure 1.1 in Chapter one provided a diagram of the full analytical model put forward in this book. Figure 4.1 presents that same diagram but specifically highlights the main connections that we expect to be present between the various environmental and contextual aspects and the four components that comprise the decision to join a political organisation.[10] As we can see, environmental (macro- and meso-) factors intervene in the final decision to join a political association mainly through their effect on the subjective evaluations of the costs and benefits that an individual expects to derive and bear from co-operation with the organisation (Hansen 1985).

The expected impact of the individual contribution is of the utmost relevance in the rational calculus of co-operation because it has a direct effect on the motivating capacity of the collective benefit to spur individual action. Only when citizens perceive or believe that they can have a real impact on the provision of the common good that is sought can this be a sufficient motive for co-operation – as long as the costs are not higher than the value placed on the good. In sharp contrast to the common 'turnout paradox', the value of p may vary greatly from one political organisation to another, depending on (a) the size of the organisation and (b) the 'size' of the common good that it seeks.[11] Thus, confronted with the decision to join a political organisation, some individuals may have good reasons to believe that their participation may be decisive or, at least, relevant to achieving the common goal; while others may find themselves in the situation commonly expected by the logic of collective action.

To a large extent, which of these two expectations and beliefs prevails in each country will be determined by the average (membership) size of the political organisations of the given nation and by the environment in which they act.[12] Hence, the organisational structures prevalent in each society can have an important impact on the participative decisions of their citizens. Especially important is the nature of the associational ecology and whether it tends to favour the mushrooming of local organisations or, rather, limits collective action at the local level in favour of higher levels of territorial aggregation. The degree of concentration at the local community level will have an impact on the average size of organisations and on the possibility that the good sought can be obtained by small groups.[13] In addition to the size of the political organisations, mobilisation strategies by organisations themselves will surely make a difference, as the perceptions of individual influence on collective action are moulded by the public discourse of organisations.[14] And political organisations, frequently, actively aim at shaping these beliefs through their slogans, mottos and campaigns: '*sí se puede*', 'yes, we can', and 'you can make a difference' are recurrent mobilising slogans around the globe.

On the other hand, as we have discussed on previous pages, how many other citizens will also co-operate will affect the expected benefits of co-operation, as well as the expected impact of the individual contribution in obtaining the common good. Yet these expectations are, frequently, formed through subjective perceptions based on imperfect information. The political context can have a substantial impact on these perceptions, given that organisational traditions and the past history of co-operation will be reflected in optimism or pessimism about the number of people who will also co-operate.[15]

Individuals in countries with a long tradition of political membership and of organisational co-operation to seek common goods will have reasons to be optimistic about the capacity of organisations to sustain collective action and, thus, they will be optimistic about their likely effectiveness in obtaining the common good. In the opposite case, the citizens of less participative societies will have few reasons for optimism and, thus, will be less likely to regard optimistically the willingness of other individuals to co-operate.[16] Consequently, we can think of this situation as an n-players iterated prisoner's dilemma, such that past experiences of co-operation will determine the prevailing co-operation strategies in successive games (Axelrod 1984, Taylor 1976: chapter 4). And, because the expected rewards from collective action are dependent on the number of other individuals who participate (Oliver 1984, Chong 1991: 115), if citizens believe that other individuals will not join political organisations in sufficient numbers, they will be less inclined to do so themselves.[17]

But, further to its effect on perceptions of the likely impact of individual contributions and of the likely number of participants, other aspects of the political context will also directly influence the capacity to achieve the common good sought. In this regard, political opportunity structures (POS) will condition to a great extent how permeable the political system is to the demands of organised groups. All other factors being equal, if political structures can easily and quickly accommodate the various interests expressed through organised action, citizens will have more incentives to create political organisations and to join them.[18] If the efforts of co-operating in collective action are deemed to be in vain, individuals will find few reasons to bear the costs derived from co-operation. Additionally, some political and institutional configurations directly promote more than others the creation of political organisations and interest groups, by means of providing various sorts of aids and subsidies (see Hansen 1985, Skocpol 2003: 206–9).[19]

The political context and the expected costs of joining political organisations
The costs of co-operation with political organisations are also noticeably affected by various aspects of the political environment. On the one hand, mobilisation by organisations reduces the transaction costs of joining them (Wielhouwer & Lockerbie 1994 and Rosenstone & Hansen 1993), while also reducing the costs of obtaining information about the existing political organisations, what they offer, how they work, their location, etc. Undoubtedly, if organisations devote resources and efforts to recruiting new members it is more likely that individuals will respond positively than if they never receive such requests.[20] And, because a great deal of these recruitment efforts originate in the primary reference group of the recruited individuals, social pressure and norms will contribute even more to the success of the mobilising effort.

Moreover, depending on how political organisations target their recruitment efforts towards different groups in the population, mobilisation processes can have varying interactive effects with individuals' resources to reduce – or otherwise – the costs of joining a political organisation.[21] In the United States, scholars have extensively documented the 'mobilisation bias' in different sorts of political organisations – from parties to environmental groups – as they target mostly the wealthier and highly educated. Yet other countries need not follow the same logic – as mobilisation strategies are context-dependent – but there is little cross-national research in this area to make any strong claims. In any case, the most relevant conclusion is that mobilisation efforts are likely to interact with individual resources in their impact on the costs of joining a political organisation.

Mobilisation strategies are, however, not the only contextual factor that can have a relevant impact on the cost structure of co-operation. The POS exerts a substantial influence on the cost structure of collective action. If political institutions and structures are hermetic and impermeable to the social demands of groups and individuals, the costs of action increase because citizens will need to dedicate more resources and efforts to achieve their goals. Not only will the overall costs of organised co-operation increase but individuals will also need a wider variety of resources – economic, social and cognitive – to be able to contribute effectively to collective action.

In short, by providing more open or closed channels to decision-making processes, the POS may contribute significantly to increasing or decreasing the costs of co-operation. Countries with a more open POS are, thus, expected to promote higher levels of political membership, while nations with a more closed POS are expected to incite citizens to join political organisations less. But also, the POS will have an interactive impact on the cost structure of political membership, through the mediation of individual resources. A more closed POS will make the resource-rich much more capable of bearing the costs of co-operation than the resource-poor, whereas a more open POS will foster a more equal access to decision-making processes, rendering social resources less necessary for political action. Thus, an open POS is expected to have an equalising effect on political membership and a closed POS to bring about the opposite result.

Finally, the organisational history of a country can also have a decisive impact on the organisational costs of collective action. Olson (1982) suggests that the number of organisations increases over time in stable societies as, once a group has overcome the fixed costs of mobilisation and of the creation of an organisation, this tends to last over time. Stinchcombe (1965: 152) makes a similar claim: organisational experience determines the capacity to create new organisations, while it also increases the resources available to do so.

Past research in the field of social movements has also demonstrated that inter-organisational networks are crucial for the emergence of new groups and actors (Curtis & Zurcher 1973, Snow, Zurcher & Ekland-Olson 1980: 797ff., Morris 1984, Kriesi & van Praag 1987, Klandermans 1989, Fernández & McAdam 1989, McAdam & Fernández 1990). Inter-organisational networks, coalitions and alliances between organisations provide material (money, infrastructure, etc.) and social (experience, leadership, access to means of communication, etc.) resources, which are essential to the emergence of new organisations and also serve to extend the scope of communication of new demands and of recruitment networks (Klandermans 1989: 306). As a result, the pre-existence of consolidated organisational structures of 'traditional' organisations (political parties, unions, religious associations and churches) contributes to reducing the initial investment costs of the creation of new organisations, thus facilitating organised collective action. Consequently, there is a certain element of path dependency and structural inertia that contributes to certain nations being able to sustain high levels of political membership through time. Organised collective action is costly but, when the structural foundations of political organisations are laid, these structural investments are a valuable capital for future collective action.

In summary, this section has discussed the micro-mechanisms that can account for the macro to micro transition between the political context – a set of macro-level properties – and citizens' decisions to join political organisations. Chapters five and six will discuss many of these links in greater detail when presenting the specific indicators chosen for empirical analysis.

The remaining part of this chapter will succinctly address the role of micro-contexts – especially personal networks – in accounting for political membership. While the analytical model presented in Chapter one reserves a special role to micro-contexts in the explanation of decisions to join political organisations, unfortunately, the cross-national empirical data that are available are insufficient to include this set of factors in the core parts of this study. The major cross-national surveys that are employed in this volume – the WVS, the EBs, the ESS – do not include relevant items that capture the nature of the influence of personal networks in individual decisions to join political organisations. Hence, the next section will present the scattered evidence that supports our claims about its real impact on political membership.

A NOTE ON THE ROLE OF MICRO-CONTEXTS: SOME EMPIRICAL EVIDENCE ON PERSONAL NETWORKS AND POLITICAL MEMBERSHIP

The study of the impact of micro-contexts on citizens' political behaviour covers a wide range of social influences and communication interactions that are increasingly recognised as fundamental but are, nonetheless, difficult to measure empirically and to disentangle. As we discussed in the first sections of this chapter, in its origins, contextual analysis placed processes of 'social resonance' (Sprague 1982) at the core of its models. Thus, the social setting and the immediate social context were viewed as the main driving forces for citizens' behaviour. Neighbourhoods and workplaces were the social settings where social interaction took place and where patterns of political agreement and disagreement shaped the political mentality of individuals.

Over time, scholarly attention has been diversified in many ways.[22] On the one hand, the range of settings that are deemed relevant has substantially widened, to include the school, the church and the recreation areas. On the other hand, it has moved beyond the analysis of 'social spaces' to embrace a more flexible approach that takes into account the multiple and complex social relations in which individuals engage, thus focusing on personal networks and social ties as well. Thus, contemporary studies of the 'social logic' of politics cover a wide range of settings and social relationships: the closest family ties, friendship bonds, class-based links and the context of the workplace, ego-centred discussion networks, online communities, etc. (Zuckerman 2005).

There are three main mechanisms that link micro-contexts to political participation: (i) socialisation and learning processes; (ii) flows of information and of communication; and (iii) recruitment and mobilisation processes. In many cases, they will be jointly operating during social interaction and, thus, it is relatively difficult to distinguish them empirically.

Micro-contexts and personal networks are, first and foremost, the social spaces where political socialisation takes places – where values, social norms and attitudes are shared and learnt. Within the family and the household, appropriate social roles are defined and this, certainly, includes clear cues about how to behave politically. Parent-child socialisation processes provide the set of values, attitudes and habits with regard to political participation, at the same time that they provide (or otherwise) the socio-economic resources that will facilitate engaging in public affairs (Verba, Schlozman & Burns 2005). In some family contexts, civic and political engagement is learnt as the normal way of engaging with the wider society, while in others it is actively discouraged. Equally, the school and the workplace provide contexts where additional skills and social values and norms are transmitted – and sometimes enforced.

Beyond these socialising properties, social ties and networks facilitate the exchange of communication and the distribution of incentives for participation (Granovetter 1983, Knoke 1990c, Opp & Gern 1993, Gould, 1993). Wider interpersonal links foster the flow of information and reduce its costs while, at the same time, providing wider and more up-to-date information (Granovetter 1973, Huckfeldt & Sprague 1995). In fact, past research has suggested that less intimate contacts might have a stronger persuasive impact than family and close friends (Huckfeldt & Sprague 1991). Equally, heterogeneity in personal networks is related to diversity in the communication cues received, as it limits the redundancy of the information flow that could result if network members have homogenous interests. Hence, contact with a wider and more varied range of people will provide greater opportunities for participation, as information of a more varied nature will travel faster and more effectively through these weak ties (Kotler-Berkowitz 2005).

Closely related to this flow of information and cues is the relevance of micro-contexts and personal networks as primary *loci* of recruitment processes. Recruitment processes are strongly determined by structural proximity, availability and affective interaction, because recruitment is much more effective when

Table 4.1: Family ties and political membership in selected western countries: percentages of political membership of main respondent (*ego*) by party or union membership of *alter* within household

	Someone else in household is a party member?				Someone else in household is a union member?			
	Yes	No	Cramer's V (Sig)	No. cases	Yes	No	Cramer's V (Sig)	No. cases
France	33	12	0.12 (0.00)	1000	35	12	0.14 (0.00)	1000
Belgium	40	25	0.06 (0.06)	995	25	26	0.01 (0.78)	997
Netherlands	52	38	0.05 (0.13)	1001	50	37	0.10 (0.00)	1000
W. Germany	33	24	0.04 (0.20)	988	18	25	0.05 (0.09)	993
Italy	26	19	0.06 (0.06)	1000	29	18	0.09 (0.00)	1000
Luxembourg	43	41	0.02 (0.77)	300	39	41	0.02 (0.78)	300
Denmark	75	67	0.05 (0.13)	1001	76	60	0.17 (0.00)	1000
Ireland	30	17	0.06 (0.04)	1000	13	18	0.05 (0.15)	1000
United Kingdom	45	26	0.08 (0.00)	1298	29	27	0.02 (0.58)	1295
Greece	29	12	0.14 (0.00)	1000	28	12	0.10 (0.00)	1000
Spain	17	8	0.06 (0.08)	1000	12	8	0.04 (0.24)	1000
Portugal	17	5	0.08 (0.01)	996	8	5	0.04 (0.25)	998

Source: Eurobarometer 34 (1990), own elaboration.
Note: the values are the percentage of main respondents who are members of any political organisation (trade union, political party, human-rights groups, environmental or consumer organisations), conditional on any other household member being a party or trade union member.

potential participants are in direct contact with recruitment agents (Snow, Zurcher & Ekland-Olson 1980: 787–9). Personal networks and micro-contexts, therefore, help bridge the gap between political organisations' mobilising strategies and citizens. In this sense, individuals with more extensive networks and ties will be more likely to be asked to participate, if only because participants tend to recruit primarily from people they are most frequently in contact with, and from those who are similar to themselves (Granovetter 1983, Popielarz, McPherson & Drobnic 1992). Moreover, past research has shown that invitations to participate are more likely to come from people whom we know and, in turn, we are more likely to accept these invitations from the people we know (Verba, Schlozman & Brady 1995).

With this set of hypotheses, we now turn to evaluate the scarce cross-national evidence of the link between personal networks and political membership. The main difficulty lies in finding surveys that include data that allows us to measure political membership adequately – i.e. those with a reasonable number of political organisations listed – while also including relevant indicators of the political engagement of the respondent's acquaintances. In our case, the most interesting set of propositions would relate the involvement of respondents' personal networks in organisations to their engagement with political organisations. This would justify the assumption that processes of social influence – socialisation, the flow of information, or recruitment – underlie this outcome.

Table 4.1 provides mixed evidence about the relevance of family influences on political membership.[23] Eurobarometer 34, in 1990, asked respondents about their own membership of listed associations and organisations[24] and also asked them if any individuals in their households – other than themselves – were at that time members of a political party or a trade union. Thus, given the findings of past research in this field, we would expect that respondents – *ego* – who share their households with relatively politicised and committed individuals – the *alter* – will be more likely to join a political organisation themselves.

Nevertheless, while there is some evidence that this is the case, this is by no means a universal relationship in European countries. The association between the party membership of a family member and *ego's* membership of any political organisation is statistically significant for p≤0.10 in most countries but the association coefficients are quite modest in most cases. However, an interesting pattern emerges, as we cannot help but notice that the relation between the politicisation of family members and the respondents' engagement is more common in South European countries. And the impact of *alter's* engagement on *ego's* political membership is generally higher when the former is a party member than when she joins a union.

The results are not substantially different when we distinguish between 'traditional' and 'new' political membership for *ego*, although the association is somewhat weaker for the latter (Table 4.2). And, in fact, association coefficients are only systematically significant and sizeable when the *alter* and the *ego* belong to

Table 4.2: Association between party membership of *alter* and various forms of political membership of *ego*: Cramer's V coefficients

	With *ego*'s membership of any 'traditional' political organisations	With *ego*'s membership of any 'new' political organisations	With *ego*'s party membership
France	0.10 (0.00)	0.11 (0.00)	0.22 (0.00)
Belgium	0.10 (0.00)	0.02 (0.48)	0.13 (0.00)
Netherlands	0.08 (0.01)	0.05 (0.11)	0.14 (0.00)
W. Germany	0.07 (0.04)	0.02 (0.50)	0.10 (0.00)
Italy	0.04 (0.23)	0.06 (0.04)	0.13 (0.00)
Luxembourg	0.10 (0.10)	0.06 (0.27)	0.23 (0.00)
Denmark	0.05 (0.11)	0.05 (0.12)	0.36 (0.00)
Ireland	0.05 (0.15)	0.01 (0.76)	0.02 (0.58)
United Kingdom	0.06 (0.03)	0.05 (0.07)	0.32 (0.00)
Greece	0.15 (0.00)	0.04 (0.27)	0.20 (0.00)
Spain	0.05 (0.11)	0.05 (0.09)	0.06 (0.05)
Portugal	0.06 (0.08)	0.06 (0.06)	0.02 (0.58)

Source: Eurobarometer 34 (1990), own elaboration.
Note: the values are the Cramer's V association coefficients with the significance p value. 'Traditional' political organisations are trade unions, and political parties; while 'new' political organisations are human rights groups, environmental or consumer organisations.

Table 4.3: Summary of results of logistic regression on *ego's* party membership: unstandardised coefficients for *alter's* party and trade union membership

	Alter is a member of a party	Alter is a member of a trade union	Number of cases
France	2.39 **	-0.40	847
Belgium	1.08 *	0.26	717
Netherlands	2.13 **	-0.19	931
W. Germany	1.58 **	-0.15	843
Italy	1.01 **	0.54	771
Denmark	2.83 **	-0.33	886
Ireland	0.14	0.66	834
United Kingdom	3.40 **	-0.10	1176
Greece	1.66 **	-0.26	830
Spain	1.72 **	0.06	733
Portugal	-16.16	-17.28	685

Source: Eurobarometer 34 (1990), own elaboration.
Note: the logistic regression included as controls the following attributes of the respondent: education level, working situation, ideology, marital status, gender, age, postmaterialism, and religious practice. Luxembourg has not been included due to the low number of cases retained in the analysis.

the same organisation. Thus, the engagement of a family member in a political party makes *ego* more likely also to be a member of a party, but not necessarily of other political organisations. And the same happens with family transmission of trade union membership. This would indicate that the impact of social interaction might have limited transferability to other forms of political engagement, at least in the case of membership in political organisations.

Once we control for the impact of respondents' resources and dispositions, our findings suggest that the social transmission of party membership within the household is quite substantial in many countries (Table 4.3).[25] For example, in the United Kingdom, the probability of a 50-year old highly educated working male with centre-right ideological leanings, who is married and is not religious, and who lives with no party member in his household being a party member is 0.18. For a Briton with exactly the same attributes who lives with a party member in his house-hold the estimated probability of being a party member as well is 0.87! This is, cer-tainly, quite a substantial effect. In other countries the impact is smaller but still con-siderable: a change in probability from 0.11 to 0.52 in the Netherlands and from 0.09 to 0.20 in Italy. Only in Ireland and Portugal is the coefficient not significant.

Thus, the (limited) cross-national evidence available suggests that personal net-works are of substantial importance for understanding the processes through which citizens join political organisations. Yet, the mechanisms can be multiple. It might well be that the underlying process is one of homophily, that individuals with sim-ilar political affiliations tend to marry each other. Because the survey does not dis-close who this household member is, we cannot really know. But the results in Table 4.4 can provide some hints about this, even if only for the Spanish case. These findings seem to suggest that the effect of family ties is relatively similar

Table 4.4: Family ties and political membership in Spain, 1997 (percentages)

Family member active in politics, present or past		Respondent is a member of any political organisation		
		No	Yes	No of cases
Father currently active in politics	No	83	17	2472
	Yes	62	38	18
Mother currently active in politics	No	83	17	2482
	Yes	63	37	8
Sibling currently active in politics	No	83	17	2460
	Yes	63	37	30
Spouse currently active in politics	No	83	17	2469
	Yes	57	43	21
Grandparent active in politics in the past	No	83	17	2474
	Yes	63	37	16
In-law currently active in politics	No	83	17	2467
	Yes	65	35	23
Cousin currently active in politics	No	83	17	2462
	Yes	61	39	28
Any close relative (father, mother, grandparent,	No	83	17	2408
sibling, son/daughter, or spouse) currently active in politics	Yes	62	38	82
Any distant relative (uncle/aunt, cousin,	No	83	17	2403
in-laws, nephew, etc.) currently active in politics	Yes	70	30	87
Any close relative (father, mother, grandparent, sibling,	No	83	17	2374
son/daughter, or spouse) active in politics in the past	Yes	73	27	116
Any close relative (father, mother, grandparent, sibling,	No	83	17	2400
son/daughter, or spouse) active in politics in the past	Yes	75	24	90

Source: Study no. 2240 of the Spanish CIS (1997).

across different types of family relations. Individuals with a family member active in politics – contemporaneously or in the past – are around twice as likely to be members of a political organisation as those with no relative active in politics. Spouses are somewhat more relevant in their impact and the effect of a currently politically active relative is more significant than that of one whose activity is past. But, in general terms, the effect seems to be strikingly similar.

In summary, micro-contexts are likely to have a non-negligible impact on citizens' decisions to join a political organisation, especially personal networks. Processes of socialisation, information flow and explicit recruitment make individuals who are in contact with political members more likely to join political organisations themselves. The fact that we cannot adequately incorporate these sets of processes jointly with other factors in our model should not lead us to disregard them in future research – hopefully, with better data.

CONCLUSIONS

The main purpose of this chapter has been to discuss the various issues that are relevant when considering the impact of contextual factors on individual political participation – in our case, membership of political organisations. As we have seen, various contexts and environments are likely to have an impact on the decisions individuals make about joining political organisations and these can be identified at various levels of analysis – individual, territorial, organisational, and institutional.

While recognising that various other contexts might be relevant in the analysis of political membership – notably the micro-contexts of local communities and of personal networks – the cross-national data that is available will limit our capacity to explore all this complexity simultaneously. Thus, the remaining parts of this work will restrict the analyses to two sets of contexts that we can measure reasonably well: the institutional or macro-level context and the mobilisation or meso-level context.

Consequently, Chapters five and six discuss in great detail the main hypotheses and indicators of the meso- and macro-level contexts that will be put to test in bivariate and multivariate analyses of individual political membership. Subsequently, Chapter seven puts the full model of resources, attitudes, mobilisation and opportunities to the test, using multilevel modelling.

For all of the remaining chapters we restrict the measurement of political membership to 18 western democracies included in the 1990–93 World Values Survey (WVS). This cross-national survey has been chosen – in preference to more recent ones – for several reasons. Firstly, the second wave of the WVS is the cross-national study that combines the inclusion of a large number of western democracies, with a sufficiently detailed and complete list of political associations. Maximising the number of countries included in the analyses is fundamental to maximising the variation of contextual variables and, thus, to obtaining results which will be as robust as possible – given the limited number of higher-level units.[26]

In any case, the research questions that motivate this study are not fundamentally affected by the date of collection of the survey data. If the aspects of the political context that are considered have an impact on individual political membership they are likely to be rather stable in the short-medium term. Moreover, the more recent survey data presented in Chapter two has already provided sufficient evidence that cross-national variations in political membership are stable and similar through time. Hence, there is no reason to believe that our results would significantly vary had any other equally suitable but more recent survey been used.

NOTES

1   Przeworski (1974: 34) also makes a distinction between the 'social context' and the 'political context' that is substantially different from the one that will be used in this book. For Przeworski, the social context is the aggregate distribution of the set of socially relevant individual characteristics of the social groups studied. For example, if we are explaining electoral turnout, an element of the social context is the social class that prevails in each

neighbourhood – this is what Sprague (1982) describes as 'social resonance'. And the political context is the aggregate distribution of the very behaviour and attitudes that we wish to explain – what Sprague (1982) terms 'behavioral contagion'. In our example, the political context is the distribution of electoral turnout in the voter's neighbourhood. Thus, for Przeworski (1974), the social and political contexts are simply the product of the aggregation of individual characteristics and behaviour; their effect on the behaviour or the attitudes of a given individual is due to social interaction.

2   Choosing the national level of aggregation and measurement of institutional variables does not imply eliminating subnational institutions from the analysis. We will just not aim to explain intra-national variation.

3   Many scholars have taken this view of rational choice theories of political behaviour in the past, without necessarily following an orthodox rational choice 'methodology' (see Knoke 1990c, Hardin 1991, Schlozman, Verba & Brady 1995, Verba, Schlozman & Brady 1995 and 2000, Whiteley 1995, Pattie, Seyd & Whiteley 2004).

4   See Moe's (1980a and b) interesting analysis of the tendency individuals have to overestimate their ability to have an influence on the final outcome of collective action.

5   Elster (1989: 37) claims that obtaining the public good is a continuous function of the number of agents who take part.

6   See Elster (1989: chapter one) to get a general vision of the distinct links that may be established between the number of agents that co-operate and the distribution of costs and benefits of collective action. For this reason, the parabolic function included in Equation 4.3 is only one of the possible alternatives to describe this relationship. Klandermans (1997: 26 ff.) also discusses various aspects that have an influence on the expectations of the success of collective action, among which is the number of persons who participate in the action. Nevertheless, Klandermans does not limit himself exclusively to the framework of rational choice and combines this with value-expectancy theory, which is more common in social psychology.

7   This is why Equation 4.3 includes these parameters in the section related to benefits.

8   Other aspects commonly considered in models of collective action are not too relevant in the case of co-operation with political organisations. Thus, the role of negative selective incentives – or sanctions – for not co-operating is negligible for most political organisations, given the voluntary nature of membership and their limited capacity to impose penalties on free-riders.

9   Both the estimation of the probability that other individuals will also co-operate, and the estimation of the impact of the individual's contribution, can be misguided by erroneous or misinformed individual perceptions or beliefs, in line with notions of practical rationality (see Verba, Schlozman & Brady 2000: 245).

10 In this chapter, only the general links and micro-mechanisms of the various contextual factors with the decision to join a political organisation are discussed. Chapters six and seven discuss in more detail the specific hypotheses that pertain to each set of macro- and meso-factors, while also presenting the specific indicators that are used to measure these environmental structures and processes.

11 Olson (1965) stressed the importance of both aspects. He mentions that, although small groups may provide incentives to individual participation due to the greater chances to have an impact on the course of collective action – but also thanks to social control, and the

greater risks of defection – if we are dealing with a lumpy good, small groups may have difficulties in providing the good itself, as too many resources are needed.

12 Recent data from a study of organisations in 23 communities of varying size in six European countries (Germany, Denmark, Spain, Great Britain, the Netherlands and Switzerland) collected by the network Citizenship, Involvement and Democracy of the European Science Foundation indicate that, in fact, there are substantial differences in the number of members political associations have in cities of a similar size. For example, the political associations of Sabadell (Spain) have an average number – even after trimming the 5 per cent of extreme cases – of only 107 members, while those of Berne (Switzerland) have an average of 1,498. And the (5 per cent trimmed) average size of explicitly political associations is substantially larger than that of the typical local association, as in these same cities the overall average size of associations varies from 48 members in Sabadell to 309 in Berne.

13 Whiteley (1995: 214) offers a similar argument: '... if collective goods are provided in significant amounts at the local level by a relatively small number of actors, then the small size of the group will promote co-operation. In this situation the collective good will very likely be provided, and the actors will participate.'

14 There are numerous studies that show that individuals tend to over-estimate the likelihood that their contribution will have an impact on the final outcome (see, for example, Muller & Opp 1986, Coleman 1990: 14, Baumgartner & Leech 1998: 71). And some scholars argue that it is unproblematic to conceptualise rationality as dependent on the beliefs and perceptions of the agent, rather than on 'real' probabilities. See Elster (1989: chapter three) for a summary of the various forms of problematic rationality.

15 Introducing optimism about others' behaviour into the equation does not necessarily imply assuming the existence of some sort of 'collective rationality' if the individual's expectations are informed by past collective behaviour. See a discussion of this in Orbell & Dawes (1991: 526) and in Ainsworth (2000).

16 Muller & Opp (1986 and 1987) refer to a similar process of evaluation of the probability of success of political protest from the past success of similar initiatives.

17 This argument only partially contradicts Oliver's (1984) findings. In her study, activists are pessimistic about token member's contributions and free-riding – and this is why they become active – while token members are optimistic about others' efforts in the provision of the collective good – based on their experience with activists. However, it is reasonable to assume that, because there are more token than active members in every society, it is the perception of token members – and similar individuals – that matters the most for the overall collective outcome.

18 Ainsworth (2000: 100) predicts that, after successfully achieving collective goods through interest group organisations, the 'external' efficacy of all citizens should increase, regardless of whether they joined or free-rode. They will also increase their sense of 'internal' efficacy, as their strategies towards collective action – joining or freeriding, depending on the individual – proved to be the correct ones.

19 Both Hansen (1985) and Skocpol (2003) discuss the crucial role of public subsidies – frequently, in the form of tax exemptions – and of foundation patronage, in promoting the emergence and continuation of public-interest groups and organisations in the United States.

20 Even if their data do not explicitly address organisational participation, Verba, Schlozman &

Brady (1995: 134–6) show that between 10 and 30 per cent of Americans receive requests to participate in collective action. Of these, between 30 and 60 per cent responded positively to the requests and decided to participate. In general, Verba, Schlozman & Brady's study highlights the importance of recruitment processes for citizens' participation in politics. Individuals who are not recruited into political action are less likely to participate on their own initiative.

21 Skocpol (2003: 232–6) provides a nice summary of the ways in which this mobilisation bias operates and how it is substantially shaped by the form recruitment strategies adopt.

22 Huckfeldt (2007) offers an exceptionally clear and succinct overview of the evolution and angles of this subfield of research in political behaviour. It is pointless to repeat this overview here.

23 We will assume that most household members are part of the respondent's family.

24 The list of organisations can be found in Table 2.2 in Chapter two.

25 To avoid yet another big table with lots of coefficients, we only present the coefficients for *alter's* party and trade-union membership. We have controlled for a number of relevant variables in all countries and the full results are available upon request.

26 The 1995–97 wave of the WVS only included nine western countries, while Eurobarometers 47.2 (1997) and 49 (1998) include the then 15 member countries of the EU, but the questionnaire limited excessively the number of political associations listed (see Chapter two). The data of the study Citizenship, Involvement and Democracy (2000–2003) also includes only nine West European countries. Finally the data of the first round of the European Social Survey (2002) does include a substantial number of West European countries but it inadequately lumped together various associations that differ substantially with regard to their political and non-political goals. A detailed analysis of the suitability of various cross-national surveys for the study of membership can be found in Morales (2002).

chapter five | the effect of meso-contexts: the patterns and structures of mobilisation

INTRODUCTION

Very frequently, citizens participate in public affairs just 'because someone asked' (Verba, Schlozman & Brady 1995, Klandermans 1997: 67) yet research on the impact of mobilisation structures and efforts on citizens' political participation is not very abundant. Nevertheless, some previous research has demonstrated how mobilisation processes account for why and when citizens get involved in politics (Pollock 1982, Klandermans 1984 & 1997, Briet, Klandermans & Kroon 1987, Klandermans & Oegema 1987, Klandermans & Tarrow 1988, Klandermans 1997, Knoke 1990, Rosenstone & Hansen 1993). All political organisations make some effort – large or small – to recruit new members and some organisations place recruitment strategies at the core of their organisational efforts (Harasse 1996, Jordan & Maloney 1997, Johnson 1998).

Thus, in our study of political membership we will be interested in ascertaining how mobilisation processes affect citizen participation and, additionally, whether mobilisation patterns account for the different levels of political membership in western democracies.

There are not many definitions of mobilisation.[1] Tilly (1978: 69) defines mobilisation as 'the process by which a group goes from being a passive collection of individuals to an active participant in public life'. But maybe the simplest and most suitable definition for this research is the one proposed by Rosenstone & Hansen (1993: 25): 'Mobilisation is the process by which candidates, parties, activists and groups induce other people to participate.'[2] Nettl (1967: 32–3), however, characterises mobilisation by the presence of an attitudinal component – a commitment to action – and a behavioural component – the transfer of this commitment into an observable action or behaviour. This conceives of mobilisation as a process that unfolds in distinct phases: (1) the development of the values and the goals that mobilisation requires, (2) action by leaders and institutions to mobilise individuals and social groups, (3) collective organisation to achieve these aims, (4) the creation of a symbolic reference frame that allows the transmission of the values and aims being mobilised, and (5) the patterns of social interaction that produce effective mobilisation.

Similarly, Nedelmann (1987) distinguishes three dimensions of mobilisation activities: cognitive, affective and instrumental. The first and the third dimensions mentioned by Nedelmann are of special interest to this study, as they agree with Klandermans' (1997: 7) distinction between the processes of cognitive or consensus mobilisation and of mobilisation into action. The former contribute to the creation of an ideological support base, while the latter transform diffuse ideological support into explicit support, through the creation of structures, direct induction into action and by the creation of opportunities for participation. However, both processes are closely linked. Cognitive mobilisation and the elaboration of collective-action frames allow mobilisation into action; and explicit mobilisation into action contributes to constructing and publicising collective-action frames. Even if ideological mobilisation is necessary for citizen mobilisation, however, only mobilisation into action can convert potential mobilisation into effective mobilisation (Kriesi 1993, Klandermans 1997).

Klandermans (1997: 22 ff.) mentions three elements that intervene in the dynamic of effective mobilisation into collective action: the creation or existence of recruitment networks, the motivation for participation provided by mobilisation agents and the facilitation of participation by the reduction of barriers to collective action.

The existence or creation of recruitment networks is fundamental because it transforms the potential for mobilisation, through the formation of common ideological frames. This requires solid inter-organisational networks, as well as the development of sufficiently widespread organisational structures, both at the national and the local level, in order to recruit a large number of citizens.[3] The more widespread these networks are, the greater the reach and the success of mobilisation initiatives.

Activities organised by social movements and political organisations are valuable instruments for motivating co-operation and reducing the barriers to action. This is especially true of non-conflictual activities – such as exhibitions, festivals or the distribution of information and publications – since these initiatives heighten the visibility of organisations and bring them closer to citizens (Rochon 1988: 116). A stimulus to join can result merely from associations becoming more visible, as Hansen points out (1985: 83).

Koopmans (1996: 35) argues that mobilisation by new social movements (NSMs) has a direct impact on the number of citizens who join NSM organisations (NSMOs). This is due both to cognitive mobilisation efforts by NSMs and to their success in adding new issues on the political agenda, as well as to explicit mobilisation into action. Yet, this is not necessarily due to confrontational mobilisation strategies. In fact, Koopmans (1996: 41) argues that there is a negative relationship between the frequency and radicalism of the means of confrontational protest mobilisation and political membership. The least conflictual western nations are also those with higher levels of membership in political organisations. And this is closely related to the degree of openness of their respective political systems and the Political Opportunity Structures (POS): when the POS is open and inclusive, social movements do not need to resort to more radical forms of political action and it is strategically more practical for them to develop stable and solid organisational structures. When the POS is closed, less conventional protest is a more efficient strategy, to which associations have more frequent resort and, consequently, the creation of organisational structures becomes more costly.

As we discussed in Chapter four, organisational structures and mobilisation processes have an impact on individuals' decisions to join political organisations, primarily through affecting perceptions of the efficacy of individual action and of participation costs. Both effects are, to a large degree, related to the information provided by organisations when they mobilise and recruit. Firstly, organisational infrastructures, as well as mobilising, and recruitment activities, provide citizens with information on the very existence of organisations and on their political aims. This greatly contributes to reducing the costs of joining, as they reduce the transaction and information costs each individual has to bear.

Secondly, mobilisation by political organisations also provides substantive information on the issues at stake, thus reducing further the information costs involved in taking sides on those issues. Finally, mobilisation by organisations contributes to increasing the sense of efficacy of individual action, as it frequently provides information on the results of past actions, while also offering an optimistic vision of the likely results of collective action.[4]

Despite the clear relevance of mobilisation processes in explaining political participation, there is little research that systematically analyses the connection between cross-national variations in mobilisation and citizens' political participation in a large number of countries.[5]

This chapter is devoted to the systematic analysis of the connection between mobilisation patterns and structures and the levels of political membership in western democracies. To this end, we will explore three different dimensions of mobilisation: direct mobilisation through structures and actions; indirect mobilisation through cognitive processes and the construction of identities; and the legacy of historical traditions of mobilisation.

Generally, the theoretical expectation extracted from prior research is that higher levels of mobilisation by political organisations will translate into higher levels of political membership; this hypothesis must be qualified on occasion, though, depending on the specific type of mobilisation we are dealing with.

DIRECT MOBILISATION AND ORGANISATIONAL VISIBILITY: ORGANISATIONAL STRUCTURES AND MOBILISING ACTION

Intentional mobilisation and recruitment strategies are certainly of the utmost importance to our understanding of what leads people to join political organisations. These strategies vary substantially, depending on where they are enacted – in the public or the private sphere – and on the way the information used for recruitment is transmitted – through face-to-face interaction or mediated messages (see Snow, Zurcher & Ekland-Olson 1980: 790). Yet, the survey data usually

Table 5.1: Recruitment processes into local associations, percentages

Municipality/ District	Self-initiated		Interper-sonal	Organisational				Total N of cases
	Own initiative	Influenced by mass media reports	Encouraged by relatives, friends, colleagues	Intentional recruitment (mail or phone campaigns)	Influenced by organi-sational media or contacts with organisa-tion	Through activities	Work profes-sional relations	
Alcalá de Henares	14	2	60	2	5	15	2	100 221
Andoain	17	0	73	0	0	10	0	100 30
Deusto (Bilbao)	11	0	60	0	2	24	2	100 140
Caldes de Montbui	14	1	64	0	8	14	0	100 45
Sabadell	9	0	70	1	3	16	0	100 422
Gracia (Barcelona)	13	2	65	2	5	11	2	100 333

Source: Survey of *Organisational Members*, 2002 (CID Project, Spain). Own elaboration. Each individual reports only about the primary association through which he or she has been interviewed.

Table 5.2: Paths to joining associations

	Barcelona	Madrid
Own initiative	16	9
After media report or ad on the organisation	5	3
A relative or friend asked to join	41	31
After a phone or mail request by the organisation	5	4
After reading material published by the organisation	9	6
After attending a local event or meeting by the organisation	3	3
Any other situation	6	3
Total no. of cases	881	884

Source: *Survey of Individuals*, 2007–08 (LOCALMULTIDEM Project, Spain). Own elaboration. Figures are the percentages of individuals in the total sample who have joined any association and reported each category as the main process of joining, and thus this represents 'successful' mobilisation. Each individual reports about any association he or she is a member of.

employed for analysing political behaviour seldom incorporate systematic coverage of recruitment processes, and certainly never in cross-national survey studies.[6] Given the survey data available, it is thus difficult to link mobilisation strategies and processes to individual behaviour in a significant number of countries.

Nonetheless, the fragmentary evidence available does indicate that recruitment into organisations is very much dependent on someone asking, and on organisational activity. Tables 5.1 and 5.2 show the results of two different surveys in Spain that enquired about the processes by which citizens first joined an association.[7]

In addition to the fundamental role of interpersonal face-to-face recruitment – which adds to the findings presented in the last section of Chapter four – recruitment into associations is also largely dependent on organisational efforts and activities.[8] Even if membership campaigns are not the most effective means of recruitment, the organisation of activities and the publication of various materials has a substantial impact on decisions to join. These results support the findings by Snow, Zurcher & Ekland-Olson (1980) on the emergent and interactional character of the process of recruitment:

> it is important to emphasise that people seldom initially join movements *per se*. Rather they typically are asked to participate in movement activities. Furthermore, it is during the course of initial participation that they are provided with the 'reasons' or 'justifications' for what they have already done and for continuing participation. [...] We would thus argue that the 'motives' for joining or continued participation are generally emergent and interactional rather than prestructured. They arise out of a process of ongoing interaction with a movement organisation and its recruitment agents. (Snow, Zurcher & Ekland-Olson 1980: 795)

Besides, a certain organisational infrastructure is needed to carry out mobilisation activities. Knoke (1990b) repeatedly shows that organisations with policy goals that undertake political mobilisation require greater economic and human resources. Political mobilisation is capital-intensive; thus, associations with political goals have an incentive to recruit more members or – alternatively – to become wealthier. But the capacity to recruit new members is also dependent on the economic and human capital stocks that the organisation has already amassed. In this context, territorial and infrastructure expansion become crucial to membership growth. There are two main reasons why political associations might not expand their infrastructures and memberships over time: either they do not have the resources to do so or they simply do not wish to do so. In both situations, the mobilisatory capacity of these associations will be reduced more than would that of organisations with infrastructures all over the country.

In this regard, both organisational infrastructures and organisational activities are crucial for membership recruitment and expansion. And, for this reason, we will focus on both aspects when measuring the mobilisation context of western democracies. In the next pages, a number of indicators will attempt to measure the spread of organisational infrastructures in each country, as well as the intensity and type of organisational activities and actions. However, fully measuring the distribution of organisational infrastructures in any given country is an impossible task, even for a single case study, and we will need to rely on *proxies*.

In our case, the best available indicator or *proxy* is the organisational density of political parties: the number of party branches per one thousand inhabitants.[9] The use of this indicator as a *proxy* assumes that its variation across European

Graph 5.1: Organisational density of political parties in Europe

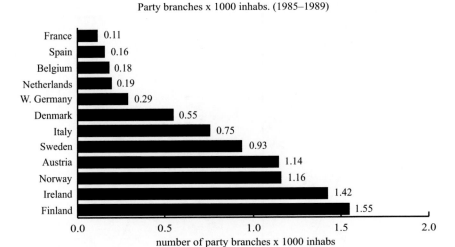

Party branches x 1000 inhabs. (1985–1989)

countries reflects in some way the variations in the organisational density of the whole set of political organisations. In other words, it assumes that those countries where political parties have a more solid and widespread organisational infrastructures are also the countries where the rest of the political organisations have more consolidated organisational infrastructures.

Unfortunately, information on the number of party branches is not available for all West European countries, nor for the United States or Canada, given their different styles and structures of partisan organisation.[10] Graph 5.1 illustrates the substantial variation that is found in the organisational density of European political parties.

The organisational spread of European parties differs substantially across countries, and varies from more than one and a half branches per thousand inhabitants in Finland to the very few 0.1 branches per thousand inhabitants – or one branch every ten thousand inhabitants – in France. Clearly, the organisational density of parties is generally higher in Scandinavia but is also higher in Ireland, Austria and Italy; and it is much lower in France, Spain, Belgium, the Netherlands and Germany.

The connections between organisational infrastructure and recruitment success set out previously would lead us to expect that this organisational density is linearly and positively related both to traditional and new political membership, if parties' organisational spread is a good proxy for the overall extension of political organisations over the country. At a minimum, it should be positively related to party membership. Graph 5.2 shows, however, that the bivariate relationship between party organisational density and political membership is not linear. In fact, the relation is more clearly curvilinear and is different for party membership and for 'new' political membership. The organisational embeddedness of political

Graph 5.2: Political membership and organisational density of political parties in Europe

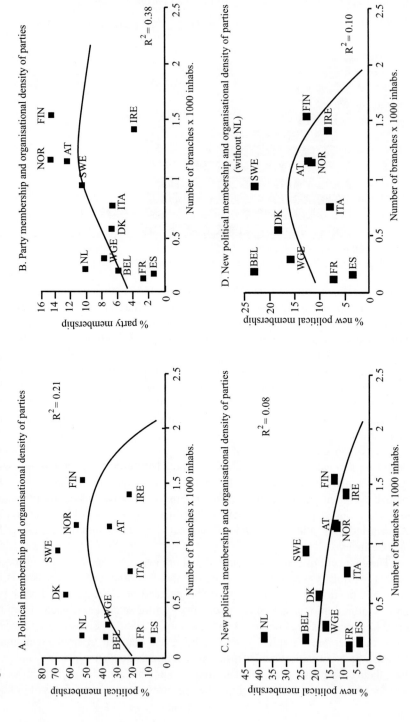

parties is positively but moderately related to individual partisanship but not so much to membership of NSMOs. In the latter case, if at all, strong party infrastructures seem to lead to a smaller inclination to join NSMOs.[11]

But, as we have discussed, the visibility that organisational infrastructure and branches provide is not the only valuable means of membership recruitment; we should also consider the activities that organisations perform. As regards direct mechanisms of face-to-face public mobilisation – such as the distribution of leaflets in the streets, the organisation of public events, demonstrations, etc. – the available comparative data are also limited and derive exclusively from studies of protest-events.

Kriesi *et al.* (1995) carried out a pioneering study of the levels of protest in Europe, based on information available in the daily press. Their database, which collected all the protest-events related to social movements (excluding economic strikes) that were reported in Monday's edition of a national newspaper and which took place between 1975 and 1989, is, unfortunately, limited to four countries: the Federal Republic of Germany, France, the Netherlands and Switzerland.[12]

More recently, a group of American researchers led by Ron Francisco developed a study with similar aims but using different data-collection strategies: the *European Protest and Coercion Dataset* (EPCD), 1980–1995.[13] This dataset – the one primarily used here – collects all the protest and repression events, including economic ones, that were reported by a wide range of national and local communication media in 28 European countries.[14] The nature of the data collected through this project makes it the most complete to date for research into the level and type of protest mobilisation in Europe.[15] Some estimates indicate that the media report only between 4 and 10 per cent of all the protest actions that occur in a given territory (Koopmans 1999: 96, note 10), but, rather than the absolute number of protest actions, here we are primarily interested in the differences across countries in the number and types of protests, as well as the political actors who initiate them.

We can, nevertheless, compare the data available in each database for the four countries included in both studies: Germany (FRG), France, the Netherlands and Switzerland.[16] Limiting ourselves to the 1985–9 period – the same included earlier for the indicator of organisational density – Graph 5.3 compares the results from both protest-event datasets.

The results clearly illustrate that the two methods of data-collection for protest-events result in strikingly contrasting conclusions. *A priori*, given the methodology, we would expect the EPCD to report systematically more protest-events than did Kriesi *et al.* This is indeed the case for France and, to a much smaller degree, for Germany and the Netherlands. However, for reasons that are not apparent, the ECPD automated system of protest-event data-collection massively under-reports protest in Switzerland.

The huge difference for France can be explained by the fact that Kriesi's team excluded all actions related to labour strikes or those of an economic nature, while the data from Ron Francisco include these types of events. Actually, as one of the

Graph 5.3: Comparison of the results of the two datasets for four countries, 1985–9

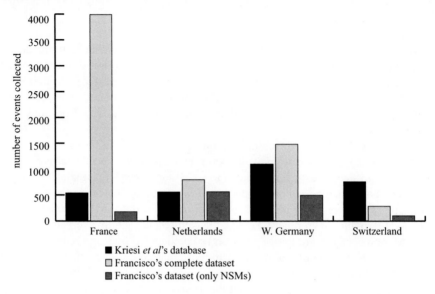

researchers in Kriesi's team explains (Koopmans 1999: note 17), the protest-event data collected by this team reflect, primarily, protest mobilisation by social movements and, above all, by NSMs. For this reason, it is preferable to compare Kriesi *et al.*'s dataset with the subsample of protest action collected in Ron Francisco's dataset, whose main actors are part of NSMs (right-hand column for each country). Yet, the different overall results reveal that the two studies do not uncover the same events, as evidenced by the Swiss case.[17] And this should probably lead us to be cautious about the results obtained with automated systems of protest-event coding, such as that of the ECPD.

Nevertheless, Francisco's dataset of protest-events is the only one available for a large number of western democracies and, hence, it will be the primary source of information for the indicators of mobilisation used hereafter.[18] With this data, a general indicator of the relative number of protests in each country can be computed for the period 1985–9, which is immediately prior to the survey employed – the 1990–93 World Values Survey (WVS).[19] We can also distinguish between different types of protest, depending on the type of action involved and on the degree of conflict. Following the distinction made by Kriesi and his colleagues (1995), three additional indicators were computed to reflect the number of protest actions in the form of demonstrations, confrontation and violence. Demonstrative protest involves some kind of non-violent collective demonstration with low levels of confrontation – for example, demonstrations, petitions, large-scale meetings, festivals, etc. Confrontational protest entails a higher degree of confrontation with the authorities or with opposing groups but stopping short of physical violence – for

Table 5.3: Indicators of direct mobilisation: number of protests in Europe, 1985–9

Country	Total protest (1985–1989)		Demonstrative protest		Confrontational protest		Violent protest		Population	
	Absolute number	n/log pop.	Absolute number	n/log pop.	Absolute number	n/log pop.	Absolute number	n/log pop.	1000s	Log pop.
Austria	158	40.7	98	25.3	45	11.6	11	2.8	7,570	3.9
Belgium	697	174.3	69	17.3	550	137.6	78	19.5	9,960	4.0
Canada	n.a.	n.a.	n.a.	n.a.	n.a.	n.a.	n.a.	n.a.	25,880	4.4
Denmark	585	157.6	31	8.4	510	137.4	44	11.9	5,140	3.7
Finland	329	89.0	12	3.2	314	85.0	3	0.8	4,950	3.7
France	3991	840.7	419	88.3	3303	695.8	269	56.7	55,860	4.7
W. Germany	1479	309.0	670	140.0	655	136.9	154	32.2	61,024	4.8
Great Britain	7561	1595.0	182	38.4	7212	1521.4	100	21.1	54,989	4.7
Iceland	122	51.0	8	3.3	108	45.1	5	2.1	248	2.4
Ireland	1660	467.5	145	40.8	1474	415.1	39	11.0	3,553	3.6
Italy	609	128.0	148	31.1	400	84.1	61	12.8	57,400	4.8
Netherlands	794	190.5	95	22.8	659	158.1	36	8.6	14,750	4.2
Norway	353	97.4	20	5.5	330	91.1	1	0.3	4,202	3.6
Portugal	384	95.6	32	8.0	317	79.0	33	8.2	10,350	4.0
Spain	2522	549.3	585	127.4	936	203.9	1001	218.0	38,996	4.6
Sweden	425	108.3	44	11.2	335	85.3	19	4.8	8,415	3.9
Switzerland	282	74.0	106	27.8	125	32.8	21	5.5	6,470	3.8
United States	n.a.	n.a.	n.a.	n.a.	n.a.	n.a.	n.a.	n.a.	245,560	5.4

Source: *European Protest and Coercion Dataset* (1980–1995). Own elaboration. Key: n.a.= no information available.

example, boycotts, hunger-strikes, sit-ins, etc. Lastly, violent protest actions are all those which involve some degree of violence against persons or property.[20]

Table 5.3 presents these various indicators of direct mobilisation but, as the overall amount of protest is partly due to the population size of each country, our indicators need to take this element into account.[21] And Graph 5.4 shows the relative distribution of these three forms of protest in each of the 16 European countries for which data are available. In most countries, the most common type of protest action involves some kind of confrontation with the authorities or with opposing groups.[22] Only in Austria and West Germany are demonstrative protest actions more common. Additionally, in most countries there is a significant number, albeit a minority, of violent actions.

Our expectations about the relation between levels of direct mobilisation – as measured by the level of protest – in a country and the level of political membership are multiple. On the one hand, Koopmans (1996) argues that the frequency of protest is inversely related to the degree of development of NSMs and to levels of political membership. Hence, countries where more intense protest is frequent are also those where the NSMs have not gained much ground because the traditional social cleavages (class, religion or centre-periphery) have still not been pacified and institutionalised; and this acts as a deterrent to participation through

Graph 5.4: Distribution of protest actions by types, 1985–9

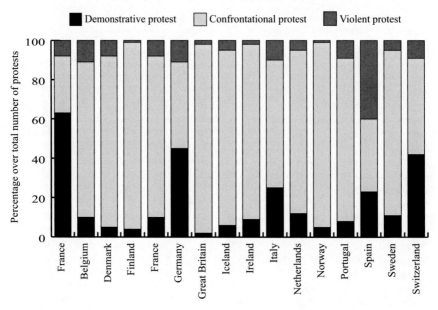

conventional and stable structures: political organisations. At the same time, the literature on the impact of mobilisation patterns on political participation leads us to expect that membership of NSMOs will be higher in those countries where the latter have greater visibility. In other words, if NSMs are more frequently the main initiators of collective action, participation in 'new' political associations will be higher. The results of the bivariate analyses presented in Graphs 5.5 and 5.6 support both hypotheses.

Graph 5.5: Negative association between protest and political membership

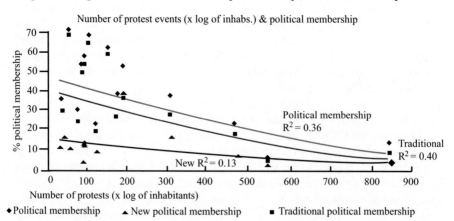

Graph 5.6: Positive relation between the visibility of NSMs and new political membership

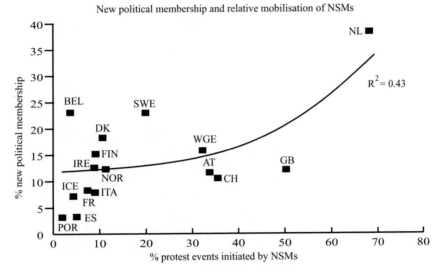

New political membership and relative mobilisation of NSMs

Indeed, as previous research on social movements has suggested, higher levels of social conflict hinder the development of more stable forms of participation, such as political membership. The negative relationship between protest and membership of political associations is, nevertheless, stronger for traditional political associations than for 'new' political organisations.[23]

Yet, when NSMs are responsible for a greater share of this social conflict, this fosters membership of NSMOs. NSMs mobilise in ways other than just protest and, in turn, not all protest actions are organised by NSMs (Rucht, Koopmans & Neidhardt 1999: 9). When protest is the result of the mobilisation of new issues and actors, this contributes to the expansion of 'new' political associations and of their membership. But when protest is primarily linked to the traditional *cleavages*, the result is that conflict leads to citizens refraining from joining political organisations.

Thus, the available data seem to support two provisional conclusions. On the one hand, the level of visibility and of direct mobilisation by political organisations has an impact on citizens' decisions to join these organisations, though in many cases this relationship is not necessarily linear. As a result, where parties are better distributed in the territory they tend to attract more members and, where NSMs are especially active in mobilising protest, the membership of 'new' political organisations blossoms. On the other hand, an excess of conflict and unrest is indicative of the lack of pacification of the traditional social and political cleavages and this, in turn, restrains political membership in general.

COGNITIVE MOBILISATION:
CLEAVAGE AND POLARISATION STRUCTURES

Cognitive mobilisation processes play a fundamental role in the creation of the conceptual frameworks for action. They allow the creation of collective identities and of reference frameworks, as well as the establishment of conceptual connections that link collective action to the desired political and social changes.

Ideally, testing the impact of cognitive mobilisation processes implies measuring the set of collective identities and reference frameworks for action that prevail in each country. However, this is impractical in a comparative study of a large number of nations; we will have to settle for an approximation of different degrees of cognitive mobilisation: ideological polarisation.

In a certain sense, the degree of ideological polarisation is an indirect indicator of the level of cognitive mobilisation carried out by the political agents of a given society. And, in turn, this can have consequences for the level of political membership. For example, Kalyvas (1997) describes how the political strategies of polarisation pursued by PASOK and *Nea Demokratia* in Greece during the mid 1980s led to a considerable increase in party identification and affiliation in that country.

There are, nonetheless, various ways in which we can define ideological polarisation. First, we need to define the ideological dimensions around which polarisation (or its absence) develops. Usually, the focus is on the ideological dimension resulting from class divisions: the left–right divide. However, polarisation in contemporary western democracies is not only (and in some cases not even mainly) based on the left–right dimension.[24] Thus, we should also take into account other dimensions of political competition and other social cleavages: for example, the religious cleavage, the regional or nationalist cleavage, etc.

Once again, data limitations prevent us from using direct indicators of religious and ethno-regional polarisation. The lack of cross-nationally standardised scales around these two dimensions means that indicators of social segmentation or heterogeneity will have to be employed as proxies of the degree of polarisation around these cleavages.[25]

Past research in the field of political participation suggest that social segmentation increases citizen participation. For example, Huntington & Nelson (1976: 103) claim that social segmentation increases political participation because it favours residential segregation, intensifies collective or group consciousness and stimulates the organisation of the distinct collectivities in associations. Some of these ideas are confirmed by Oliver (1999), who argues that social heterogeneity is linked to the existence of higher levels of conflict and political competition for scarce resources; this, in turn, encourages citizens to participate in public issues.[26]

In addition, social segmentation has an impact on the mobilisation capacity that all sorts of political organisations have (Oberschall 1973: 129). Kriesi (1993: 13) clearly emphasises this relationship between segmentation and mobilisation when he argues that a 'closed group is above all mobilisable by its own political organisations [...] the closure of social relationships is very likely to imply the stabilisation of mobilisation capacities not only for specific parties, but also for given interest groups and social movements.'

However, not all types of social conflict, segmentation or polarisation will have positive consequences on citizens' participation in political associations. Kriesi *et al.* (1995: 5–25) claimed that the centrality and polarisation of traditional class conflicts are counterproductive to opportunities for mobilisation by NSMs; and that, in those countries where class conflict has been pacified through the expansion of the welfare state, 'new' political organisations have had more space to articulate new conflicts. Thus, the intensity of the class cleavage is inversely related to the strength of the NSMs.

Ideological polarisation around the left–right divide can be measured in different ways. We may distinguish between party-system polarisation and citizens' polarisation. Although these are, undoubtedly, related (Sani & Sartori 1983: 308), the political elites have a certain capacity to generate depolarising dynamics through institutional mechanisms. In fact, a wide range of political and social institutions have been created in western societies to pacify social conflicts institutionally (see Lijphart 1975, 1977 and 1999).

To measure the degree of citizens' polarisation on the left–right dimension, we use the variance in respondents' self-positioning in the left–right scale, for each of the national samples in the 1990–93 WVS.[27] Higher values of the variance indicate greater heterogeneity in the ideological positions of citizens and, hence, more

Table 5.4: Indicators of citizens' and party system polarisation, 1986–90

	Citizen polarisation [a]	Party system polarisation [b]
Iceland	4.85	24.2
Portugal	4.54	16.5
Spain	4.53	7.2
Italy	4.48	34.2
Finland	4.45	21.1
Sweden	4.39	5.6
Switzerland	4.36	8.5
Norway	4.16	16.3
Belgium	4.12	2.7
Netherlands	3.98	1.8
France	3.88	21.4
Great Britain	3.62	0
Denmark	3.59	24.6
Ireland	3.39	4.9
United States	3.21	0
Austria	3.01	0.7
W. Germany	2.87	0.6
Canada	2.75	2.1

[a] Variance of ideological self-placements. Source: WVS 1990–93, my own elaboration.

[b] Percentage of the vote for extreme parties (communists, populists and extreme right). Source: Lane & Ersson (1999: 145), extended to Canada and the US.

Graph 5.7: Citizen and system polarisation: bivariate relations

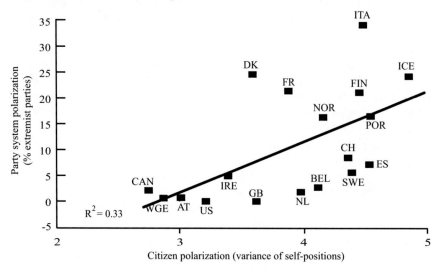

polarisation around the main dimension of political competition in western societies.[28]

In turn, party-system polarisation has been measured with a simple indicator proposed by Lane & Ersson (1999: 145): the percentage of votes obtained by the parties positioned at the extremes of the ideological spectrum (communists, populists and extreme-right parties). Other indicators of party-system polarisation were considered and discarded because they showed a weaker connection to political membership (Morales 2004: 321–9).[29] Table 5.4 shows the distribution of these two indicators of polarisation.

The use of separate indicators of citizen and system polarisation is justified by the fact that, although related, they are empirically distinct. Indeed, bivariate analyses of the two indicators reveal that the relation between the two forms of polarisation is moderate and limited and that it is mediated by the effects of electoral systems (Graph 5.7).

According to the hypotheses previously outlined, we would expect that both citizen and party-system polarisation would foster political membership. Polarisation contributes to citizens' clearly distinguishing among the various political options and policy goals and facilitates mobilisation by political organisations.[30] However, social movement scholars have argued that the salience of the traditional class cleavage limits the organisational development of NSMs (Kriesi et al. 1995). Given that the salience of the class cleavage is also reflected in the level of ideological polarisation in the left–right dimension, we expect the latter to be inversely related to the percentage of membership in NSMOs.

Graph 5.8 presents the bivariate relationships between the indicators of citizen and party-system polarisation and, first, the percentage of membership of political associations and, second, the percentage of membership in 'new' political organisations. The results indicate that ideological polarisation – whether among citizens

Graph 5.8: Ideological polarisation and political membership

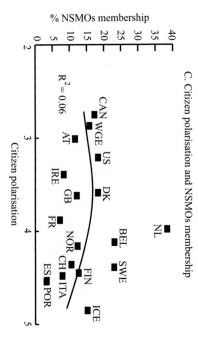

A. Citizen polarisation and political membership

—— Excluding Southern Europe   —— All countries

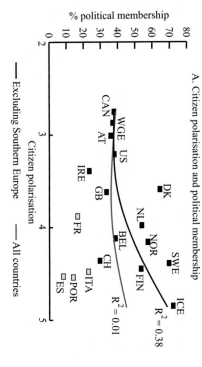

B. System polarisation and political membership

—— Southern Europe apart   —— All countries

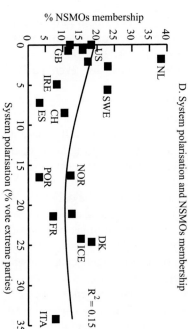

C. Citizen polarisation and NSMOs membership

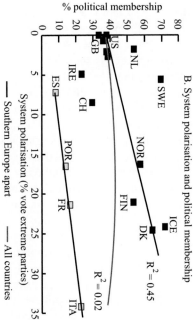

D. System polarisation and NSMOs membership

Table 5.5: Indicators of social segmentation (1981–7)

	Effective number of linguistic groups	Effective number of ethnic groups	Effective number of religious groups
Austria	1.02	1.01	1.36
Belgium	2.17	2.35	1.60
Canada	2.33	3.49	3.07
Denmark	1.05	1.02	1.06
Finland	1.14	1.13	1.24
France	1.32	1.17	1.23
Great Britain	1.15	1.48	1.65
Iceland	1.06	1.06	1.11
Ireland	1.11	1.08	1.13
Italy	1.16	1.04	1.00
Netherlands	1.14	1.08	3.19
Norway	1.05	1.04	1.13
Portugal	1.02	1.02	1.06
Spain	1.79	1.65	1.02
Sweden	1.20	1.26	1.14
Switzerland	2.13	2.13	2.12
United States	1.27	1.35	2.26
W. Germany	1.16	1.15	2.45

Source: Cox & Amorim Neto (1997).

or at the party-system level – contributes to mobilising citizens to join political associations. This positive relationship is much clearer when we identify South European nations (France, Spain, Italy and Portugal) separately, because those countries systematically show lower levels of political membership, even if a similar positive relation also holds for them.

In the case of 'new' political organisations, the results confirm the existence of a certain negative association between ideological polarisation on the left-right dimension and membership of NSMOs; but it is so weak that it is hardly relevant.

In summary, ideological polarisation in the main dimension of political competition – the left-right divide – is connected to higher levels of political membership, albeit not necessarily for all types of political organisations.

Yet, as we have discussed before, the left-right divide is not the only relevant basis for social conflict and polarisation; and we also need to look at other cleavages. However, in the case of ethnic, linguistic and religious divisions, no comparative data on the positions of citizens, nor of political parties, is available for the 1980s, and we cannot compute similar indicators of polarisation. Hence, we will use a number of indices of the presence of these cleavages as proxies. Bartolini & Mair (1990) have emphasised that the existence of social differences does not automatically transform into political mobilisation around them. But, as a general rule, in the western nations we are studying, ethnic, linguistic and/or religious differences have indeed been politically mobilised. However, this does not always

Graph 5.9: Social segmentation and political membership

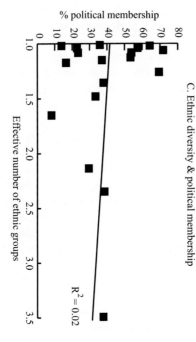

A. Linguistic diversity & political membership

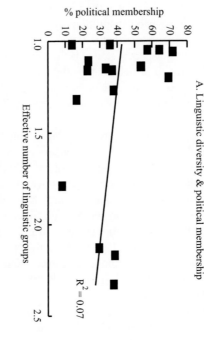

B. Religious diversity & political membership

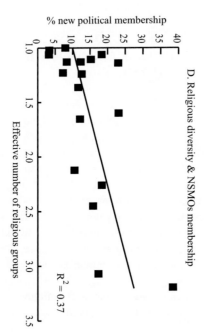

C. Ethnic diversity & political membership

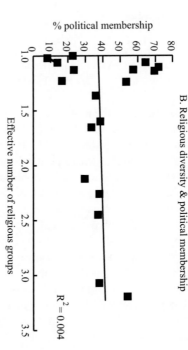

D. Religious diversity & NSMOs membership

result in greater polarisation around these cleavages, as in many countries these divides have been institutionally pacified. Table 5.5 presents the indicators of social segmentation that will be employed.

The first aspect to notice is the limited variation in the effective number of linguistic groups, which is only slightly higher for the ethnic and religious composition. We expect social segmentation around these three cleavages to have similar effects to left-right polarisation. The results in Graph 5.9 do not support these expectations.

The association between ethnic, linguistic and religious heterogeneity and political membership is very weak and inconsistent. The only exception is the relation between religious pluralism and membership of NSMOs. Religious segmentation might operate in such a way that it multiplies the support of organisations linked to NSMs. Past research has stressed the role played by organisations with religious roots in the emergence and development of social movements – especially the peace movement – in European countries such as the Netherlands (Kriesi & van Praag 1987). Often, the NSMOs replicate religious cleavages, for example, between Catholics and Protestants; thus giving rise to a larger number of organisations. And, frequently, churches act as *loci* of mobilisation and recruitment into NSMOs.

In any case, these bivariate results indicate that polarisation around the left–right divide might contribute to citizens' joining political organisations in higher numbers, while religious pluralism might promote membership of NSMOs. There is no evidence that ethnic or linguistic heterogeneity has any impact on political membership.

THE ORGANISATIONAL HERITAGE OF THE PAST: CONSOLIDATING MOBILISATION STRUCTURES

The final aspect of the mobilisation context that will be analysed is the historical tradition of political mobilisation. This might have an impact on current levels of political membership through various mechanisms.

First, in countries where political mobilisation has been sustained over time, networks and infrastructures of mobilisation develop and this contributes to further (present and future) mobilisation. Inter-organisational networks and resources for action foster the emergence and development of new groups, organisations and movements that may resort to existing infrastructures to carry out their own activities. In this sense, the fruits of past co-operation and mobilisation are transferred to the present, thanks to the resources available to new organisations. Hence, the costs of citizen organisation will be lower in countries with numerous pre-existing organisational resources and infrastructures.

That past and present mobilisation are connected by the accumulation of organisational resources has been suggested, albeit not systematically tested, by various scholars. Stinchcombe argued that:

Because literacy, urbanisation, money economy, political revolution, and *previously existing organisational density* affect the variables leading to high motivation to found organisations and the variables increasing the chances for success of new organisational forms, they tend to increase the rate at which new organisational forms are developed. Such, at least, is the current theory, which remains at a relatively low level of verification. (1965: 153 emphasis added).

And Olson (1982) claimed that the number of organisations increases over time in stable societies: once they have overcome the fixed costs of mobilisation, organisations tend to perpetuate themselves, thus giving rise to an accumulation of groups and associations over time. According to Olson, collective co-ordination, being costly, requires a long gestation period, in the sense that it does not spontaneously come about under every circumstance; once it has, however, it establishes the bases to reproduce itself and multiply the self-organisation of social groups.

In this line, Walker (1991: chapter 5) provides data in support of some of these hypotheses. His study of interest groups in Washington DC illustrated the importance of the support of established organisations for the creation of new ones. Associations frequently help to create new ones, with the aim of generating wider organisational networks that will strengthen their positions when defending causes that are fairly 'volatile', or when defending social sectors that are particularly disadvantaged.

On the other hand, past experiences in mobilisation and collective co-ordination have an impact on present behaviour, through the creation of a certain culture of co-operation and mobilisation. If organisations with political objectives have been successful in recruiting members and mobilising citizens in the past, citizens will develop positive orientations towards collective action, as well as a set of beliefs about its effectiveness and suitability for achieving collective goals.[31] A lack of substantial past experience of political membership is likely to render citizens sceptical about collective action.

Although both mechanisms are likely to operate simultaneously, in this work we will focus on the structural component of historical legacies:[32] the prior existence and accumulation of infrastructures and resources for action and co-operation to facilitate the future development of political organisations and, therefore, promote political membership.

One way of operationalising these structural legacies of past mobilisation is to consider the levels of organisational development of those political organisations that have been historically more important: political parties and unions. Thus, the main indicators of organisational legacies that will be used in this study are the membership figures of political parties and trade unions in each country during the period 1945–60.[33] This period is the most relevant for the study of organisational legacies and historical mobilisation, because World War II led to important changes in the structure of politics and political organisations; and because, from the 1960s onwards, participation in parties and unions began – in general terms –

to decline, but at a different pace in the various countries. Therefore, an indicator that covered a longer period could be distorted.

It is important to emphasise that the expected spillover effects affect all types of political associations, both traditional and 'new'. Research on NSMs shows that there is no radical separation between these two types of political organisations and that organisational interconnections are important to understand the success or failure of mobilisation (Kriesi & van Praag 1987, Schmitt 1989). Good relations between new and traditional political organisations lead to an increase in the available resources for action. In this vein, Klandermans' work confirms the relationship between traditional and new political organisations and supports the hypothesis of the importance of organisational structural legacies:

> To a large extent, the formation of movement networks is accomplished by co-optation of indigenous organisations (church parishes, chapters of unions, political parties, or women's organisations, community organisations and so on). [...] By co-opting, let's say, a national church organisation a movement gains access to church parishes all over the country. [...] Similar examples can be given of movements that successfully co-opted such organisations as political parties and labour unions. (1997: 66)

Table 5.6: Indicators of organisational legacies

	Party membership (average 1945–60) [a]	Party membership × 1000 inhabs. (average 1945–60) [a]	Union membership (1950) [b]	Union membership × 1000 inhabs. (1950) [b]
Austria	1,106,531	159.6	1,290,581	186.1
Sweden	1,101,000	157.0	1,298,300	185.1
Denmark	598,000	140.0	656,400	153.7
Finland	440,500	109.9	n.a.	n.a.
Norway	324,000	99.2	488,400	149.6
Italy	3,989,000	84.7	5,830,410	123.8
Netherlands	680,000	67.2	1,023,040	101.2
Great Britain	3,250,000	64.8	7,827,900	156.2
Belgium	463,462	53.6	887,319	102.7
France	924,000	22.1	3,600,000	86.1
Ireland	59,000	19.9	113,789	38.4
W. Germany	1,072,422	15.7	5,454,183	79.8
Portugal	0	0	0	0
Spain	0	0	0	0
Canada	n.a.	n.a.	1,006,000	71.8
Iceland	n.a.	n.a.	n.a.	n.a.
Switzerland	n.a.	n.a.	443,500	94.1
United States	n.a.	n.a.	16,300,000	107.0

Sources: [a] Katz & Mair (1992). For Belgium, data from 1960; for Denmark, data from Scarrow (2000: 89) and an average for 1950–1960. [b] Ebbinghaus (1993); Statistics Canada; US Department of Labor.

Graph 5.10: Organisational legacies and political membership

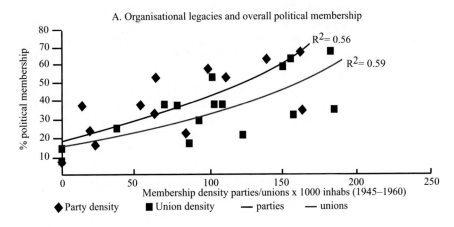

A. Organisational legacies and overall political membership

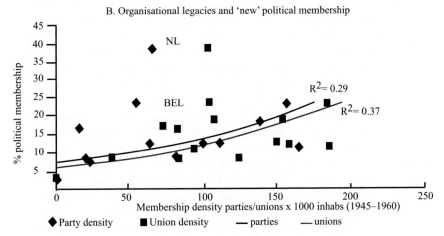

B. Organisational legacies and 'new' political membership

Table 5.6 shows the distribution of the two indicators of membership density used to measure the organisational legacies in each country. Previous research leads us to expect that past levels of membership density of parties and unions will be positively related to more recent levels of political membership in its different forms.

Indeed, the reduction in investment costs provided by pre-existing structures and organisational traditions is especially important for the emergence and development of NSMOs, since these frequently lack start-up resources and have less access to public funding. Therefore, we should expect that both party and union density in the past will also be strongly related to recent levels of NSMO membership.

Graph 5.10 provides results that support these hypotheses. Diagram A indicates that there is evidence of a strong positive relationship between party and union density in the mid twentieth century and overall levels of political membership in the early 1990s. Furthermore, these results suggest that the historical strength of political parties is slightly more important for current levels of political membership than that of trade unions. In the case of 'new' political membership, the predictive capacity of organisational legacies is, understandably, weaker.[34] Nonetheless, the association between historical legacies and present behaviour is still remarkable; and much more so when we disregard the outlying case of the Netherlands.

These results suggest that historical legacies of mobilisation and organisation are important to our understanding of current participation patterns and that we should not overlook the impact of the accumulation of resources and infrastructures for action over time.

MOBILISATION AND POLITICAL MEMBERSHIP: A MULTIVARIATE EXPLORATION

In the preceding sections we have identified three different aspects of mobilisation processes that are of some relevance to the study of cross-national patterns of political membership: (1) direct mobilisation patterns and structures, as measured by the territorial density of party branches and by protest action; (2) patterns of cognitive mobilisation, as indicated by ideological polarisation and cleavage segmentation; and (3) the organisational legacies of past political mobilisation.

The various bivariate analyses shown in this chapter suggest that these three aspects of the mobilisation context are related to cross-national variations in political membership. Thus, a wider organisational spread of political parties, and a greater visibility of new social movements (NSMs) as the instigators of collective action, encourage citizens to join political organisations in general and 'new' political organisations particularly; whereas extreme social unrest hinders organisational membership. In turn, various aspects relating to cognitive mobilisation have inconsistent effects on political membership: ideological polarisation in the left-right divide is positively related to high levels of political membership; but the mobilisation of other cleavage dimensions is not necessarily related to citizens' organisational behaviour. Whereas religious pluralism seems to favour organised political participation, this is not the case with ethnic or linguistic segmentation. Finally, we have found some evidence that the organisational legacy of past mobilisation might have a positive effect on present levels of political membership.

Yet, all these results were based on analyses restricted to the aggregate level of countries and disregard individual-level factors. In this final section, the contextual indicators of mobilisation are confronted to individual attributes in several multi-level models of political membership. Due to the restrictions imposed by the limited number of countries included in this study, only the indicators that have shown some relevant bivariate association with political membership in preceding analyses are employed (Table 5.7).

The results shown in Table 5.8 take into account all the indicators of mobilisation discussed in this chapter.[35] Because some of these variables are strictly related

Table 5.7: Summary of indicators of the mobilisation context

Country	No. of party branches per 1,000 inhabitants (1985–9)	No. of protests / population (log)	Percentage of protest initiated by NSM actors	Citizen polarisation	Party system polarisation	Effective no. of religious groups	No. of union members per 1,000 inhabitants (1950)
Austria	1.14	40.73	33.8	3.01	0.70	1.36	186.10
Belgium	0.18	174.33	3.7	4.12	2.70	1.60	102.71
Canada	n.a. (0.70)	n.a. (310.51)	n.a.	2.75	2.10	3.07	71.80
Denmark	0.55	157.64	10.6	3.59	24.60	1.06	153.69
Finland	1.55	89.05	8.8	4.45	21.10	1.24	n.a. (102.21)
France	0.11	840.72	4.4	3.88	21.40	1.23	86.07
Great Britain	n.a. (0.70)	1595.0	50.3	3.62	0.00	1.65	156.16
Iceland	n.a. (0.70)	50.95	9.2	4.85	24.20	1.11	n.a. (102.21)
Ireland	1.42	467.53	7.4	3.39	4.90	1.13	38.40
Italy	0.75	127.97	9.0	4.48	34.20	1.00	123.77
Netherlands	0.19	190.50	68.2	3.98	1.80	3.20	101.16
Norway	1.16	97.42	11.3	4.16	16.30	1.13	149.59
Portugal	n.a. (0.70)	95.64	2.0	4.54	16.50	1.06	0.00
Spain	0.16	549.33	5.1	4.53	7.20	1.02	0.00
Sweden	0.93	108.28	19.9	4.39	5.60	1.14	185.10
Switzerland	n.a. (0.70)	74.0	35.5	4.36	8.50	2.12	94.06
USA	n.a. (0.70)	n.a. (310.51)	n.a.	3.21	0.00	2.26	107.05
West Germany	0.29	302.54	32.2	2.87	0.60	2.45	79.77

Sources: see Tables 5.3 to 5.6.
Notes: n.a. = information not available. The figures in brackets are the average values for all other countries that have been used to replace these missing values in some of the analyses that follow.

to unionisation, the analyses are done separately for two different operationalisations of the dependent variable: with and without union membership.[36] Furthermore, because union membership is particularly high in certain countries – notably Scandinavian nations – this also allows testing our contextual hypotheses without the distortion that this particular aspect may introduce. As we shall see, although the exclusion of union membership does not substantially change the results in many cases, in others it does. The full models adopt the following functional form:

$$\text{Logit}\,(\pi_{ij}) = \gamma_{00} + \sum_{h=1}^{r}\beta_{h0}\,x_{hij} + \sum_{k=1}^{q}\gamma_{0k}\,z_{kj} + U_{0j} + \sum_{h=1}^{p}U_{hj}\,x_{hij} \qquad \text{(Equation 5.1)}$$

where, i = individual i, for I = 1, 2, 3, ..., n;
j = country j, for J = 1, 2, 3, ..., N;
$\pi_{ij} = p_{ij}/1\text{-}p_{ij}$, and $p_{ij} = \text{prob}(y_{ij}=1)$, for y=1 (member of a political organisation);
β = parameters estimated at the individual level (level 1);

Table 5.8: Mobilisation context and political membership: complete models

Variables	Baseline model (with unions)	Full model (with unions)	Baseline model (without unions)	Full model (without unions)
Intercept	-2.32	-2.32	-3.72	-3.73
Fixed parameters (indiv. level)				
Education	0.94	0.94	1.26	1.25
Employment situation (ref= +30h)				
Works <30 h.	-0.27	-0.27	0.15	0.15
Inactive	-0.67	-0.67	-0.25	-0.25
Unemployed	-0.62	-0.62	-0.32	-0.32
Age	4.18	4.15	3.92	3.89
Age (squared)	-4.31	-4.29	-3.65	-3.63
Woman (ref=man)	-0.14	-0.13	n.s.	n.s.
With partner (ref=without partner)	n.s.	n.s.	n.s.	n.s.
Church attendance	-0.26	-0.26	n.s.	n.s.
Religious membership	1.09	1.09	1.02	1.02
Interest in politics	0.57	0.57	0.74	0.74
Political efficacy	0.27	0.27	0.37	0.37
Inter-personal trust	0.16	0.16	0.24	0.23
Values index (ref=materialist)				
Mixed	0.14	0.14	0.14	0.14
Post-materialist	0.50	0.50	0.50	0.50
Attitude to social change (ref= conservative)				
Radical	n.s.	n.s.	0.21	0.22
Reformist	0.14	0.14	0.11	0.11
Fixed parameters (country level)				
No. political party branches (x1000 inh.)		1.83		0.91
No. political party branches (squared)		-1.09		-0.44
No. protests relative to population		n.s.		n.s.
Citizen polarisation		n.s.		3.63
Citizen polarisation (squared)		n.s.		-0.46
Party system polarisation		n.s.		n.s.
Effective no. of religious groups		n.s.		0.39
Tradition of participation (union members x 1000 inhabs. in 1950)		0.005		0.002
Random parameters (country level)				
$u_{ij} \sim N (0, \Omega u)$: Ωu †	0.48-0.89	0.37-0.59	0.25-0.37	0.14-0.37
$u0_{ij}$ [intercept] *	0.89 (0.94)	0.59 (0.77)	0.37 (0.61)	0.37 (0.61)
$u1_{ij}$ [education]*	0.22 (0.47)	0.21 (0.46)	0.27 (0.52)	0.27 (0.52)
$u2_{ij}$ [church attendance]*	0.12 (0.34)	0.11 (0.34)	0.10 (0.31)	0.8 (0.28)
$u3_{ij}$ [gender]*	0.05 (0.23)	0.05 (0.23)	0.08 (0.28)	0.08 (0.28)
Intra-class correlation + †	0.13-0.21	0.10-0.15	0.07-0.10	0.4-0.10
R2 dicho§ †	0.19-0.17†	0.24-0.23	0.21-0.20	0.26-0.24
% unexplained level 2 variance †	10-18†	8-12	6-8	3-8
Number of cases (no. of countries)	20,815 (17)	20,815 (17)	20,815 (17)	20,815 (17)

Source: Individual variables are from the 1990–93 WVS, for contextual variables see the preceding tables.
Notes: All coefficients indicate the change (increase or decrease) in the natural logarithm of the odds ratio (p/1-p) of the dependent variable (membership of any political association = 1, non-membership = 0) when

x_h = variables measured at the individual level (level 1), for h = 1, 2, 3, ..., r; and the subset with random coefficients is h = 1, 2, 3, ..., p;

γ = average parameters estimated at the country level (level 2);

z_k = variables measured at the country level (level 2), for k = 1, 2, 3, ... q; and

U = parameters of the variation or error at the country level (level 2).

The two models support some of our previous bivariate results and highlight the relevance of mobilisation processes in accounting for cross-national patterns of political membership. Yet the findings regarding the impact of mobilisation factors are slightly different, depending on whether we include or exclude union membership from our indicator of political membership. Whereas the individual-level components of the model are relatively stable, the country-level elements show important differences, according to the way we operationalise the dependent variable. High levels of unionisation in some European countries conceal the positive effects of citizen polarisation and of religious pluralism on political membership. Thus, when union membership is excluded from our dependent variable, all three dimensions of mobilisation processes – structural, cognitive, and historical – have a significant impact on cross-national variations of political membership.

In countries where political parties are better spread in the territory – an indicator that we use as a proxy of the overall visibility of all types of political associations – citizens are more likely to join political organisations. However, this relation is curvilinear, in such a way that the highest values of partisan organisational embeddedness slightly depress overall levels of political membership. A curvilinear effect is also evident for citizen polarisation but, in this case, the impact is much stronger (see Graph 5.11). In countries where polarisation around the left-right divide is more acute, citizens are much more likely to join political organisations. Finally, historical legacies have some impact on current levels of political membership but it is moderate.

A last aspect to underline is that mobilisation factors reduce the remaining unexplained cross-national variation, whether we include or exclude union membership from the dependent variable. This reduction in unexplained variation is larger for individuals with the highest values for variables with random parameters: women, highly educated individuals and frequent church-goers.

In short, despite the limitations of the available indicators of mobilisation

---

the explanatory variable increases by one unit. All the ordinal and quantitative variables at the individual level – except for age – have been recoded so that 0 represents the minimum value and 1 the maximum. The contextual variables are centred around their means, so that the value 0 corresponds to the average value of the variable for the 17 countries. Only the significant coefficients are shown for p≤0.10. The significant coefficients for p≤0.05 are underlined, and for p≤0.01 they are shown in bold. N.s. = not statistically significant for p≤0.10. * For the variance parameters coefficients the component is expressed in variance terms, with the standard deviation values shown in brackets. + Proportion of the total residual variance attributable to the variation between countries. § R2 for multilevel binomial regressions (see the details on calculation and interpretation in Snijders & Bosker 1999: 225–6). † The first figure corresponds to calculations with all the variables associated with random coefficients set at their maximum value (1), while the second corresponds to the equivalent calculation setting variables at their minimum value (0).

Graph 5.11: Estimated effects of various aspects of the mobilisation context

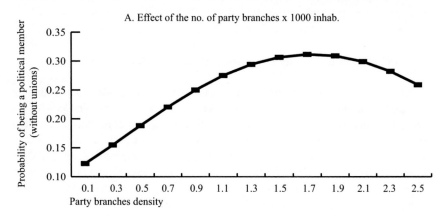

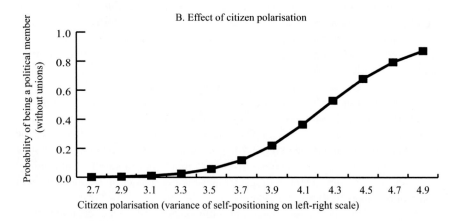

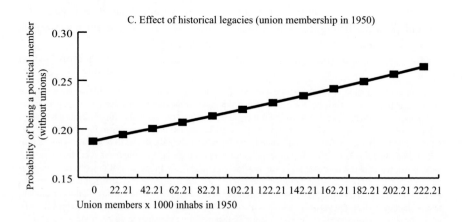

processes, our model for political membership clearly improves when we take into account the context of political mobilisation in which citizens make their decisions to join a political association.

CONCLUSIONS

This chapter has shown that there is enough empirical evidence to justify a detailed analysis of the impact of mobilisation processes on individual decisions to join political organisations. The patterns of political mobilisation that prevail in each nation are closely connected to the propensity of their citizens to join a political association. Clearly, our measures of political mobilisation are imperfect and – in most cases – only approximate the real underlying mobilisation structures and processes that are to be found in each country. Yet, our results should encourage the systematic measurement and analysis of mobilisation factors if we are to gain a fuller understanding of what makes western citizens join political organisations.

Another fundamental aspect of mobilisation processes that we could not include in this study, for lack of information, is the set of specific recruitment strategies that political organisations use in each country. Rothenberg's model (1988, 1989 and 1992) describes the process of approaching and joining political associations as an 'experiential search' and this suggests that the decision to join a political group is very contingent on the recruitment strategies that citizens are exposed to. As Johnson (1998: 60) argues, very frequently

> collective interests do not explain group membership – recruiting activity does. […]people who have an interest in a collective good do not tend to be 'self-starters' who seek out and join groups. Instead they must be sought out, pursued, enticed, and persuaded.

And Johnson's data show that recruitment efforts and strategies widely vary across organisations, depending on their size and their degree of professionalisation.

There are no comparative data on the variation in recruitment strategies by political organisations, if producing such data is at all possible. But the scattered information available in cross-national studies such as the *Citizenship, Involvement and Democracy* project suggests that associations whose primary goal and sector of action are political are much more engaged in mobilising and recruiting members than other associations; and that the patterns of mobilisation and recruitment of associations vary substantially across contexts in Europe (see Lelieveldt *et al.* 2007). A passing observation by anyone who has spent some time in several western countries would conclude that, indeed, recruitment strategies by political organisations vary considerably across countries.

For example, the likelihood of being approached by an activist of an environmental association, human-rights organisation or any other sort of public-interest group in the streets is substantially different in large European capitals such as

London, Amsterdam or Madrid. Italians are reminded every year of the period for renewing their party and union membership cards by billboards in the streets and advertisements in newspapers;[37] whereas Spaniards never come across such public and periodic requests to join political parties and only sporadically for unions. A final example – that readers who have lived in the United States may relate to – is the widely different chances of receiving a request by post or telephone to contribute money for a campaign or an organisation in America compared to most European countries. Many Americans are bombarded with such petitions – amidst many other commercial approaches – while this is much less common in Europe.

Hence, we cannot uncover many aspects of the mobilisation structures and processes that are of interest to this study with the available cross-national information. However, the findings presented in this chapter show that the patterns and traditions of mobilisation of each society do have a relevant impact on citizens' propensity to join organisations that seek political goals. And, it is very likely that the limitations imposed by the available data make our conclusions about its impact more conservative than they might otherwise be.

NOTES

1   See Nedelmann (1987) to obtain a summary of the most important definitions of mobilisation to date.

2   Tilly's definition is intentionally broad because his intention is to cover different types of mobilisation and collective action (see 1978: 84). And Nedelmann's definition (1987: 185) – 'the development of relationships between different types of actors in the social and political system' – is too vague for the purposes of this research.

3   Skocpol (2003) discusses how the large American civic organisations purposefully created a wide network of local branches and organisations in order to sustain large and influential national organisations.

4   As an illustration, Amnesty International systematically emphasises the past success of petitions and protest letters to the competent authorities in order to prevent actions that violate human rights, such as carrying-out the death penalty. To this aim, they illustrate past success stories, often with pictures of the people who have benefited from mobilisation, with the aim of humanising what would otherwise just be a cold set of statistics. This, undoubtedly, allows potential participants to fully grasp the usefulness of their co-operation, especially when this may seem as little effective as sending a letter.

5   Koopmans' (1996) study analyses only six European countries and it is limited to the aggregate level. Rosenstone & Hansen (1993), Kriesi (1993) and Klandermans (1997) only study one case: the United States for the former and the Netherlands for the latter two.

6   A partial exception is the American Citizen Participation Study of 1990, see Verba, Schlozman & Brady (1995).

7   The study reported in Table 5.1 was part of the project *Political Participation and Social Capital in Spain* (SEC 2000-0758-C02), funded by the Spanish Ministry of Science and Technology and co-ordinated by Prof. José Ramón Montero, in co-operation with the ESF

Citizenship, Involvement and Democracy network. The study reported in Table 5.2 is part of the project *Multicultural Democracy and Immigrants' Social Capital in Europe* (LOCAL-MULTIDEM), funded by the European Commission (CIT5-CT-2005-028802) and the Spanish Ministry of Education (SEJ2005-07733/CPOL) and co-ordinated by the author.

8   Clearly, these surveys only allow conclusions to be drawn about the Spanish case and are not sufficient for generalisations about other societies. Nevertheless, there seems to be a quite systematic pattern across various contexts in Spain that would suggest a certain stability that is context-independent.

9   An attempt was made to construct another *proxy* indicator that was more specific to 'new' political organisations with data on the organisational density of large environmental and human-rights organisations present in all western democracies (e.g. Amnesty International, AI, and Greenpeace, GP); but, unfortunately, most of the national organisations of AI and GP do not keep data on the number of branches or local groups that existed by the end of the 1980s. And, in some cases, they did not even keep membership records for that period.

10 The main source for this information is Katz & Mair (1992), although it has been complemented by other sources.

11 But it is more likely that party infrastructures are, indeed, not good proxies for NSMOs infrastructures.

12 Nevertheless, in more recent times other researchers have reproduced the study in other countries, among them Spain (see Koopmans 1996 and 1999: 90–1). But this data was not readily available.

13 Information on this project and the data can be obtained on the web page: http://web.ku.edu/ronfran/data/index.html. Gerner *et al.* (1994) describe the original system of data-collection on events (KEDS). See, for example, Francisco (1996) for an application of the data different to that which is presented in the pages below.

14 The research project uses Lexis-Nexis as the main source of information and through this service it accesses the Reuters database with 400 publications, as well as the agency's local, regional, and global teletext services.

15 Undoubtedly, this type of data source has limitations that are common to the project led by Kriesi, given that the media and communication agencies introduce biases related to the attention they pay to protest-events. The debate on the use and the limitations of journalistic information for research on collective action is wide, and samples of it can be found in Rucht & Ohlemacher (1992), Fillieule (1996), Hug & Wisler (1998), Tarrow (1999), Rucht & Neidhardt (1999), Koopmans (1999) and, in general, many of the chapters in the book edited by Rucht, Koopmans & Neidhardt (1999).

16 I am sincerely grateful to Hanspeter Kriesi for granting me access to their dataset, and to Ron Francisco for making available to the public the data collected through his project.

17 The lower number of total events in Germany, France and Switzerland for NSMs that result from the analysis of Ron Francisco's dataset might be due to my coding decisions with regard to the main actors, which probably excludes many actions that might have been included in Kriesi and his colleagues' codings. See Morales (2004: Appendix 4) to obtain more information on the codes used for the analysis of the data collected by Ron Francisco.

18 As Koopmans (1999) points out, all the analyses of protest-events underestimate the real protest that occurs. Yet, what is of interest here is not so much the exact number of protest-events that

took place in each country but the relative differences that exist across the European countries.

19 A five-year period has been chosen to minimise the measurement errors that may appear from using a single year for the calculations, if exceptionally strong (or weak) mobilisations occur in some countries for that specific year.

20 See Kriesi *et al.* (1995: 267–8) to obtain a more detailed description of the type of protest actions that are included in each category, and Morales (2004: Appendix 4) for the exact codes considered within each category for Francisco's ECPD dataset.

21 The population size is transformed by its base-10 logarithm for variance stabilisation.

22 These results must be interpreted with care, given that media biases result in the greater likelihood of confrontational protest-events being reported.

23 Separate analyses (not shown here) confirm that higher degrees of confrontation strengthen this negative relationship.

24 Besides, the fundamental cleavage around which this ideological distinction emerges does not have to be social class; it can be based on cleavages of another political nature (Kalyvas 1997: 98).

25 Similar methods were used by Bartolini & Mair (1990) and Billiet (1997).

26 But see Putnam (2007) for a contrasting view, primarily arguing that racial diversity – as produced by immigration – might hinder social trust and, thus, social capital.

27 On a scale that ranges from 1 (extreme left) to 10 (extreme right).

28 It is also common to use variance-related indicators when measuring polarisation at the party-system level (see Taylor & Herman 1971 and Hazan 1995).

29 These other indicators employed the variance in parties' ideological positions – using Hazan's (1995) formula – as measured by experts' surveys (Huber & Inglehart 1995, Castles & Mair 1984) and occasionally, when data was not available in the former, party-manifesto codings provided by Budge *et al.* (2001).

30 Yet, polarisation could also lead to a retreat from the public arena, if it carries the risk of extreme social conflict.

31 This type of outcome is suggested by Axelrod's iterated prisoners' dilemma (1984).

32 As opposed to the cultural or attitudinal component of historical legacies just outlined.

33 The membership density of parties and unions has been calculated over the total population and not over the number of electors and active population respectively.

34 We should remind the reader that the indicator of general political membership includes membership of political parties and unions, so it is only natural that the relation of dependency between past and present values is much higher in this case than for NSMOs alone.

35 Given that the number of countries that can be used for the analyses is limited, a set of manual step-wise procedures have been used to identify the final models. The indicators were first introduced separately in 'thematic' blocks (i.e. direct mobilisation, cognitive mobilisation and historical legacies) and only those with a statistically significant effect were retained for more complex models. The logic of this modelling procedure can be seen in greater detail in Morales (2004: chapter seven). Some methodologists have expressed concern about the estimation of models with a small number of higher-level units. Some scholars argue that there needs to be at least 15–20 cases per higher-level variable (see Snijders & Bosker 1999) and some argue that this figure should be increased to 50 (Maas & Hox 2005). Yet, the problem remains when a small number of higher-level units are the only

available information. A number of leading political methodologists suggest that ignoring the multi-level structure is worse than the problems of power and robustness of estimators with small sample sizes (see the special issue of *Political Analysis*, vol. 13 (4) of 2005). And while various methods are proposed to overcome this limitation of the higher-level sample size, some of the pieces in that special issue show that the substantive results of the models might not differ much (Duch & Stevenson 2005), and that two-stage models are not always to be preferred to single-stage multi-level models (Franzese 2005 and Beck 2005). Finally, a number of pieces published in the top journals in political science use the same estimation methods we use here (see, for example, Rohrschneider 2002). The important thing to bear in mind is that the standard errors of the country-level parameters in this and equivalent analyses in this study might be biased.

36 Because the dependent variable is a dichotomous indicator, this means that – when excluding union membership from the operationalisation – a given individual who is a union member will only be identified as a 'political member' if she is also a member of the other political organisations included in our definition (see Chapter two for the detailed list). In other words, individuals who are only union members will not be identified as 'political members' in this alternative operationalisation.

37 Many associations and organisations in Italy have yearly membership drives or *campagne di tesseramento*. Political parties and trade unions are the most visible ones but big associations or umbrella organisations such as ARCI are also very active in trying to recruit and keep members every year.

chapter six | macro-contexts: the effect of institutions on political membership

INTRODUCTION

The context in which citizens are embedded shapes, in various important ways, the opportunities they have to participate and the requests they receive to do so. The last section of Chapter four briefly explored how micro-contexts – their personal networks and their political leanings – moulded citizens' engagement in political organisations, while Chapter five provided some evidence that mobilisation processes and structures are crucial determinants of cross-national variations in political membership. This chapter analyses the impact of the macro-context on individual political behaviour. More specifically, we will discuss how institutional factors – and, in particular, a set of institutional features that define political opportunity structures – affect the decisions citizens make to join (or not join) political organisations. To this purpose, the chapter first identifies and describes the dimensions of the institutional setting of western democracies that are of primary relevance for the study of political membership. We will then move to a discussion of the main empirical indicators that allow us to measure each of these dimensions; and we will explore their bivariate relation to political membership at the aggregate country-level. The final section assesses the impact of each of these dimensions on individual political membership, with a multi-level model that jointly considers individual attributes and the various relevant aspects of the institutional macro-context. With these analyses, this chapter will provide consistent evidence to support the claim that the openness of political systems determines in important ways the cross-national patterns of political membership in western democracies.

POLITICAL OPPORTUNITY STRUCTURES: THE *OPENNESS* OF THE POLITICAL SYSTEM

Political opportunity structures (POS) are thought to play a central role in explaining the birth, development and success (or failure) of social movements.[1] Yet, the concept of a POS has become, too frequently, a catch-all or umbrella category that limits its analytical usefulness (Gamson & Meyer 1996: 275). There are multiple definitions of a POS. Probably one of the best known is that offered by Sidney Tarrow (1994: 85)[2] as the 'consistent – but not necessarily formal or permanent – dimensions of the political environment that provide incentives for people to undertake collective action by affecting their expectations for success or failure'.[3]

Tarrow's definition, like most of those first proposed, suffers from a certain vagueness and is excessively inclusive: any element of the political environment can be part of the POS. To a certain extent, Kitschelt's (1986: 58) definition is more precise: 'Political opportunity structures are comprised of specific configurations of resources, institutional arrangements and historical precedents for social mobilization, which facilitate the development of protest movements in some instances and constrain them in others.'

Furthermore, Kitschelt's conception of a POS is more systematic, as it distinguishes two sets of factors that determine the openness or 'closedness' of political systems to new actors and challengers: aspects related to input procedures and those that determine the outputs of the political system. Input procedures condition the access that citizens and organised groups have to the process of political agenda-setting; thus, they structure the procedural impact of social movements. Output-related procedures determine the substantive impact and the final success of collective action. Kitschelt's distinctions are useful for this study because both the opportunity structures related to inputs and those related to outputs shape the expected costs and benefits of collective action and, hence, the organisational strategies that citizens adopt.[4]

Fortunately, research on social movements over the last decade has resulted in a certain consensus over the set of basic elements that compose the POS. Thus, generally, the POS includes: (1) formal institutions, (2) the informal processes that take place in those institutions, and (3) the alliance opportunities that organisations and social movements face (McAdam 1996: 27, Rochon 1998: 200). This means that the POS is conceived of as dynamic in nature rather than being a static or constant property of the context.[5] Certainly, some elements give continuity to the configuration of the POS – mainly political institutions – but internal dynamics and informal processes also contribute to the configuration of the final opportunities that movements and citizens confront (Kriesi et al. 1995: 33).

For our specific purposes, the interest of these approaches lies in the fact that these aspects of the political context of collective action should be useful not just to explain the success or failure of social movements; they are also likely to contribute to varying degrees of citizen participation in those same movements (Kriesi & van Praag 1987, Koopmans 1996, Dekker, Koopmans & van den Broek 1997, Klandermans 1997). Given that the POS shapes the cost and benefit structures of collective action, it helps us better understand, all at once, the mobilisation strategies of social movements, their results and their popular support.

As an illustration of the analytical potential of the concept of POS for the study of individual political engagement, Kriesi (1996) employs the notion to explain the different organisational support of social movements in France, Germany, the

Netherlands and Switzerland.[6]

In summary, there is a wide range of dimensions or elements of a POS that have been identified in social movements studies.[7] But not all of them are equally relevant to the purposes of this work. For example, while informal processes and alliance structures or opportunities are of great interest for the analysis of specific cases of collective action, they are much less so when our main concern is to explain patterns of membership in political associations. Consequently, we will narrow our focus to the most institutionalised and stable components of the POS, since institutions – without being immobile – are relatively constant over time and common to all associations.[8] The most stable elements of the POS are the most relevant for this study, because cross-national variation in the levels of political membership in western democracies is relatively stable over time (see Chapter two).

Therefore, we need to clearly define what specific aspects of the institutional POS we will consider. Kriesi *et al.* (1995) also focus on institutional structures and distinguish between strong and weak states, depending on their degree of autonomy, and their ability to act. This characterisation is applied to three different political arenas: the parliamentary, the administrative and the direct-democratic one. Thus, they classify the institutional configurations of the four countries they study – France, Germany, the Netherlands and Switzerland – depending on: (1) the degree of centralisation of the state, (2) the level of functional separation of powers, (3) the proportionality of parliamentary representation and the number of parties, (4) the system of interest-representation in the administrative arena, and (5) the availability of mechanisms of direct democracy. In fact, these five institutional dimensions can be conceived of, for our purposes, as the core elements that define the degree of *openness of the political system* of each society.[9]

A political system is more open or more closed depending on the degree to which its political institutions incorporate or exclude citizens' associations and demands for influence (Rochon 1998: 202). As a result, the openness of the political system will shape citizens' propensity to join political associations in various ways.

First of all, political associations are, to a large extent, the main actors in the process of demand-creation, articulation and aggregation.[10] Because the degree of openness of the political system is a powerful incentive (or disincentive) to collective action, and for membership in associations in particular (Knoke 1990: 189), it shapes the development of new demands: the more open a political system is to new demands, the greater their legitimacy and support among the population.

Secondly, greater openness to new demands and challenges will help new actors achieve their goals and this increases the expected benefits of collective action. If the political system is responsive to the requests of its citizens and of the organisations they create in order to express their demands and concerns, individuals will have convincing reasons to regard associations as useful tools to achieve their objectives.

Undoubtedly, the degree of openness of political systems is a multidimensional notion, as the same political system might be open in certain aspects and closed in others. We, therefore, need to specify the various elements that form the different dimensions of openness of a political system. To this aim, we adapt Kriesi *et al.*'s

(1995) and Rochon's (1998: chapter seven) proposals and distinguish between:
(1) The *access points* to the political system;
(2) the *fragmentation* of the political elites; and
(3) the *porousness* of the decision-making system.

THE ACCESS POINTS OF THE POLITICAL SYSTEM

A first dimension that defines the degree of openness is access to decision-making processes, which will depend largely on the number of decisional nodes or, to use Rochon's term (1998), on institutional pluralism. And the number of access points will depend on (a) the degree of political decentralisation, and (b) the availability of institutions of direct democracy.

The degree of political decentralisation
Alexis de Tocqueville (1980: 100–1) explained that the degree of political decentralisation of the United States was one of the factors that promoted the wide development of associations in that country.[11] Knoke details the mechanisms that account for this link:

> American interest-group proliferation is encouraged by a federal constitutional structure and electoral systems that fragment power among hundreds of separate policy domains. Each domain comprises a sub-government consisting of congressional subcommittees, government bureaus, and interest-group clientele that resist the intrusion of a strong central authority (Knoke 1990a: 189)

Thus, political organisations are created at every one of these layers of government, to formulate demands, support some decisions and oppose others. And, although geographical decentralisation is fundamental, it is not the only form of decentralisation (or de-concentration) that is relevant. De-concentration and functional autonomy also multiply access nodes. Thus, in consociational political systems, such as the Dutch, the Belgian and the Austrian, the state has given up the management of certain functions and services of a semi-public nature to private organisations, such as churches, economic associations and recreational associations

Hence, the proliferation of access points that political decentralisation favours is likely to contribute to the multiplication of groups and organisations that will take advantage of the opportunities to influence decision-making processes. In turn, this increases the chances that citizens will join those organisations. However, some scholars have argued that a high level of decentralisation may also have a negative effect on organised collective action, as it complicates the allocation of responsibilities and increases the information costs of collective action (Klandermans 1997: 193).

Yet, all in all, decentralisation and functional de-concentration brings the government closer to its citizens and this is expected to promote citizens' engagement in political affairs.

Thus, the hypotheses that connect these different aspects of decentralisation lead us to expect that levels of political membership will be higher in countries with:

(a) higher levels of political decentralisation;

(b) more de-concentration or functional autonomy; and

(c) more autonomous local governments.[12]

There are various options for the operationalisation of the concept of decentralisation (Rodden 2004). A first possibility is to focus on the distribution of functions between different levels of government (Council of Europe 1988, Norton 1991, Blair 1991, Sharpe 1993). However, measuring governmental functions directly is a complex endeavour that does not provide very clear information, because the powers in some subject areas are shared by various levels of government and the degree to which the exercise of a specific area-jurisdiction leads to real autonomy in decision-making varies greatly. As several scholars have argued (Tarrow 1977, Smith 1985, Page 1991, Norton 1993), even in those cases where the relation between local/regional governments and central government is one of high formal dependency it is not true that the former lack any discretion or capacity to make decisions. Consequently, most scholars have opted to measure the functions and the autonomy of sub-national government indirectly, using local and regional governments' expenditure and their ability to raise and determine taxes as the best proxies (Stoker 1991, Page 1991).[13]

Table 6.1: Indicators of decentralisation

Country	% local expenditure over total public expenditure in 1989 [a]	Lijphart's federalism-decentralisation index (1971–96) [b]
Austria	14.8	4.5
Belgium	12.74	3.2
Canada	25.29	5
Denmark	51.66	2
Finland	40.14	2
France	15.22	1.3
Great Britain	24.57	1
Iceland	21.99	1
Ireland	24.81	1
Italy	28.97	1.5
Netherlands	30.02	3
Norway	32.79	2
Portugal	10.63	1
Spain	22.78	3
Sweden	35.47	2
Switzerland	21.91	5
United States	41.06	5
W. Germany	12.49	5

Sources: *a* OECD National Accounts (1993); *b* Lijphart (1999: 313).

Graph 6.1: Political membership and institutional pluralism

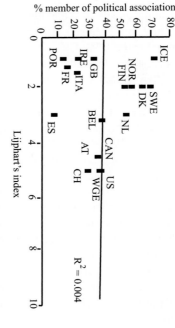

A. Political Membership and Political Decentralisation

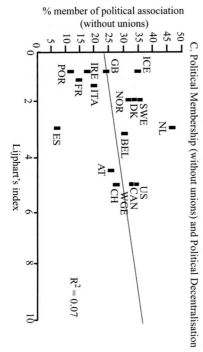

C. Political Membership (without unions) and Political Decentralisation

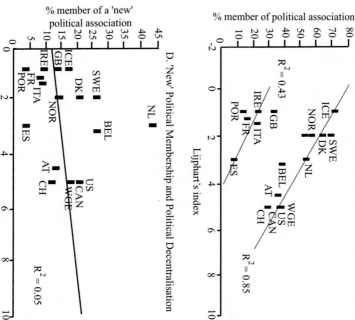

B. Political Membership and Political Decentralisation (2 groups of countries)

D. 'New' Political Membership and Political Decentralisation

An alternative approach is to use global indicators that take into account the general institutional structure and to score countries on the basis of their constitutional structure and the organisation of the various levels of government (Bennett 1993a and b, Sharpe 1993, Lane & Ersson 1999, Lijphart 1999).[14]

Table 6.1 shows the indicators used to measure these aspects of political decentralisation in each nation. The data on spending[15] are only available at the local level[16], as regional data are only included in the national accounts of the OECD for federal states. As regards Lijphart's index, some clarifications are essential. This index ranges from 1 to 5, and assigns values to each country depending on Lijphart's own assessment of whether it constitutes a centralised unified (1), unified and decentralised (2), semi-federal (3), federal and centralised (4), or federal and decentralised (5) state.[17]

Graph 6.1 illustrates the connection between political decentralisation and the level of political membership in western democracies. Dispersion diagram A presents the bivariate association between Lijphart's index and the percentage of membership of political organisations for the 18 western countries included in the 1990–93 WVS. As we see, the linear relationship with political membership is rather weak. This seems to be due to the interference of another contextual variable that distinguishes between two groups of countries, among which decentralisation and political membership seems to be inversely related. A visual inspection of the distribution of countries in the scatterplot might indicate that high levels of unionisation in Scandinavian countries are the source of this negative relation. However, when we exclude unions, the results do not vary drastically (diagram C). This inverse relation between the degree of institutional decentralisation and membership of political groups, if confirmed, would weaken the theoretical hypotheses that link greater political decentralisation with a proliferation of political groups and, therefore, with greater participation.

Yet, the importance of institutional pluralism or de-concentration has been most emphatically claimed for the study of the emergence and development of new social movements (NSMs). Thus, we also check its impact on membership of new social movement organisations (NSMOs). Diagram D seems to indicate that, in this case, the two subgroups of countries disappear and, though quite weak, the relation between decentralisation and membership is positive.

We have, however, another indicator of decentralisation that specifically measures local autonomy (spending ability). Graph 6.2 presents the bivariate relation between political membership and the indicator of the financial autonomy of municipalities. Consistent with hypotheses in the literature, the relation between local autonomy and membership of political groups is clearly positive.

We will assess again the impact of decentralisation in the last section of this chapter, when we will look at the various institutional variables with multivariate models. We now turn our attention to the other aspect that determines the plurality of access points to the political system: the existence and development of institutions of direct democracy.

Graph 6.2: Relation between political membership and local financial autonomy

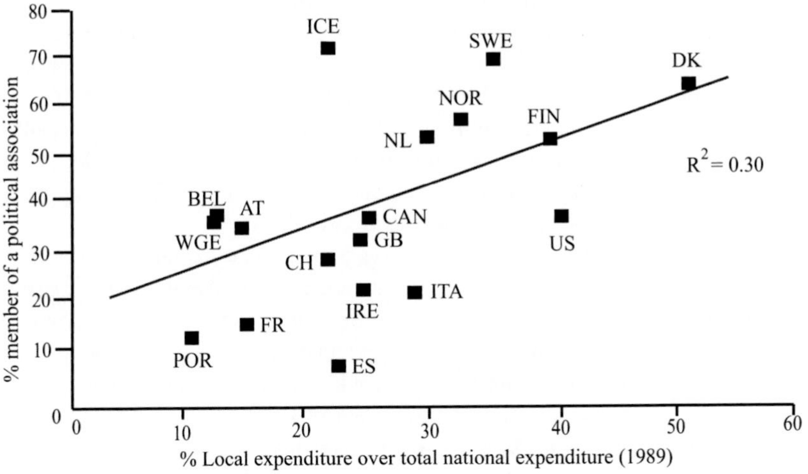

The chart plots % member of a political association (y-axis, 0 to 80) against % Local expenditure over total national expenditure (1989) (x-axis, 0 to 60). Countries plotted: ICE, SWE, DK, NOR, FIN, NL, BEL, AT, WGE, CAN, GB, CH, US, IRE, ITA, FR, POR, ES. $R^2 = 0.30$

The availability of institutions of direct democracy

The capacity to influence decision-making processes by means other than electing representatives can also foster political membership in various ways. Institutions of direct democracy promote the creation of organisations in order to mobilise, first, citizens' support to comply with the legal requirements to call a referendum or popular initiative and, later on, the votes in support of their preferred option. As Boehmke points out (2002), direct democratic institutions offer various additional opportunities to citizens' organisations to influence the decision-making process, as it offers them an alternative mechanism to the traditional activities of lobbying and, secondly, it gives them more bargaining power with the political authorities as they can use the threat of a referendum campaign.[18] Boehmke (2000) also predicts that, given that the expected benefits of mobilisation are, *ceteris paribus*, larger where institutions of direct democracy exist, the number of interest groups will multiply in these societies.

Kriesi & Wisler (1996: 22) point out that, in addition, institutions of direct democracy lower the costs of individual participation in collective action as, being regulated and conventional processes, the risks of repression decrease. At the same time, in many cases, the participants only have to sign the petitions, which involve a minimal cost.[19] Additionally, around a campaign in favour of (or against) a referendum a large number of political actors and organisations are mobilised, and they all gain greater visibility, as do the causes they defend. This fact also contributes to reducing the information costs for citizens who are interested in the issues that each organisation defends.

The dynamism that the processes and institutions of direct democracy bring with them is also likely to encourage citizen participation in political organisations through indirect mechanisms related to the strategies of the organisations. For example, social movements are forced to moderate their repertoires and, mainly, to develop and consolidate their organisational structures to be able to use these resources in mobilisation (Kriesi & Wisler 1996: 23). This strategic necessity to develop organisations leads them to try to capture activists and members who will contribute time and money to their plebiscitary campaigns. Furthermore, the very dynamic of how referenda are run invariably leads to the emergence of organisations opposed to those who initiated the campaign (Boehmke 2002: 831). Hence, institutions of direct democracy favour the emergence and mobilisation of groups that would otherwise probably not have been mobilised.

But, for the effects on organised collective action, what matters is not only the presence or absence of institutions of direct democracy but also the specific institutional configuration of these processes. Therefore, the specific conditions and regulations of direct democratic processes are of special importance, as these are what determine the additional opportunities they provide and the costs organisations have to bear if they want to resort to them (Kriesi & Wisler 1996: 25, Boehmke 2002: 830). Thus, the few available studies on the connection between direct democracy and political participation[20] leads us to expect that levels of political membership will be higher in countries where the regulation of popular initiatives and direct democracy is more permissive and shifts the balance of power in the ultimate decision to voters.

Most western democracies have included at least some mechanisms of direct democracy in decision-making processes, through referenda or popular legislative initiatives. Butler & Ranney (1978) offer a typology of referenda: (a) those controlled by the government, (b) those which are mandatory under the constitution, and (c) those initiated by popular petition and initiative.[21] The main distinction is in the source of the initiative: the constitution, the head of state, the government, the parliament or a section of the electorate. Nevertheless, a second criterion for distinguishing between types of referenda is based on the type of decision that is subject to popular consultation. Thus, Uleri (1996) proposes a classification of referenda and popular initiatives that consists of: (a) referenda/initiatives that promote a decision; and (b) referenda/initiatives that control a decision and, among the latter, (i) referenda that allow for the rejection of decisions not yet implemented (*rejective vote*), and (ii) referenda that allow for the rejection of decisions already implemented (*abrogative vote*).

For our comparative study, these distinctions need to be transformed into indicators that can be used in further analyses. Table 6.2, details the elaboration of such an indicator by assigning numerical scores to the classification proposed by Bogdanor (1994) and the calculation of an overall additive index.

As we can see in Graph 6.3 the association between a greater availability of institutions of direct democracy and political membership is negative for all operationalisations of political membership. The intensity of the bivariate relation in fact decreases when we exclude unions and also when we only look at 'new' political organisations. And this inverse relation does not seem to be produced for any of the outliers. The results are relatively stable when we exclude the Dutch case – with relatively higher levels of political membership once unions are excluded –

Table 6.2: Formal regulation of referendum (until 1990)

Country	Referendum mentioned in constitution (0-1)	Referendum required for constitutional amendments (0-2)	Constitutional provision for referendum in non-constitutional legislation? (0-1)	Who is entitled to trigger the referendum? (0-4)	Provision for qualified majority? (0-1)	Referendum consultative or binding? (0-1)	Additive index
Switzerland	Yes (1)	Yes (2)	Yes (1)	Electorate (4)	Yes (0)	Binding (1)	9
Italy	Yes (1)	No[d] (1)	Yes (1)	Electorate (4)	Yes (0)	Binding (1)	8
Spain	Yes (1)	Yes[e] (1.5)	Yes (1)	Gov or LM (2)	No (1)	Binding (1)	7.5
Austria	Yes (1)	Yes[a] (1.5)	Yes (1)	Gov or LM (2)	No (1)	Binding (1)	7.5
France	Yes (1)	No[b] (0.75)	Yes (1)	Gov (1.5)	No (1)	Binding (1)	6.25
Denmark	Yes (1)	Yes (2)	Yes (1)	LM (2)	Yes (0)	Consult. (0)	6
Ireland	Yes (1)	Yes (2)	Yes (1)	H & LM (1)	Yes (0)	Binding (1)	6
United States*	--	--	--	--	--	--	5.8
Federal level	No (0)	No (0)	No (0)	Nobody (0)	Nobody (0)	Nobody (0)	0
State level	Yes (49=0.98)	Yes (49=1.96)	Yes (24=0.41)	Electorate (24=1.64)	No (0.41)	Binding (0.41)	5.8
Portugal	Yes (1)	No (0)	Yes (1)	H (1)	No (1)	Binding (1)	5
Finland	Yes (1)	No (0)	Yes (1)	Gov (1.5)	No (1)	Consult. (0)	4.5
Sweden	Yes (1)	No (0)	Yes (1)	Gov or LM(2)	Yes (0)	B. & c. (0.5)	4.5
Iceland	Yes (1)	No[c] (0.2)	Yes (1)	H (1)	Yes (0)	Binding (1)	4.2
Canada	No (0)	Yes[f] (1.25)	No (0)	Gov (1.5)	No (1)	Consult. (0)	3.75
Norway	No (0)	No (0)	No (0)	Gov (1.5)	No (1)	Binding (1)	3.5
W. Germany	Yes (1)	No (0)	No (0)	Nobody (0)	No (1)	Binding (1)	3
Belgium	No (0)	No (0)	No (0)	Gov (1.5)	No (1)	Consult. (0)	2.5
Great Britain	No (0)	No (0)	No (0)	Gov (1.5)	No (1)	Consult. (0)	2.5
Netherlands	No (0)	No (0)	No (0)	Nobody (0)	Nobody(0)	Nobody (0)	0

a For a total reform of the constitution. A partial reform could be put to a referendum by a petition of a third of the members of each house. b As one of the alternatives. The other is holding a joint session of the two houses and passing it with a majority of 3/5. c Only to alter the position of the established Lutheran church. d As one of the alternatives, if requested by half a million voters, one-fifth of the members of either of the houses, or five regional assemblies. But a referendum cannot be called if the amendment has been approved by a majority of two-thirds in both houses. e For a total reform and for partial reforms that affect certain fundamental sections. Other decisions can be put to a referendum if it is requested by one-tenth of the members of either house. f A referendum is necessary in the provinces of Alberta and British Columbia for the houses to approve a constitutional amendment at the federal level.
* For the US we distinguish between federal and state regulations. The row corresponding to the state level presents the number of states with each regulation and the corresponding value projected to the national level (once weighted for the proportion of the US population affected by the regulation). Gov= Government; LM = Legislature minority; H = Head of State.
Sources: Own elaboration from information in Bogdanor (1994: 26–7) for European countries. For Canada and the US the scoring has been assigned from information by the *Centre d'études et de documentation sur la démocratie directe* (2003), and the I & R Institute (2003b).

and the relation is still negative.

It is not obvious what the underlying mechanism of this negative relation between political membership and direct democracy might be. What is certain is that the frequency of use of referenda has no relationship at all to political membership – at least in these countries.[22] It is unlikely that the mere availability of institutions of direct democracy that empower citizens to participate in the decision-making process would, in itself, have a negative effect on citizens' participation in political

Graph 6.3: Political membership and the regulation of direct democracy

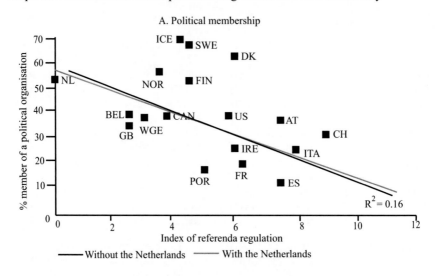

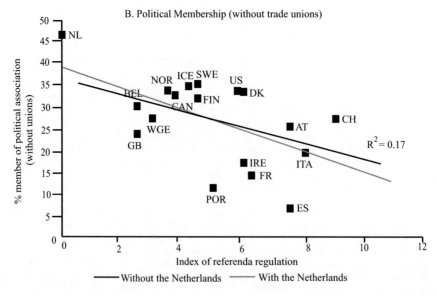

Graph 6.3: Cont.

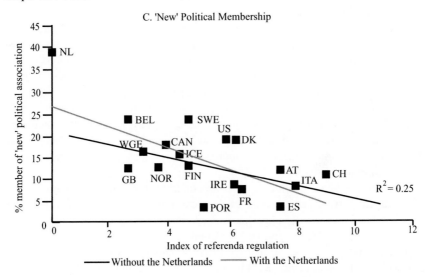

C. 'New' Political Membership

Without the Netherlands —————— With the Netherlands

organisations. And it is true that – because the Swiss survey under-reported membership of NSMOs – it is likely that the relation approaches zero instead of being negative. It is also the case that only in three countries – Italy, Switzerland and the US – are ordinary citizens entitled to promote a referendum. Hence, it may well be that variations in the different situations in which calling for a referendum is allowed might not be consequential enough to provide further participation opportunities, if citizens are not included as initiators of the process, because political elites are seldom inclined to initiate plebiscitary processes unless they have to, or unless they anticipate clear political gains from the outcome. Thus, rather than interpreting these results as indicative of a negative relation to political membership, we should probably only conclude that direct democratic institutions – as such – do not promote individual engagement in political organisations in any clear way.

THE FRAGMENTATION OF POLITICAL ELITES

The second dimension that defines the degree of openness of a political system is the extent to which its political elites are fragmented. Political pluralism increases with the fragmentation of elites, which means that established political actors will be more inclined to respond to new social demands and less able to limit their articulation (Kitschelt 1986: 63). Two main mechanisms link a higher degree of fragmentation with a greater openness to new demands. On the one hand, greater political fragmentation tends to trigger centrifugal political competition, making political leaders appropriate the demands of new organisations more readily and play the part of 'people's tribunes' (Tarrow 1994: 88, Rochon 1998: 201). This, in turn, allows outsiders to forge alliances with members of the political elite, there-by increasing their own impact (Rucht 1996). On the other hand, greater elite frag-mentation tends to be associated with reduced political and electoral autonomy, due to the need to forge coalitions and alliances with other parties, who are also subject to their own internal and electoral dynamics.[23] In highly fragmented party systems, party elites need to compromise with other coalition partners and this will make all of them vulnerable to pressures from each other's constituencies. Consequently, political elites will be more flexible when confronted with popular demands and new challengers (Koopmans & Rucht 1995), especially when these are accompanied by protest and unrest. Both mechanisms operate in such a way that collective action is likely to be more successful, thus increasing the expected benefits of collective action.

The fragmentation of elites can be measured by the degree of fragmentation either of the party system or that of the government. Clearly, both aspects are closely related – especially in parliamentary systems – as a fragmented party sys-tem will more frequently produce coalition governments. Results presented in Morales (2004: 291–4) show that the effective number of parliamentary parties calculated by Lijphart (1999: 312) best represents the latent variable of elite frag-mentation; hence, it is used as the primary indicator in this study (Table 6.3).

The results of previous studies, as well as the general hypotheses discussed, lead us to expect a positive relation, or at the least a curvilinear one,[24] between elite fragmentation and political membership, and that this relation will be more intense for membership of 'new' political organisations.

Table 6.3: Fragmentation of elites

Country	Effective number of parliamentary parties 1971–96
Switzerland	5.57
Belgium	5.49
Italy	5.22
Finland	5.17
Denmark	5.11
Netherlands	4.68
Iceland	4
Norway	3.61
France	3.54
Sweden	3.52
Portugal	3.33
W. Germany	2.84
Spain	2.76
Ireland	2.76
Austria	2.72
United States	2.41
Canada	2.35
Great Britain	2.2

Source: Lijphart (1999: 312).

Graph 6.4: Political membership and elite fragmentation

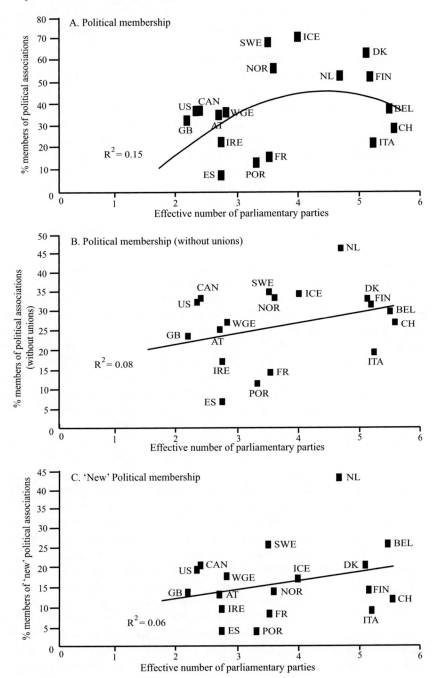

An examination of the bivariate relation between the number of effective parliamentary parties and political membership – in its different operationalisations – shows a positive but moderate association (Graph 6.4). In all cases, variation around the average effect is large. And, although research in the field of social movements has shown that their mobilisation is related to traditional politics, both in the parliamentary arenas as well as in the extra-parliamentary ones (Kriesi *et al.* 1995: xii), and that the fragmentation of elites is related to the ability of NSMs to achieve their goals, our results seem to indicate that this connection is moderate and seems to interfere with other relevant contextual aspects. However, the analyses presented in Chapter seven will show that the relation between elite fragmentation and political membership is much more intense and clear once we control for other individual and contextual variables and when we exclude unions from the operationalisation of the dependent variable.

THE POROUSNESS OF THE SYSTEM OF INTEREST-REPRESENTATION

A fundamental problem when studying the effect of interest-representation systems lies in the multiple concepts and approaches that have been used in political science to analyse interest-representation systems. Although the prevailing approach distinguishes between pluralist and corporatist or neo-corporatist systems, the content and definition of both concepts is far from unequivocal or consensual (Lane & Ersson 1999: chapter seven, Siaroff 1999). In fact, the main limitation of this distinction is that it is sometimes used to describe complete interest-representation systems (Schmitter 1988) or the overall interaction system between the public and the private sectors (Lehner 1987 and 1988) and, on other occasions, to classify different methods of policy-making – especially economic policies – or even different degrees of economic integration (Siaroff 1999).

These varying definitions of the pluralist-corporatist continuum and the frequent lack of precision when creating empirical indicators, may lead to confounding patterns of interest mediation that have distinct impacts on the degree of porousness of the decision-making system. So, what are the elements of pluralist and corporatist systems that entail greater porousness in the interest-mediation system?

On the one hand, porousness largely depends on the degree of openness of the various decision-making arenas to a plurality of groups and organisations. In this sense, we should distinguish between pluralist systems that provide access to a multiplicity of players and systems with monopolistic tendencies that limit access to a select group of actors and organisations. In general, research on social movements assigns to pluralist interest-representation systems and to "weak" administrative systems a greater capacity to incorporate new demands (Kitschelt 1986, Kriesi *et al.* 1995: 31 ff.). When the bureaucratic structure of the state is fragile and lacks consolidated coordination and decision-making mechanisms as well as professionalisation, interest groups have more chances to influence decision-making processes. However, what is an advantage in enabling the action of organised groups becomes a disadvantage when the state has to implement decisions already adopted, even those that favour citizens' organisations: there is, thus, a trade-off between access and efficacy (Kitschelt 1986, Kriesi *et al.* 1995).

Furthermore, pluralist systems incorporate a wider range of demands, as no group has a privileged or preferential position in the representation system. Monopolist systems, on the other hand, privilege economic interest groups – mainly unions and business organisations – when adopting decisions, which often leads to the exclusion of other players and political organisations outside these policy domains.

On the other hand, the porousness of the interest-representation system also depends on the degree to which the access of interest groups is institutionalised and forms part of the normal *modus operandi* of the decision-making process. Formal structures, such as committees or commissions, for debate, negotiation or consultation on policy decisions can channel new demands through institutional mechanisms that set the rules for inclusion and for the resolution of conflicts and disagreements (Lehner 1987, Lane & Ersson 1999: 226–34). Hence, the distinction between *consensual* and *conflictual* representation systems taps into this element.[25] Consequently, representation systems that combine pluralism in interest-representation with predominantly consensual representation will be, *a priori*, the most porous and accessible to organised citizen demands and groups.

The reality is that both aspects of interest-representation systems are empirically linked. In other words, neo-corporatist systems tend to adopt consensual styles and procedures, while pluralist systems are often characterised by more

Table 6.4: Indicators of the porosity of interest-representation systems

Country	Condensed index of corporatism (Siaroff)
Austria	5
Norway	4.92
Sweden	4.81
Netherlands	4.27
Denmark	3.58
Finland	3.46
Switzerland	3.37
W. Germany	3.31
Iceland	3
Belgium	2.75
Ireland	2.05
Great Britain	1.58
Italy	1.58
France	1.46
Canada	1.1
United States	1.1
Spain	1
Portugal	1

Source: Siaroff (1999: 180)

Graph 6.5: Corporatism and political membership

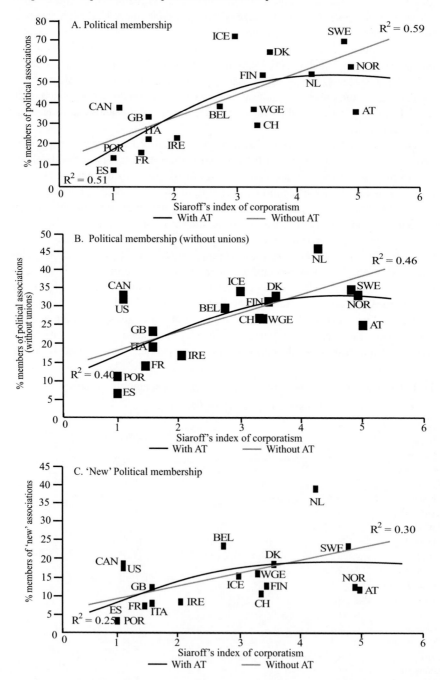

conflictual methods of decision-making.[26] Partly, this empirical coincidence is due to historical factors that have led to the establishment of certain rules of social bargaining in the employment sector and have also produced wider bargaining systems in other policy domains (Schmitter 1988, Siaroff 1999).

The close connection between corporatism and consensual systems of interest-representation is reflected in the high correlation between the various indexes available in the literature. Lane and Ersson's (1999: 235) corporatism index, Siaroff's (1999: 180) condensed index of corporatism, Lehner's (in Siaroff 1999) index of public-private interaction and Siaroff's (1999: 192) condensed index of consensual interest representation are all highly correlated, with coefficients ranging from 0.71 to 0.92. For our analyses we have selected Siaroff's condensed index of corporatism, because it is the one that shows highest correlations with all the other three indicators (Table 6.4).

Siaroff's condensed index of corporatism is a summary of 13 other indices of corporatism, many of which focus on the degree of monopolistic power of the larger unions and business associations in decision-making processes in the economic and social policy fields.[27]

Graph 6.5 describes the relation between corporatism and membership of political organisations. Given that corporatist institutions are closely linked to the structure and organisational capacity of unions, it is crucial to inspect the bivariate relations with and without membership of unions, as well as for membership of political organisations linked to NSMs.

As we can see, in all three cases the association is positive and curvilinear, and more corporatism does not translate into higher percentages of political membership after a certain point. Furthermore, Austria is somewhat of an outlier and, when we remove it from the analyses, the relation is no longer curvilinear but neatly linear.[28] Therefore, these results provisionally support the hypothesis that consensual and non-monopolistic systems of interest-representation foster the formation and development of numerous political organisations that represent different types of interests and causes. However, as this scholarly literature also hints, too much corporatism may not always be good, as it might limit the ability of political organisations that are unrelated to the economic sphere to act and develop, given the monopolistic role of unions and business organisations.

In summary, descriptive bivariate analyses indicate that political decentralisation is only partially related to engagement in political organisations. Whereas greater autonomy of municipalities seems to be associated with higher political membership, that is not the case with overall decentralised and federal states. In turn, institutions of direct democracy are, at best, not having any impact on organised political involvement and may even hinder it. Thus, overall, they matter little for involvement in political organisations. In contrast, the other two dimensions of openness – the fragmentation of political elites and the porousness of interest representation systems – seem to be clearly related to political membership. In the last section of this chapter we assess the impact of all these institutional factors once individual attributes are controlled for.

THE OPENNESS OF POLITICAL SYSTEMS AND POLITICAL
MEMBERSHIP: A MULTI-LEVEL ANALYSIS

Throughout this chapter, we have focused our attention on three main elements that define the openness of political systems: (1) the plurality of points of access to the political decision-making system, (2) the fragmentation of political elites, and (3) the porousness of the administrative decision-making process. The latter two, at least, seem to be related to political membership in western democracies.

However, these results are still only partial, since some of these relationships may turn out to be spurious when we take into account the effect of the resources, the social status and the civic and political orientation of citizens, as well as their variations across countries. Table 6.5 shows four multilevel models of political membership that include and exclude, respectively, union membership from the operationalisation of the dependent variable. The baseline models only include individual-level variables, and serve as reference points for evaluating the better adjustment of the full models – which incorporate the variables relating to the context of the openness of political systems – to the data.[29] Thus, the full models adopt the functional form of Equation 6.1, as described in equation 5.1.

$$\text{Logit }(\pi_{ij}) = \gamma_{00} + \sum_{h=1}^{r}\beta_{h0}\,x_{hij} + \sum_{k=1}^{q}\gamma_{0k}\,z_{kj} + U_{0j} + \sum_{h=1}^{p}U_{hj}\,x_{hij} \qquad \text{(Equation 6.1)}$$

The first thing to note is the substantial improvement in the proportion of country-level variance accounted for by the variables that measure the openness of the political system. This is particularly notable in the case of the model that excludes union membership, as we can see from the decrease in the variance of the intercept parameters.

The inclusion of the variables of openness does not, however, reduce the variation in the coefficients for education, church attendance and gender. This confirms the results shown in Table 3.13 (Chapter three), which showed that education was an important factor of inequalities in participation in many countries,

---

Notes to Table 6.5
Source: Own elaboration using data from the 1990–93 WVS. All coefficients indicate the change (increase or decrease) in the natural logarithm of the odds ratio (p/1-p) of the dependent variable (membership of any political association = 1, non-membership = 0) when the explanatory variable increases by one unit. All the ordinal and quantitative variables at the individual level have been recoded so that 0 represents the minimum value and 1 the maximum. The contextual variables are centred around their mean, so that the value 0 corresponds to the average value of the variable for the 17 countries. Only significant coefficients are shown for p≤0.10. Significant coefficients for p≤0.05 are underlined, and for p≤0.01 they are shown in bold. N.s. = not statistically significant for p<0.10. * For the variance parameters coefficients the component is expressed in terms of the amount of variance, with the value in standard deviations shown in brackets + Proportion of the total residual variance due to the variation between countries. § R2 for multilevel binomial regressions (see the details on calculation and interpretation in Snijders & Bosker 1999: 225–6). † The first figure corresponds to calculations with all the variables associated with random coefficients set at their maximum value (1), while the second corresponds to the equivalent calculation setting variables at their minimum value (0).

Table 6.5: Political membership and the openness of the political system: individual and contextual effects

Variables	Baseline model (with unions)	Full model (with unions)	Baseline model (without unions)	Full model (without unions)
Intercept	-2.32	-2.32	-3.72	-3.72
Fixed parameters (indiv. level)				
Education	0.94	0.94	1.26	1.25
Employment situation (ref= +30h)				
Works <30 h.	-0.27	-0.26	0.15	0.16
Inactive	-0.67	-0.67	-0.25	-0.25
Unemployed	-0.62	-0.62	-0.32	-0.31
Age	4.18	4.16	3.92	3.91
Age (squared)	-4.31	-4.29	-3.65	-3.63
Woman (ref=man)	-0.14	-0.14	n.s.	n.s.
With partner (ref=without partner)	n.s.	n.s.	n.s.	n.s.
Church attendance	-0.26	-0.25	n.s.	n.s.
Religious membership	1.09	1.09	1.02	1.02
Interest in politics	0.57	0.57	0.74	0.74
Political efficacy	0.27	0.27	0.37	0.37
Inter-personal trust	0.16	0.16	0.24	0.23
Values index (ref=material.)				
Mixed	0.14	0.13	0.14	0.14
Post-materialist	0.50	0.49	0.50	0.50
Attitude to social change (ref= conservative)				
Radical	n.s.	n.s.	0.21	0.22
Reformist	0.14	0.14	0.11	0.11
Fixed parameters (country level)				
General decentralisation		n.s.		n.s.
Local autonomy		0.04		n.s.
Formal regulation of direct democracy		n.s.		-0.7
Effective number of parties		n.s.		0.12
Effective no. of parties (squared)		n.s.		n.s.
Corporatism index (Siaroff)		0.65		0.13
Corporatism index (squared)		-0.09		n.s.
Random parameters (country level)				
uij ~ N (0, Ωu): Ωu †	0.48-0.89	0.26-0.57	0.25-0.37	0.16-0.17
u0ij [intercept] *	0.89 (0.94)	0.57 (0.76)	0.37 (0.61)	0.17 (0.41)
u1ij [education]*	0.22 (0.47)	0.21 (0.46)	0.27 (0.52)	0.27 (0.52)
u2ij [church attendance]*	0.12 (0.34)	0.11 (0.33)	0.10 (0.31)	0.09 (0.29)
u3ij [gender]*	0.05 (0.23)	0.04 (0.21)	0.08 (0.28)	0.08 (0.28)
Intra-class correlation + †	0.13-0.21	0.07-0.15	0.07-0.10	0.05-0.05
R2 dicho§ †	0.19-0.17†	0.27-0.25	0.21-0.20	0.55-0.55
% unexplained level 2 variance †	10-18†	5-11	6-8	2-2
Number of cases (no. of countries)	20,815 (17)	20,815 (17)	20,815 (17)	20,815 (17)

Graph 6.6: Political membership and the availability of direct democratic institutions

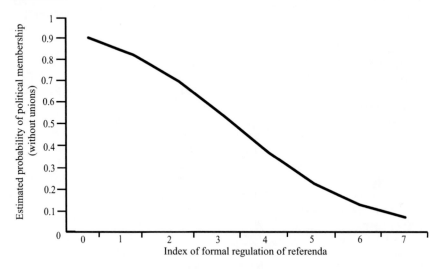

though not in countries as Sweden, Belgium or Austria, for example.

Turning our attention to the fixed parameters, as for the models presented in Chapter five, the individual-level variables are largely unaffected by the inclusion of the country-level ones. Hence, the main aspects that the models reveal are the effects of the openness variables. In this regard, we first notice that the variables relating to openness that are relevant for political membership change depending on the inclusion or exclusion of union membership. Thus, the degree of local autonomy ceases to have any impact when we exclude unions, while we find a highly negative effect of the availability of direct democracy institutions (Graph 6.6) and a moderately positive effect of the effective number of parliamentary parties. Only the degree of corporatism has a clear impact on political membership, either with or without unions, though it is considerably smaller in the latter case (Graph 6.7).

Although at first sight it may seem that the effect of some of the openness variables is at best moderate, we should bear in mind that, as a general rule, the effect of contextual variables on an individual's behaviour is always smaller than the effect of the individual's attributes, given the significant variation in individual behaviour within each particular country.

In short, the institutional elements of western democracies that shape the degree of openness of the political system to citizens' demands contribute considerably to improving our understanding of political membership among individuals and, above all, across countries.

Graph 6.7: Political membership and corporatism

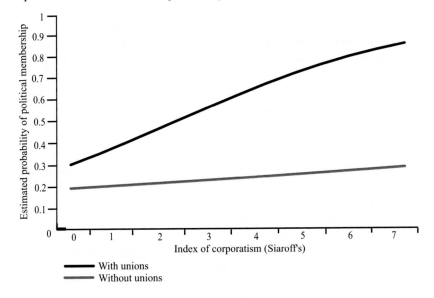

With unions
Without unions

CONCLUSIONS

This chapter has shown that several aspects that are linked to the POS of western democracies – especially, the degree of fragmentation of the political elites, and the porousness of the system of interest-representation – can help us account for cross-national variations in political membership in these nations. The findings presented in this chapter thus justify the inclusion of these sets of factors in a more complete model of what makes western citizens join (or not join) political organisations.

Further to this, it is important to mention that there are some other features of the institutional context of western countries that could not be analysed here, despite their relevance in shaping citizens' opportunities to join political organisations. For example, due to a lack of adequate data, it was not possible to study the extent to which different levels of 'patronage' (Walker 1991) in each society affect the tendency to form and join political and advocacy associations.

It would also have been especially interesting to examine whether cross-national variations in political membership are linked to the different approaches to public subsidies for associations. As many scholars have made clear, a solution to the collective-action dilemma is the intervention of an external agent, who enables co-operation by means of positive or negative incentives (Ordeshook 1986: 206–25, Laver 1997: chapter three). The state can – and very frequently does – play a determining role in the promotion of political membership, not only through the creation of means and channels for participation but also by explicitly supporting the creation and subsistence of organisations that collaborate with various public agencies in the provision of services or in decision-making processes.[30]

In conclusion, the results presented in this chapter show that political opportunity structures have a relevant impact on citizens' propensity to join organisations that seek political objectives. These findings – along with those discussed in the previous chapter – lead us to the final stage of this study. In the next chapter we build on the partial results presented in this chapter and Chapter five and confront the main significant elements of the meso- and macro-contexts with the individual-level variables, in order to fully develop our analytical model of political membership.

NOTES

1 See, among others, Kitschelt (1986), Kriesi (1989), Tarrow (1994), Koopmans (1995), Kriesi *et al.* (1995), della Porta & Rucht (1995), and Rucht (1996).

2 The concept was first introduced by Eisinger (1973: 25): 'the degree to which groups are likely to be able to gain access to power and to manipulate the political system'.

3 In Tarrow (1996: 54) a slightly modified version of this definition is offered: '[the] consistent – but not necessarily formal, permanent, or national – signals to social or political actors which either encourage or discourage them to use their internal resources to form social movements'.

4 Kitschelt (1986) shows how assimilative strategies are more frequent in the antinuclear movement of countries with more open POSs as regards *input*; while movement strategies tend to be *confrontational* in countries with more closed POS. Although Kitschelt does not refer to this, it implies that collective action via stable and effective organisations will be more attractive in the former than in the latter, where citizens will invariably need to resort to protest to get their voices heard.

5 Various scholars distinguish between stable and dynamic elements of the POS. See, for example, della Porta & Rucht (1995), Rucht (1996), Kriesi *et al.* (1995).

6 In some instances, Kriesi (1996: 161–3) uses survey data and indicators of membership similar to those used in this study, thus establishing a clear precedent for the analyses presented in this chapter with a larger number of western democracies. Nevertheless, the limited number of countries studied by Kriesi – four – reduces the capacity to check the hypotheses generated by the literature on the effects of the POS systematically. On many occasions the existence of patterns of behaviour that deviate from the expectations raise doubts as to whether these are outliers or whether the hypotheses should be rejected. This happens, for example, when Kriesi tries to explain the scarce professionalisation of Swiss social movements (p. 173), of alliance structures with the left in the Netherlands (note 21), or the limited relations between Swiss social movement organisations and political authorities.

7 See, for example, Kriesi *et al.* (1995: xiii ff.), McAdam (1996: 27), Klandermans (1997: chapter seven), Rochon (1998: chapter 7).

8 Stability and generality distinguish institutions from other components of the POS, namely processes and alliance structures (Rochon 1998: 200).

9 This classification coincides with the dimensions of the POS that McAdam distinguishes (1996). Rochon (1998: chapter seven), in turn, distinguishes between institutional pluralism and institutional porousness, in such a way that the former is defined by the number of decision

nodes that exist in the political system and the latter depends on how far movement organisations can form part of the decision-making system. In my opinion, both pluralism and institutional porousness point in the same direction: the accessibility or openness of the political system.

10 Frequently, political parties are regarded as the main actors in charge of demand aggregation. We should remind readers that parties are certainly included in our more general category of 'political associations'. Nonetheless, other political associations do also play a crucial role in the process of demand aggregation for specific subgroups of the public. Thus, for example, professional associations and unions not only create and articulate the demands of the groups of professionals and workers they represent, they also aggregate the conflicting demands that may arise between different sectors of the same groups.

11 More recent studies have confirmed that the degree of decentralisation influences different types of citizen participation (Mabileau *et al.* 1987).

12 In Morales (2004: chapter six) the size of municipalities was also considered but, due to its minimal connection with political membership, it has been excluded from all analyses in this study.

13 Vetter (2002a and 2002b) uses both strategies and similar indicators to those used in this study.

14 The main limitation of this option is the subjective assignment of numerical values to each country, guided by criteria that frequently are not explicit and difficult to quantify.

15 Calculated from item 38 (*Total current disbursements and net saving*) for *General government* and for *Local government* in OECD National Accounts (1993).

16 The figures for Spain and the Netherlands provided by the OECD also include those from the provincial level.

17 In Morales (2004), Lane & Ersson's (1999) autonomy index was also used, but given its high correlation with Lijphart's (0.86), only the latter was retained.

18 Thus, Boehmke argues, and his results bears this out, that the important thing for the density of the interest group sector is the possibility of using mechanisms of direct democracy and not the frequency with which they are really used. Nevertheless, this prediction is referred to the organisational level and not the individual level.

19 This does not mean that the organisation of referendum campaigns is not costly in organisational terms. In fact, as Kriesi & Wisler themselves point out (1996), the financial and organisational costs involved in these types of campaigns can lead to important participative inequalities and marginalise disadvantaged social groups even more. Boehmke (2002) also points out that the existence of institutions of direct democracy favour unequally different groups. Nevertheless his conclusions on the data of the North American states suggest that it is the most inclusive citizen interest groups, rather than particular economic interest groups that most bloom in relative terms and take advantage of the opportunities that they are given by direct democratic processes.

20 See Freitag (2006) for a similar argument about associational membership in general.

21 There is a certain debate about whether popular initiatives are a type of referendum (see Uleri 1996). This debate is irrelevant for our study, since at the moment there is no systematic information on the regulation of popular initiatives in the 18 democracies included here.

22 Results not presented here. See Morales (2004: 287–90).

23 This need not translate directly into cabinet stability.

24 The existence of a curvilinear relation between the openness of a political system and the capacity and level of mobilisation of social movements has been noted by many scholars (Eisinger 1973, Kitschelt 1986, Kriesi *et al*. 1995: 40, Tarrow 1996: 54).

25 Yet this distinction does not exactly represent what we refer to, since some conflictual systems – such as the American – still systematically resort to the creation of committees and commissions that serve to adopt decisions that are not necessarily consensual.

26 See the interesting debate related to this topic in Lijphart & Crepaz (1991), Keman & Pennings (1995) and Crepaz & Lijphart (1995).

27 The fact that these indicators primarily focus on interest groups does not prevent them from being useful as proxies of the wider interest-representation system. Schmitter (1988) makes this same assumption and Wiarda (1997: 175), additionaly, claims that corporatist systems have expanded to new areas of public policy beyond those of the traditional areas of economic policy and social policy connected to economic competitiveness (especially, education and social security).

28 Iceland and the Netherlands are also cases with some leverage in the determination of this bivariate relation. But the exclusion of the Icelandic case makes the bivariate relation between corporatism and political membership even stronger; while the exclusion of the Dutch case weakens it for its second (without unions) and third (new groups) variants.

29 Excluded from these four models are family income and the size of the community variables, because the samples from Iceland and Finland do not include them, and their inclusion in these models would entail that we would lose these two countries, thus reducing the number of countries from 17 to 15. Switzerland is excluded from all multivariate analyses because its survey omitted several items of 'new' political membership. The construction of the models – as in all other chapters in this book – has been done with great care and in several steps to minimise the problems of the limited number of countries. Thus, variables that are identified as not significant were identified as such after testing different identifications of the model.

30 See the work collected in Kuhnle & Selle (1992) on the relationship between governments and voluntary associations, as well as Walker (1991).

chapter seven | attitudes, resources, opportunities, and mobilisation: a multilevel model of political membership

> Human actions, social contexts and institutions work upon each other in complicated ways, and these complex, interactive processes of action and the formation of meaning are important to political life. (March and Olsen 1984: 742)

INTRODUCTION

Chapters five and six have presented detailed empirical evidence of how mobilisation structures and processes and institutional opportunities for participation can influence individuals' decisions to join political organisations. Separately considered, mobilisation patterns and institutional openness account for a substantial amount of the cross-national variations that we find in political membership in western democracies. This chapter takes a further step in the analysis of the impact of contextual factors on political membership and tests the theoretical and analytical model of this study in its entirety.

The various multi-level models presented in the following pages, therefore, address the analytical model of political membership outlined in Figure 7.1 – which disregards the elements of the micro-context due to lack of information. As we shall see, the hypotheses that relate the political context to political participation are indeed useful for the analysis of political membership across western democracies. Consequently, our results will show that many of the concepts and approaches that have been developed in the subfield of social movements studies are also particularly valuable for the study of individual political participation.

Finally, we will show that the impact of these two broad sets of contextual factors – mobilisation and institutional opportunities – is of a double nature. In addition to having a direct impact on individuals' decisions to join a political organisation, the contextual elements that we are considering in this study also have an indirect impact, through their interaction with individual-level attributes and resources. As we will show, there is a significant interaction effect between educational resources and institutional openness, such that greater institutional accessibility mitigates the inequalities introduced by differential educational opportunities.

Figure 7.1: The full model under test

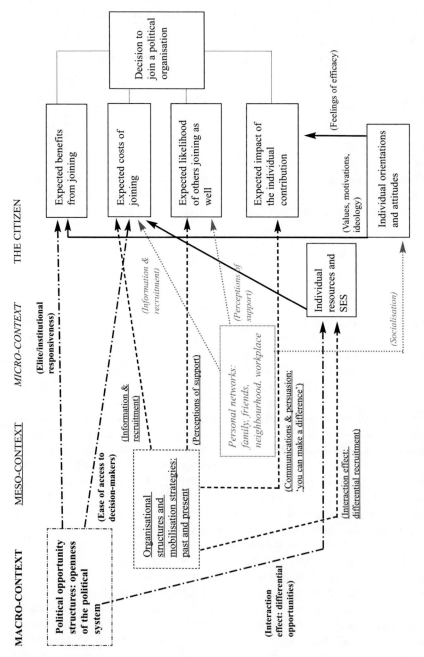

Font and line patterns identify the various levels of analysis for each set of factors: individual, micro-contextual, meso- and macro-contextual.

COMBINING INDIVIDUAL AND CONTEXTUAL FACTORS:
A GENERAL MODEL OF POLITICAL MEMBERSHIP

One of the main contributions that this study attempts to make is the proposal of an analytical framework for political participation – and, specifically, political membership – that focuses on the behaviour of individual citizens while taking into account not only their own individual characteristics but also the various aspects of the political context that may either encourage or discourage them from engaging in politics.

The analyses displayed in Chapter three confirmed that citizens join political organisations at different rates, depending on the resources they possess, their position in the social structure, and the civic and political orientations they have. In this chapter, we will show that how these individual attributes – especially educational resources – operate to make citizens more or less likely to join political associations depends also on the political context in which citizens are placed.

On the one hand, the political context provides – or fails to do so – incentives to engage in politics. As we have discussed in the preceding chapters, mobilisation efforts by organisations offer additional opportunities to gain information about the activities of the groups and to join them after explicit requests to become a member. These mobilisation efforts reduce the costs of joining but mobilisation initiatives and structures also shape perceptions of support and the likely success of the organisations, thus making membership a more attractive option. In turn, institutional settings define the range of opportunities citizens have to exert a real influence when joining a political organisation. More open institutional contexts mean that the political elites and the public administrations will be more receptive and responsive to citizens' demands and, thus, organised collective action is likely to be perceived as an effective means of political transformation. Furthermore, if access to decision-making actors and bodies is relatively easy, the costs of political action will be reduced.

Yet, one other likely impact of mobilisation patterns and institutional settings is their capacity to increase or reduce participatory inequalities among individual citizens. Incentives for participation are frequently not equally powerful for all sorts of individuals.[1] For example, we know that mobilisation strategies and patterns are sometimes biased and that organisations are more likely to recruit among the most resourceful (Rosenstone & Hansen 1993, Verba, Schlozman & Brady 1995). Equally, the reduction in the costs of accessing decision-making actors might increase the inclination to participate of certain social groups more, thus mitigating inequalities in political access. Therefore, the mobilisation and institutional contexts are not only crucial in accounting for cross-national variations in political membership but also to better understand the dynamics of unequal access to participation opportunities within and across countries. In other words, some of the features of the political context are likely to help us explain why organised political action is more egalitarian in some countries than in others.

The models shown in Table 7.1 synthesise the overall analytical model of this

Table 7.1: A general multilevel model of political membership

Variables	Baseline model (with unions)	Full model (with unions)	Baseline model (without unions)	Full model (without unions)
Intercept	-2.32	-2.31	-3.72	-3.73
Fixed parameters (indiv. level)				
Education	0.94	0.92	1.26	1.24
Employment situation (ref= +30h)				
Works <30 h.	-0.27	-0.26	0.15	0.16
Inactive	-0.67	-0.67	-0.25	-0.25
Unemployed	-0.62	-0.62	-0.32	-0.29
Age	4.18	4.15	3.92	3.94
Age (squared)	-4.31	-4.29	-3.65	-3.67
Woman (ref=man)	-0.14	-0.13	n.s.	n.s.
With partner (ref=without partner)	n.s.	n.s.	n.s.	n.s.
Church attendance	-0.26	-0.24	n.s.	n.s.
Religious membership	1.09	1.09	1.02	1.01
Interest in politics	0.57	0.57	0.74	0.72
Political efficacy	0.27	0.27	0.37	0.36
Inter-personal trust	0.16	0.17	0.24	0.23
Values index (ref=materialist)				
Mixed	0.14	0.13	0.14	0.15
Post-materialist	0.50	0.50	0.50	0.51
Attitude to social change (ref= conservative)				
Radical	n.s.	n.s.	0.21	0.24
Reformist	0.14	0.15	0.11	0.12
Fixed parameters (country level)				
Mobilisation factors				
No. political party branches (x 1,000 inhab.)		2.90		1.25
No. political party branches (squared)		-1.79		-0.75
Citizen polarisation		n.s.		-0.20
Citizen polarisation (squared)		n.s.		n.s.
Effective no. of religious groups		n.s.		n.s.
Tradition of participation (union members x 1,000 inhabs. In 1950)		n.s.		n.s.
Institutional factors				
Local autonomy (local spending)		0.02		n.s.
Siaroff's corporatism index		1.48		0.23
Corporatism index (squared)		-0.16		n.s.
Index of formal regulation of direct democracy		n.s.		-0.08
Effective no. of parliamentary parties		n.s.		0.44
Interactions between levels				
Education x level of corporatism		-0.26		-0.19
Education x effective no. of parties		n.s.		-0.30
Random parameters (country level)				
$u_{ij} \sim N (0, \Omega_u): \Omega_u$ †	0.48-0.89	0.22-0.09	0.25-0.37	0.09-0.04
u_{0ij} [intercept] *	0.89 (0.94)	0.09 (0.30)	0.37 (0.61)	0.04 (0.21)

Table 7.1: Cont.

u_{1ij} [education]*	**0.22 (0.47)**	**0.06 (0.25)**	**0.27 (0.52)**	**0.08 (0.28)**
u_{2ij} [church attendance]*	**0.12 (0.34)**	**0.10 (0.32)**	**0.10 (0.31)**	**0.06 (0.25)**
u_{3ij} [gender]*	**0.05 (0.23)**	**0.04 (0.21)**	**0.08 (0.28)**	**0.08 (0.29)**
Intra-class correlation + †	0.13-0.21	0.06-0.03	0.07-0.10	0.03-0.01
R^2 dicho§ †	0.19-0.17†	0.30-0.30	0.21-0.20	0.20-0.21
% unexplained level 2 variance †	10-18†	4-2	6-8	2-1
Number of cases (no. of countries)	20,815 (17)	20,815 (17)	20,815 (17)	20,815 (17)

Source: Individual variables are from the 1990–93 WVS, for contextual variables see the relevant tables in chapters five and six.

Notes: All coefficients indicate the change (increase or decrease) in the natural logarithm of the odds ratio (p/1-p) of the dependent variable (membership of any political association = 1, non-membership = 0) when the explanatory variable increases by one unit. All the ordinal and quantitative variables at the individual level – except for age – have been recoded so that 0 represents the minimum value and 1 the maximum. The contextual variables are centred around their means, so that the value 0 corresponds to the average value of the variable for the 17 countries. Only the significant coefficients are shown for p≤0.10. The significant coefficients for p≤0.05 are underlined, and for p≤0.01 they are shown in bold. N.s. = not statistically significant for p≤0.10. * For the variance parameters coefficients the component is expressed in variance terms, with the standard deviation values shown in brackets + Proportion of the total residual variance attributable to the variation between countries. § R2 for multilevel binomial regressions (see the details on calculation and interpretation in Snijders & Bosker 1999: 225–6). † The first figure corresponds to calculations with all the variables associated with random coefficients set at their maximum value (1), while the second corresponds to the equivalent calculation setting variables at their minimum value (0).

study. As in preceding chapters, we distinguish between two different operationalisations of the dependent variable: with and without union membership. And, to make an efficient use of the limited number of country-level units, we have only considered variables that proved to be significant in the multivariate multi-level models of the preceding chapters. The full models in Table 7.1 have the following structure:

$$\text{Logit } (\pi_{ij}) = \gamma_{00} + \sum_{h=1}^{r} \beta_{h0} x_{hij} + \sum_{k=1}^{q} \gamma_{0k} z_{kj} + \sum\sum \gamma_{hk} z_{kj} x_{hij} + U_{0j} + \sum_{h=1}^{p} U_{hj} x_{hij}$$

(Equation 7.1)

Where:
i = individual i for I = 1, 2, 3, ..., n;
j = country j, for J = 1, 2, 3, ..., N;
$\pi_{ij} = p_{ij}/1 - p_{ij}$, and $p_{ij} = \text{prob}(y_{ij} = 1)$, and y = 1 (member of a political association);
β = estimated parameters at the individual level (level 1);
x_h = variables measured at the individual level (level 1), for h = 1, 2, 3, ..., r; and the subset with random coefficients is h = 1, 2, 3, ...p; and the subset with cross-level interactions is h = 1, 2, 3, ... o;
γ = average estimated parameters at the country level (level 2);

z_k = variables measured at the country level (level 2), for k = 1, 2, 3, ..., q; and
the subset with cross-level interactions is k = 1, 2, 3, ..., s; and
U = variance or error parameters for the country level (level 2).

Thus, these models estimate the variance of countries around the average model, both in terms of the variance around the intercept (U_{0j}) and of the variance in the effect of individual-level variables (U_{hj}). Additionally, the models check for cross-level interactions of specific individual-level variables with specific country-level factors (γ_{hk}).

The full models shown in Table 7.1 confirm the substantial impact that the political context and, in particular, the degree of openness of the political system has on citizens' political behaviour. The magnitude of the effects suggests that neglecting these factors render our models of political participation largely incomplete. And the models are similar – though not identical – regardless of whether union membership is included in the operationalisation of the dependent variable.

The individual-level parameters are rather stable and change only minimally when country-level variables are included in the model. The only substantial differences emerge when comparing the two different operationalisations of the dependent variable. With union membership, all categories of employment situation, other than working full time, result in a smaller probability of joining a political organisation, while part-time employees are more likely than full-time workers to join political associations when individuals who are only union members are not included as political 'members'. Similarly, gender has a differential impact depending on the inclusion or exclusion of unions as a political organisation; and the same is true for church attendance. Political attitudes and civic orientations have a quite consistent impact, regardless of the variations in the measurement of political membership, but the impact of having an interest in politics, feeling politically efficacious and trusting others is stronger when unions are not included.

Turning our attention to the contextual factors – of primary interest in this study – our findings show that both mobilisation patterns and structures and institutional opportunities have a clear impact on political membership. Starting with mobilisation processes, the results confirm some of the preliminary conclusions discussed in Chapter five: in spite of the severe difficulties we have in systematically measuring mobilisation aspects, the capacity of political organisations to make their activities visible and recruit citizens into action matters a great deal for citizens' actual political behaviour. In particular, the effect of organisational infrastructures – here approximated with the density of party branches in each country – seems to be of utmost relevance (see Graph 7.1). A widespread and dense network of offices and infrastructures provides citizens with additional information about organisational activities and reduces the costs of joining, as groups are more visible and approachable. This effect is significant and similar regardless of the operationalisation of political membership.

The only other element of mobilisation processes that results in a significant coefficient is citizen polarisation but, in this case, the effect only emerges when

Graph 7.1: Political membership and mobilisation factors

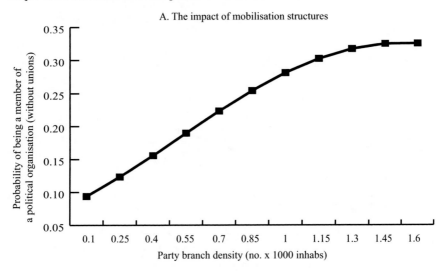

A. The impact of mobilisation structures

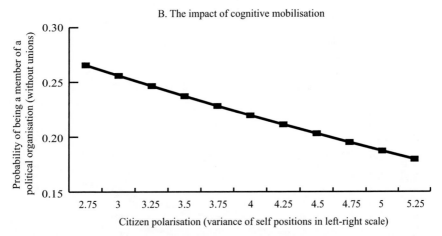

B. The impact of cognitive mobilisation

we exclude unions. Furthermore, and in contrast to our results in Chapter five, polarisation has a negative impact on political membership, once we control for institutional opportunities. This may well be due to the fact that there is a certain amount of overlap between party-system fragmentation and polarisation – with a correlation of 0.55 – and, once this institutional characteristic is taken into account, the remaining polarisation hinders political membership. This would, indeed, make a lot of sense in terms of political dynamics: citizen polarisation along the left–right divide frequently transforms in more fragmented party systems, yet the polarisation that is not absorbed by the electoral and party systems is likely to make politics highly conflictual and 'nasty', thus making citizens more unwilling to engage in political associations. In any case, the impact of polarisation

Graph 7.2: Political membership, educational resources and institutional opportunities

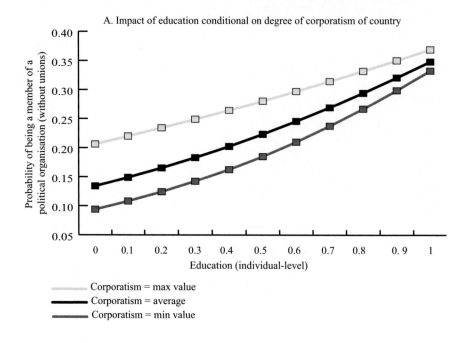

A. Impact of education conditional on degree of corporatism of country

Corporatism = max value
Corporatism = average
Corporatism = min value

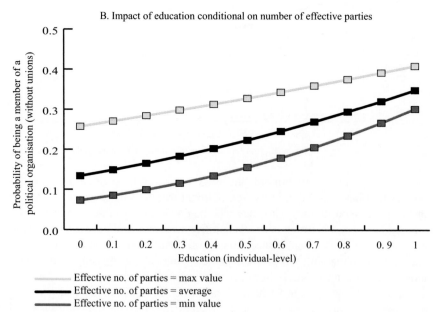

B. Impact of education conditional on number of effective parties

Effective no. of parties = max value
Effective no. of parties = average
Effective no. of parties = min value

is moderate and does not approach that of mobilisation structures.

Institutional factors are also quite important to account for cross-national variations of political membership in western democracies. Most notably, certain aspects closely related to the degree to which the political system is more open or closed to citizens' influence – such as the level of corporatism and the degree of fragmentation of the parliamentary elites – not only have a clear positive effect on political membership in western democracies but also substantially reduce inequalities introduced by differential access to educational resources.[2]

Graph 7.2 illustrates the magnitude of the impact of these two institutional properties, as well as its interaction with education inequalities, in the prediction of political membership. In both cases, the interaction with the education level of the individual is such that higher levels of corporatism or of party fragmentation reduce the impact of educational resources on the likelihood of joining a political association. Consequently, in countries with more 'open' political systems, such a crucial socio-economic resource as education is less of a discriminating factor for political behaviour. Equally, because of the nature of this interaction, this also means that lower SES-individuals are more sensitive to the institutional context, and it is for the less educated citizens that institutional openness boosts political membership the most.

How we operationalise political membership does make quite a difference for the subset of aspects of the institutional context that is of relevance. The peculiar distribution of union membership confounds some of these relationships and – quite trivially – amplifies the impact of corporatist arrangements of interest mediation, while concealing the effect of party fragmentation. Once we discount union membership from the dependent variable, the effect of corporatism is still quite prominent, but elite fragmentation – as measured by the effective number of parliamentary parties – has a more decisive impact on political membership.

Thus, citizens with low levels of educational qualifications who live in countries with a relatively corporatist system and a large number of parliamentary parties – as would be the case, for example, of the Netherlands – are only slightly less likely to join a political association than their fellow citizens with university degrees (Graph 7.3). By contrast, in countries with minimum levels of corporatism, and a reduced number of parliamentary parties – such as Canada or the United States – the less educated citizens are enormously disadvantaged in their capacity to join political groups.

As a result, the impact of the political context, particularly as regards the openness of the political system, is doubly important: on the one hand, it contributes to our understanding of why political membership is much more common in some western democracies – for example, in Scandinavian countries and the Netherlands – and much less widespread in others – Southern Europe, for example; while, on the other hand, it also accounts for the relevant cross-national variations in the social inequalities that are associated with political membership.

Even though our model is generally applicable to membership of all political organisations, many of the specific hypotheses presented and discussed in this

Graph 7.3: Political membership and openness of the political system: the combined effects of corporatism and party fragmentation

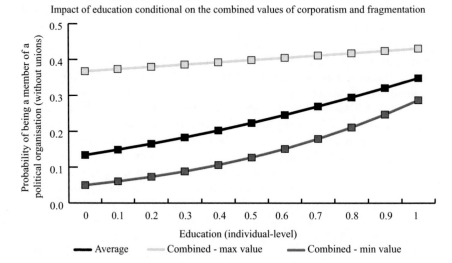

Impact of education conditional on the combined values of corporatism and fragmentation

study are especially suitable for the analysis of membership in new social movements organisations (NSMOs). Many of the ideas and theses that emphasise the importance of political opportunity structures (POS) – and, in particular, of the degree of openness of political systems and of mobilisation patterns – were originally developed in the subfield of social movements studies. Therefore, the last section of this chapter confronts the overall model with the specific case of membership of political organisations related to NSMs.

OPENNESS, MOBILISATION AND NEW FORMS OF POLITICAL MEMBERSHIP

The literature on NSMs has suggested that there is a close relationship between certain aspects of the 'openness' of the political system and the context of socio-political mobilisation, one the one hand, and the development of NSMs in western democracies, on the other. The greater decentralisation of state powers (Kriesi *et al*. 1995: 28–9), the greater availability and use of direct democratic institutions (Kriesi & Wisler 1996, Boehmke 2002), the greater fragmentation of political elites (Tarrow 1994, Kriesi *et al*. 1995, Rucht 1996, Rochon 1998) and, finally, the configuration of pluralist systems of interest representation amidst weak public administrations (Kitschelt 1986, Kriesi *et al*. 1995: 31–2) are all properties of institutional settings that facilitate access to challengers, and to citizens in general, to political decision-making structures and actors.

All of this body of research points to the fact that increased accessibility translates into a greater capacity to channel and incorporate new demands and, as a result, particularly favours the development of NSMs. In addition, research in the NSMs field has also frequently confirmed that strong and persistent mobilisation of the traditional social conflicts or cleavages – particularly that of class – limit the development of these movements (Kriesi *et al.* 1995, Koopmans 1996). We should therefore expect that greater relative mobilisation by NSMs, and the consequent decrease in the relative mobilisation in traditional conflicts and cleavages, will result in a larger proportion of citizens joining organisations linked with these movements. Equally, ideological polarisation, being an expression of the saliency of traditional ideological conflicts, should also be inversely related to membership of 'new' political groups.

The results of the multilevel models shown in Table 7.2 allow the validity of these claims to be tested. A large number of the effects that we find for membership of NSMOs are similar to those obtained for the general variable of political membership. The individual-level component of the model does not differ much from that of overall political membership when we consider this sub-group of political associations. This means that the processes that drive people to join NSMOs are not substantially different from those that make them join other more 'traditional' political organisations. The only relevant exceptions in this regard are the lack of any impact of the employment situation, and the important change in the effects of gender. In other words, working (either full- or part-time), being unemployed or being inactive in the labour market is irrelevant in terms of predicting participation in NSM organisations and, in contrast to the results for political associations as a whole, women show a greater tendency than men to join these groups.

Turning to mobilisation factors, many of the hypotheses outlined by previous research in the field of social movements seem to be quite powerful in predicting membership of NSMOs. All the relationships, when significant, are in the expected direction, except for the indicator of the density of party structures, which is inversely related to 'new' political membership. As we discussed in Chapter five, this indicator is intended to be a proxy of the level of visibility and capacity for mobilisation of all political organisations. Unfortunately, this indicator is – very likely – not particularly adequate for reflecting the cross-national variations in the organisational infrastructures of NSMs. However, we should notice that this negative impact is substantially reduced once we control for the institutional factors that relate to the degree of openness of the political system (see Graph 7.4).

However, our results only partially confirm the hypotheses regarding the negative impact of the saliency of traditional conflicts and cleavages. The absolute amount of unrest or protest shows a moderate inverse association with membership of NSM organisations, though this effect fully disappears when factors relating to the openness of political systems are included. By contrast, the other indicator relating to the centrality of traditional cleavage conflicts – the proportion of protests initiated by NSMs – shows a clear relationship in the expected direction with 'new' political membership. And this effect persists even when we include all other contextual variables in the model (Graph 7.5). Finally, as for general

Table 7.2: New forms of political membership, mobilisation and openness

Variables	Baseline model	Model 1	Model 2	Full model
Intercept	**-4.46**	**-4.47**	**-4.47**	**-4.47**
Fixed parameters (indiv. level)				
Education	**0.99**	**0.96**	**1.00**	**0.97**
Employment situation (ref= +30h)				
Works <30 h.	n.s.	n.s.	n.s.	n.s.
Inactive	n.s.	n.s.	n.s.	n.s.
Unemployed	n.s.	n.s.	n.s.	n.s.
Age	**2.38**	**2.35**	**2.38**	**2.37**
Age (squared)	**-2.27**	**-2.24**	**-2.26**	**-2.26**
Woman (ref=man)	**0.58**	**0.60**	**0.59**	**0.59**
With partner (ref=without partner)	n.s.	n.s.	n.s.	n.s.
Church attendance	n.s.	n.s.	n.s.	n.s.
Religious membership	**0.96**	**0.95**	**0.96**	**0.95**
Interest in politics	**0.45**	**0.44**	**0.44**	**0.44**
Political efficacy	**0.38**	**0.38**	**0.38**	**0.38**
Inter-personal trust	**0.25**	**0.25**	**0.25**	**0.25**
Values index (ref=materialist)				
Mixed	**0.17**	**0.17**	**0.17**	**0.17**
Post-materialist	**0.61**	**0.62**	**0.62**	**0.62**
Attitude to social change				
(ref= conservative)				
Radical	<u>0.28</u>	<u>0.28</u>	<u>0.28</u>	<u>0.28</u>
Reformist	**0.19**	**0.19**	**0.19**	**0.19**
Fixed parameters (country level)				
Mobilisation factors				
No. party branches (x 1000 inhs.)		**-3.15**		**-0.70**
No. party branches (squared)		**1.44**		n.s.
No. protests relative to population		-0.001		n.s.
% protests initiated by NSMs		**0.14**		**0.13**
% protests initiated by NSMs (squared)		**-0.003**		**-0.003**
Citizen polarisation		n.s.		n.s.
Citizen polarisation (squared)		n.s.		n.s.
Effective no. of religious groups		n.s.		n.s.
Tradition of participation (union members x 1,000 inhabs. in 1950)		<u>0.004</u>		n.s.
Institutional factors				
Local autonomy (local spending)			0.01	n.s.
Siaroff's corporatism index			<u>0.13</u>	**0.13**
Corporatism index (squared)			n.s.	n.s.
Index of formal regulation of direct democracy			-0.12	n.s.
Effective no. of parliamentary parties			n.s.	0.14

Table 7.2. Cont.

Random parameters (country level)				
$u_{ij} \sim N(0, \Omega_u): \Omega_u$ †	0.43	0.24-0.23	0.21-0.35	0.30-0.21
u_{0ij} [intercept] *	0.43 (0.66)	0.23 (0.48)	0.35 (0.59)	0.21 (0.46)
u_{1ij} [education]*	0.14 (0.37)	0.11 (0.34)	0.13 (0.36)	0.11 (0.34)
u_{2ij} [church attendance]*	0.24 (0.49)	0.25 (0.50)	0.25 (0.50)	0.25 (0.50)
u_{3ij} [gender]*	0.12 (0.35)	0.12 (0.34)	0.11 (0.33)	0.11 (0.34)
Intra-class correlation + †	0.12-0.16	0.7-0.7	0.06-0.10	0.08-0.06
R^2 dicho§ †	0.15-0.14	0.23-0.23	0.21-0.21	0.21-0.21
% unexplained level 2 variance †	11-14	5-5	5-8	7-5
Number of cases (no. of countries)	24,868 (17)	20,815 (17)	20,815 (17)	20,815 (17)

Sources and notes: see the footnote to Table 7.1. Dependent variable: member of a political association related to NSMs = 1, does not belong to any association of this type = 0.

political membership, the historical legacies of past mobilisation patterns are only very mildly – and inconsistently – related to 'new' political membership.[3]

The results of the institutional variables are strikingly similar to those we found for the general indicator of political membership (see Table 7.1). Political decentralisation is hardly relevant: the level of local autonomy is an important factor only when the mobilisation context is ignored and the overall degree of decentralisation – as measured by Lijphart's federalism-decentralisation index – is not significant at any stage of the modelling process. As for membership of all political organisations, corporatist arrangements and party-system fragmentation are the main elements of the openness of the political system that shape citizens' decisions to join NSM organisations. Interestingly enough, and contrary to what many NSMs

Graph 7.4: Membership of NSM organisations and party infrastructural density

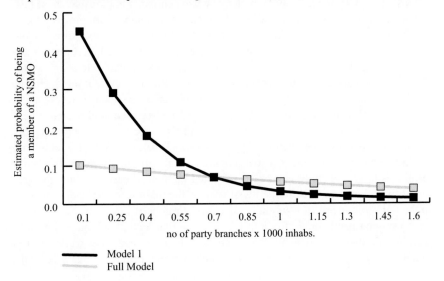

Estimated probability of being a member of a NSMO

no of party branches x 1000 inhabs.

——— Model 1
‑‑‑‑‑ Full Model

Graph 7.5: New political membership and mobilisation initiated by NSMs

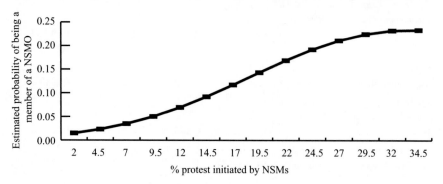

scholars might have expected (e.g. Kitschelt 1986 and Kriesi *et al.* 1995: 31), pluralist systems of interest mediation – which are frequently considered to be more
accessible for new demands and challenging actors, and related to weak administrative systems – are not facilitating the development of organisations linked to the
NSMs. It is, rather, political systems with corporatist arrangements that mildly promote higher levels of membership of this type of organisation. The explanation for
this probably lies in the fact that many of the countries with more developed corporatist arrangements are also multi-party systems. Hence, when new challengers
and issues emerge – as is the case with NSM actors and issues – the party elites are
pushed to incorporate them in some way into existing institutional arrangements;
and corporatist practices of consultation allow a relatively easy extension of the
model of interest mediation that was initially conceived for labour and business
organisations to these new political actors. Thus, corporatist arrangements and
party fragmentation jointly operate to foster membership of 'new' political organisations, though its impact is quite moderate when compared to the effect these institutional properties exert on overall levels of political membership (Graph 7.6).

Finally, the results concerning the impact of the availability of direct democratic institutions cast doubt on some of the claims made in the literature on social
movements and interest groups. We should interpret with care our own results –
given that the variability on direct democratic institutions is quite limited – but the
available evidence would suggest that, should this aspect have any effect on membership of political associations, this might well be negative, and not positive as
the studies carried out by Boehmke (2002) and Kriesi & Wisler (1996) suggest.[4]
In this case, it is possible that the hypothesis of a positive effect of direct-democratic mechanisms on citizens' participation – though consistent in theoretical
terms – is based on analyses of a very limited number of cases. In fact, the great
majority of these studies use the Swiss case as the main reference point, which –
in the light of our results – might be biasing their conclusions.

To summarise the main findings presented in this section, a model of political
membership that systematically takes into account mobilisation as well as institutional factors is helpful to gain a deeper understanding of the various aspects that

Graph 7.6: New political membership and institutional openness

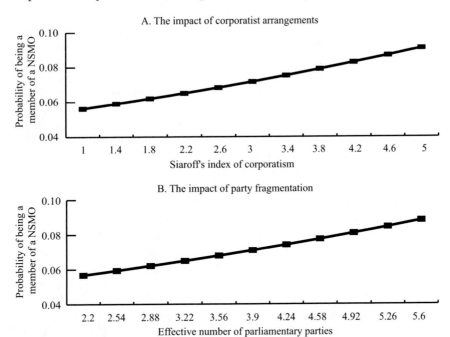

A. The impact of corporatist arrangements

B. The impact of party fragmentation

make citizens join political organisations. The model – and the range of indicators considered – is general enough to account for both 'traditional' and 'new' political membership. Hence, the body of scholarly research that has accumulated over the past few decades in the field of social movements is very useful not just for studying patterns of participation in organisations related to NSMs but also for gaining a better understanding of cross-national patterns of engagement in a wide range of political associations and groups.

CONCLUSIONS

The most general conclusion that we can draw from this chapter is that specific political settings are crucial in shaping citizens' political behaviour and that – too often – we tend to overlook the context in which citizens act and make decisions. Systematically taking into account the way in which democratic political institutions and political systems are specifically configured is fundamental to gain a fuller understanding of how citizens behave politically. It is not just the general political 'outlook' of each country (Schofer & Fourcade-Gourinchas 2001): very specific institutional arrangements have a substantial impact in how citizens relate to politics and what political organisations they choose to join (or not to join).

Specific institutional arrangements set the range of opportunities for citizens to have an impact in the decision-making processes, thus providing the incentives and disincentives for collective action. And, in response to institutional incentives and configurations, political organisations select their mobilisation and recruitment strategies. These two broad sets of contextual factors determine the real opportunities for participation that citizens have and, importantly, condition their motivation to co-operate and co-ordinate with other fellow citizens, in organisations that seek public goods and political goals. In short, mobilisation strategies and structures – on the one hand – and institutional arrangements – on the other – are crucial for citizens to be able to participate and on their finding reasons to do so.

This chapter has shown that, in particular, certain institutional settings that make political systems more or less 'open' to the demands of citizens – such as the degree of development of corporatist systems of interest representation and the degree of fragmentation of the political elites – represent powerful incentives (or disincentives) for joining political organisations. Additionally, the type and magnitude of mobilisation by political organisations are also important determinants of the extent to which citizens join political organisations and the type of organisations they choose to join. But also, and very importantly, our findings show that 'open' political systems are, put bluntly, fairer: they provide similar opportunities for influence to citizens with unequal socio-economic resources. Institutional opportunities for participation, hence, boost political membership by providing venues for the most disadvantaged citizens to have their voice heard.

The results of this study support an observation made by Brody (1978: 287) some twenty years ago: if the political context is important in explaining citizens' political participation, then the 'blame' for the lack of engagement of some (or many) of them does not lie with citizens. And if this is true, further research on how exactly the political context conditions citizens' ability to engage in the political arena should allow us to choose institutions that increase – rather than decrease – the quality of our democracies.

NOTES

1   This interaction between individual characteristics and the participative context has been analysed more systematically in the last decade, particularly in relation to electoral participation (see Oppenhuis 1995, Anduiza 1999 and Leighley 2001).

2   Other theoretically meaningful interaction terms have been explored, particularly between education and gender, on the one hand, and other context variables, on the other; and with the two operationalisations of political membership. Only those which are significant are shown. This model has also been replicated for 'new' political membership: the results are consistent, though only the interaction between education and the fragmentation of parliamentary elites is significant.

3   For the reference individual, the change from living in a country with the lowest levels of union membership in 1950 (0 members per 1000 inhabitants) to living in another with the highest value (186 per 1000 inhabitants) only transforms in an increase in the probability of

being a member of a NSM organisation from 0.05 to 0.10.

4   It is important to point out that, in the case of 'new' political membership, all of these analyses were performed without the case of Switzerland, since the questionnaire administered in this country did not include in the list of associations a significant number of organisations related to NSMs (see Morales 2004: Appendix 1). However, as Graph 6.4 shows, a correct estimation of the percentage of respondents who belong to 'new' political groups in that country would only imply that Switzerland is an outlier from the general pattern of a negative association between the availability of direct democratic institutions and membership of NSM organisations.

conclusions

Studies of non-electoral individual political participation have traditionally focused almost exclusively on the individual attributes and determinants of citizens' political behaviour. The mainstream approach to political participation has commonly emphasised the role of socio-economic (SES) factors, attitudes and values in explaining within-country variation. And, whenever cross-national differences were examined, these were attributed to varying political cultures or degrees of socio-economic modernisation. Even if several scholars have argued that the political context is crucial to our understanding of how and when citizens engage in politics,[1] and have called for a more systematic incorporation of contextual elements in our analyses of political participation, the reality is that this is rarely done. Furthermore, truly cross-national studies of non-electoral participation are relatively scarce and they almost invariably fail to take into account elements of the political context.[2] Yet, for some decades now, the scholarship on social movements has repeatedly shown that various dimensions of the political environment – and, particularly, of the mobilisation and institutional context – are critical to our understanding of collective action.

This book has tried to show that we need to go beyond the analytical approaches that reduce the explanation of political behaviour to individual factors; and it has also tried to illustrate some of the ways in which we can actually do this. Surely, citizens' resources, social status and orientations condition in important ways their predispositions to engage in political activity, as well as the opportunities they have to participate in politics. However, citizens are not in a social or political vacuum and thus their personal attributes do not have unequivocal and permanent effects. People interact with each other, with organisations and with institutions. And these interactions shape their decisions and their eventual political behaviour. The social and political context that surrounds citizens serves to structure the opportunities for participation they are presented with, as well as the expected costs and benefits from co-operation. Consequently, if we want to explain adequately why and how citizens engage in politics, we cannot ignore these contexts.

Moreover, this book has also tried to show that the theories, approaches and concepts developed by social-movements' scholars have much to offer the study of individual political participation. Although the notion of 'political opportunity structures' was developed primarily to account for the emergence, development and success or failure of social movements, the concepts and analytical categories that these approaches provide are also very useful in explaining individual political behaviour. Hence, one of the contributions that this study attempts to make is to illustrate the great potential of cross-fertilisation between these two fields of research.

The main goal of this book was to understand why some citizens join political organisations and others do not. In particular, a core aim was to explain the vast cross-national variations in membership of political associations that we find across western democracies. In doing so, this study began with the outline of an analytical model of this form of political participation that combines individual characteristics – citizens' resources, social status and civic and political orientations – with some relevant features of the political context – the patterns and structures of mobilisation and the institutional setting.

All through this study we have examined the large differences in citizens' propensity to join political organisations that exist between, for example, South European and Scandinavian countries. And we have also seen that these gaps cannot be explained by the socio-economic characteristics of the citizenry alone. In other words, citizens of South European countries are not less likely to join political groups just because they have, on average, fewer educational resources, are less integrated in the labour market, or have a more negative orientation toward politics. Certainly, these aspects contribute to such citizens' reluctance to join political associations but they do not help us much in explaining the remarkable cross-national variations in political membership that we find among western democracies. Hence, modernisation theories and the political culture approach are only of limited value in explaining these disparities across nations that are relatively similar in terms of modernisation and democratic performance.[3]

In contrast, the evidence presented in this study reveals the critical importance of the political context to gaining a fuller understanding of why more citizens join political organisations in some countries than in others. One such aspect of the political context is related to mobilisation structures and patterns. The degree to which political organisations act as effective agents of political mobilisation has an important impact on the participatory behaviour of citizens. Where political organisations display a wide organisational network, and their infrastructures are more densely distributed across the territory, citizens are more exposed to political recruitment stimuli and, hence, they participate more. Equally, in those countries where new social movements are more frequently the main actors of political action and protest, citizens are more inclined to join political associations connected to these movements.

Furthermore, the mobilisation of the left–right divide is also an important factor when explaining cross-national differences in political membership, though its effect is complex. When the institutional setting of the country is not taken into account, citizen polarisation fosters political membership; when the characteristics of the party system – especially party fragmentation – are taken into account, however, whatever polarisation remains that is not absorbed institutionally hinders citizens' political organising.

The other aspect of the political context that was systematically considered refers to the institutional characteristics that define the degree of openness of the political system. Our findings show that certain political opportunity structures foster citizens' participation in important ways. Thus, political systems that are more open to the influence of political organisations – due to the existence of corporatist and consensual arrangements of interest-representation, and to the greater pluralism and fragmentation of parliamentary representation – contribute to citizens finding greater incentives to participate in public affairs. In countries such as the Scandinavian ones, the Netherlands and Belgium, this type of configuration of political institutions has as a main consequence that political decision nodes are more accessible to the citizens that are organised in political associations. This, in turn, reduces the costs of collective action and increases the expectation of successful mobilisation.

However, we have provided evidence that not only does the political context structure the opportunities for citizens' participation but that it also interacts with citizens' resources, thus magnifying or minimising political inequalities. The more open and accessible political structures diminish the barriers and costs of participation, in such a way that individuals with fewer socio-economic resources – for example, education – are not so impeded in their ability to influence decision-making processes. On the opposite case, more closed political structures accentuate the effects of social inequalities and transform them into political inequalities.

As a result, the political context has a double impact on political membership in western democracies. On the one hand, it determines how many citizens join political organisations and, on the other, it impinges on who the participants will be. The more open political systems expand and equalise citizens' organised participation; the more closed institutional configurations reduce participation and make it more biased in social terms.

In summary, this study makes three broad sets of empirical and analytical contributions to the study of political participation in general, and to the analysis of political membership in particular. First, the multiple analyses shown in Chapter three provide abundant evidence that qualifies some recurrent assumptions in the study of political participation regarding the role of individual resources and political orientations. On the one hand, individual characteristics do not exert a uniform impact on political behaviour across western democracies. Educational resources, gender, and religious practice have widely varying impacts on citizens' propensity to join political associations. For example, in some countries a university degree clearly enhances the likelihood of joining a political group, while in other countries it has no effect whatsoever. Equally, religious practice fosters political membership in some nations but hinders it in others. On the other hand, our results show that – while important for understanding within-country variations in political membership – civic and political orientations are of little use in explaining the vast cross-national disparities in this form of political participation. In almost every country, having an interest in politics has an important effect on the inclination to join a political organisation; yet, the different distributions of political interest across western democracies cannot explain the variation in levels of political membership. And the impact of other civic and political orientations – political efficacy, social trust, and social values – is rather limited.

A second contribution of this study is its systematic consideration of important elements of the political context. Our findings underline the importance of politics – with capital letters – and, more specifically, of the opportunities for participation that mobilisation processes and political institutions grant to citizens. Unfortunately, the study of political participation has too frequently – and with the exception of research on electoral participation[4] – ignored the political nature of individual political behaviour. Yet, we show that it is possible to provide reasonable micro-mechanisms of the effect of institutional characteristics[5] and to measure them with reasonable reliability. And, while the measurement of mobilisation processes is more imperfect for comparative endeavours, there is also sufficient evidence to indicate that more careful approximations to this aspect of the political context are probably worth the effort.

The third and final contribution of this book is, in fact, a more specific derivation of the previous one. Our analyses show that the political context is fundamental in shaping how and to what extent social inequalities are transformed into political inequalities.[6] Open political systems reduce the costs of access to decision-making and, thus, provide more equal opportunities for influence to citizens with unequal socio-economic resources. As a consequence, individual resources are less of a discriminating factor for political engagement. When institutions facilitate access and influence at limited costs, citizens have more opportunities and are more inclined to join political organisations; and this overall increase in political membership is primarily due to the capacity of the most disadvantaged citizens to make their voices heard.

What are the implications of all these results for our understanding of democratic processes? On the one hand, how much organised political participation there is will shape the capacity of the citizenry as a whole to make politicians and governments democratically accountable. An active and informed citizenry will be better able to hold governments accountable for their political actions. Political organisations serve to provide greater information of what happens in the political arena, as well as to mobilise citizens into action when the reasons to do so emerge.

On the other hand, who joins political organisations has important consequences for the nature of the process of representation of political preferences. The greater the social equality of organised political action, the more likely it will be that the process of interest-representation will not introduce greater inequalities than already exist. Yet, socio-economic inequalities are not transformed into participative inequalities in the same extent in all western societies: some political institutions exert an equalising influence. This means that political institutions can generate virtuous or vicious dynamics with regard to socio-economic and political inequalities. As Verba, Nie & Kim (1978: 14–17) pointed out, for social and political equality of citizens to exist, the worse-off have to self-organise. Otherwise, the generally greater organisational resources of the wealthier social groups will act to increase participatory inequalities and, later, socio-economic inequalities. And larger social inequalities depress the political engagement of all but the most resourceful (Solt 2008). Hence, some institutional configurations can – in the long run – palliate both social and political inequalities, while the more closed political systems will – in the long term – augment both.

This leads to a debate about the role and consequences of institutional reforms. In the case of electoral participation, institutional intervention is possible through the limitation of the maximum influence – one person, one vote – as well as with the introduction of reforms aimed at guaranteeing equality of influence – such as making voting compulsory. The effect of both kinds of institutions is to equalise the political influence of citizens through their vote. However, this sort of option is not available when confronted with other forms of political participation and the potential biases they might introduce in the democratic process. For most non-electoral forms of participation it is not feasible to impose minimum or maximum limits. Thus, our capacity to directly intervene to prevent participation inequalities is fundamentally restricted to electoral participation – whether through the vote or through contributions to electoral campaigns.

The results of this study, nevertheless, suggest that there may be other forms of institutional intervention, should the goal be to further reduce political inequalities among citizens. Though it is clearly not realistic to initiate institutional reforms with the sole purpose of promoting citizens' participation in political organisations, it is nonetheless possible to orientate reforms inspired by other goals or needs in a direction that will also contribute to providing greater participation opportunities for citizens. For example, when electoral reforms are suggested for other reasons, one of the possible considerations – among others – can be the likely impact that these reforms will have on political equality in representation in the policy process, not just through elections but also through the influence that political organisations and their members exert. Thus, an additional argument in favour of adopting (more) proportional systems is its contribution to increased opportunities for the participation and influence of citizens.

In other words, the relevance of political institutions and of their effects on citizens' participation lies in the fact that the former can be designed and intentionally reformed so as to produce the intended results. The political institutions a society adopts, and the degree to which they facilitate citizens' participation, are fundamental because, as Alexis de Tocqueville (1980 [1835]: 222) claimed, they are 'the most powerful, and maybe the only means, that we retain to interest men in the destiny of their country and to make them partakers in its government'.

Finally, this study opens new lines of future enquiry. The limitations of the information available for the comparative study of the effect of mobilisation processes and political opportunity structures on individual political participation, prevent us from fully uncovering the underlying mechanisms through which these contextual factors impinge on citizens' decisions to engage in politics. What mobilisation strategies are more successful in promoting citizens' membership of political associations? Do they vary across countries? And how exactly are 'open' political systems promoting citizens' participation? Is it because they are more responsive to citizens' organised demands? If so, how exactly are governmental responsiveness and institutional design connected? This book has suggested some ways in which individual political participation and the political context are connected but we still need to refine our scholarship in this regard and systematically incorporate 'politics' in our models of political behaviour.

NOTES

1   See, among others, Conway (1989), Huckfeldt & Sprague (1993), and Leighley (1995 and 2001).

2   As an illustration, see Norris (2002) and the volume edited by van Deth, Montero & Westholm (2007). The former identifies various elements of the political context in her analytical framework – modernisation, structure of the state and mobilizing agencies – but does not assess them empirically when explaining cross-national variations in participation, except for electoral turnout. The latter edited volume does not even attempt to go beyond the mainstream individual-level model of citizen participation.

3   Of course, this is a relative notion, and western democracies are quite similar when compared to non-western democracies and to authoritarian regimes.

4   Good examples are Leighley & Nagler (1992), Kaempfer & Lowenberg (1993), Oppenhuis (1995), van Egmond, de Graaf & van der Eijk (1998), Anduiza (1999 and 2002) and Leighley (2001).

5   Contrary to what Lane & Ersson (1990) seem to suggest.

6   See Solt (2008) for a suggestive analysis of how income inequality at the country level affects income inequalities in participation at the individual level.

appendix

COMPLETE REFERENCES AND SOURCES OF SURVEYS AND DATA EMPLOYED

Andersen, Goul Jørgen; Armingeon, Klaus; Badescu, Gabriel; van Deth, Jan; Geurts, Peter; Iglic, Hajdeja; Leite Veigas, José Manuel; Montero, José Ramón; Selle, Per; Teorell, Jan; and Westholm, Anders, Citizenship, Involvement, and Democracy Survey, 2001–2003. [Computer file], 2007. Germany: Zentralarchiv für Empirische Sozialforschung, Cologne [distributor], 2007.

European Values Study Group, European Values Study, 1999/2000 [Computer file] 2003 / Release 1, The Netherlands, Germany: Tilburg University, Zentralarchiv für Empirische Sozialforschung, Cologne (ZA), Netherlands Institute for Scientific Information Services (NIWI), Amsterdam [producer], 2003. Germany: Zentralarchiv für Empirische Sozialforschung, Cologne [distributor], 2003.

Ron Francisco, European Protest and Coercion Data, 1980–1995, http://web.ku.edu/ronfran/data/index.html [electronic files], funded by the National Science Foundation (SBR 9631229).

Ronald Inglehart, et al., World Values Surveys and European Values Surveys, 1981–1984, 1990–1993, and 1995–1997 [Computer file], ICPSR version (Ann Arbor, MI: Institute for Social Research [producer], 2000. Ann Arbor, MI: ICPSR [distributor], 2000).

Roger Jowell and the Central Co-ordinating Team, European Social Survey 2002/2003, London: Centre for Comparative Social Surveys, City University (2003–2004) [Computer file and producer], Release 4 (Norwegian Social Science Data Services [distributor], 2004).

Anna Melich, Eurobarometers, 1983–1998 [Computer files], ICPSR version, (Brussels, Belgium: INRA (Europe) [producer], several years. Ann Arbor, MI: ICPSR / Koeln, Germany: Zentralarchiv fuer Empirische Sozialforschung [distributors], several years).

Marc Morjé Howard, et al., 'US Citizenship, Involvement, Democracy 2005', Georgetown University's Center for Democracy and the Third Sector (CDATS) [Computer file, producer and distributor]. The survey was funded primarily by a grant from Atlantic Philanthropies, with additional support from the Weidenbaum Center on the Economy, Government, and Public Policy at Washington University in St Louis.

Antonis Papacostas, Eurobarometer 62.2: Agricultural Policy, Development Aid, Social Capital, and Information and Communication Technology, November-December 2004 [Computer file], ICPSR version, study no. 4668 (Brussels, Belgium: TNS Opinion & Social (Europe) [producer], 2004 Ann Arbor, MI: ICPSR / Koeln, Germany: Zentralarchiv fuer Empirische Sozialforschung [distributors], 2006).

Steven J. Rosenstone, Donald R. Kinder, Warren E. Miller and the National Election Studies, American National Election Study, 1996: Pre- and Post-Election Survey [Computer file], 4th version (Ann Arbor, MI: University of Michigan, Center for Political Studies [producer], 1999. Ann Arbor, MI: ICPSR [distributor], 2000).

Universidad Autónoma de Madrid, Universidad Pompeu Fabra, and Centro de Investigaciones Sociológicas. Ciudadanía, participación y democracia, 2002. Study 2450 of the CIS (Madrid: Centro de Investigaciones Sociológicas [producer and distributor], 2003).

Sidney Verba, Kay Lehman Schlozman, Henry E. Brady, and Norman H. Nie. American Citizen Participation Study, 1990 [Computer file], ICPSR version, (Chicago, IL: University of Chicago, National Opinion Research Center (NORC) [producer], 1995. Ann Arbor, MI: ICPSR [distributor], 1995).

references

Agresti, A. (1990) *Categorical Data Analysis*, New York: John Wiley.

Ahn, T. K., Ostrom, E. & Walker, J. M. (2003) 'Heterogeneous Preferences and Collective Action', *Public Choice*, 119 (3–4): 295–314.

Ainsworth, S. H. (2000) 'Modeling Political Efficacy and Interest Group Membership', *Political Behavior*, 22 (2): 89–108.

Almond, G. A., & Verba, S. (1989) *The Civic Culture*, Newbury Park: Sage.

Anderson, C. (2000) 'Economic Voting and Political Context', *Electoral Studies*, 19 (2 & 3): 151–70.

Anduiza, E. (1999) *'Individuos o Sistemas' Las Razones de la Abstención en Europa Occidental*, Madrid: CIS.

— (2002) 'Individual Characteristics, Institutional Incentives and Electoral Abstention in Western Europe', *European Journal of Political Research*, 41 (5): 643–73.

Asher, H. B., Richardson, B. M., & Weisberg, H. F. (1984) *Political Participation, An ISSC Workbook in Comparative Analysis*, Frankfurt and New York: Campus Verlag.

Axelrod, R. M. (1984) *The Evolution of Cooperation*, New York: Basic Books.

Babchuk, N., & Edwards, J. N. (1965) 'Voluntary Associations and the Integration Hypothesis', *Sociological Inquiry*, 35 (Spring): 149–62.

Baglioni, S. *et al.* (2007) 'City Size and the Nature of Associational Ecologies', in W. A. Maloney & S. Rossteutscher (eds.), *Social Capital and Associations in European Democracies: A Comparative Analysis*, London: Routledge.

Barnes, S. H., & Kaase, M. (1979) *Political Action: Mass Participation in Five Western Democracies*, Beverly Hills: Sage.

Baron, J. (1997) 'Political Action Versus Voluntarism in Social Dilemmas and Aid for the Needy', *Rationality and Society*, 9 (3): 307–26.

Bartolini, S., & Mair, P. (1990) *Identity, Competition and Electoral Availability: The Stabilisation of European Electorates 1885–1985*, Cambridge: Cambridge University Press.

Baumgartner, F. R., & Leech, B. L. (1998) *Basic Interests: The Importance of Groups in Politics and Political Science*, Princeton: Princeton University Press.

Baumgartner, F. R., & Walker, J. L. (1988) 'Survey Research and Membership in Voluntary Associations', *American Journal of Political Science*, 32 (4): 908–28.

— (1990) 'Response to Smith's 'Trends in Voluntary Group Membership: Comments on Baumgartner and Walker': Measurement Validity and the Continuity of Results in Survey Research', *American Journal of Political Science*, 34 (3): 662–70.

Beck, N. (2005) 'Multilevel Analyses of Comparative Data: A Comment', *Political Analysis*, 13 (3): 457–58.

Beck, P. A. & Jennings, M. K. (1979) 'Political Periods and Political Participation', *American Political Science Review*, 73 (3): 737–50.

Bennett, R. J. (1993a) 'European Local Government Systems', in R. J. Bennett (ed.), *Local Government in the New Europe*, London: Belhaven Press.

— (1993b) *Local Government in the New Europe* (London, Trans.), Belhaven Press: London.

Bennett, W. L. (1975) *The Political Mind and the Political Environment*, Lexington, MA: DC Heath.

Berelson, B., Lazarsfeld, P. & McPhee, W. N. (1954) V*oting: A Study of Opinion Formation in a Presidential Campaign*, Chicago: University of Chicago Press.

Billiet, J. B. (1997) 'Political Parties and Social Organizations in Flanders', in J. W. van Deth (ed.), *Private Groups and Public Life*, London: Routledge.

Blair, P. (1991) 'Trends in Local Autonomy and Democracy', in R. Batley & G. Stoker (eds.), *Local Government in Europe: Trends and Developments*, London: MacMillan.

Boehmke, F. J. (2000) *Beyond the Ballot: The Influence of Direct Democracy on Interest Group Behavior*. California Institute of Technology.

— (2002) 'The Effect of Direct Democracy on the Size and Diversity of State Interest Group Populations', *Journal of Politics*, 64 (3): 827–44.

Bogdanor, V. (1994) 'Western Europe', in D. Butler & A. Ranney (eds.), *Referendums Around the World. The Growing Use of Direct Democracy*, London: Macmillan Press.

Boix, C. & Posner, D. N. (1996) *Making Social Capital Work: A Review of Robert Putnam's Making Democracy Work: Civic Traditions in Modern Italy,* Working Paper Series: Vol. 96/4, Cambridge: Harvard University Centre for International Affairs.

Booth, A. & Babchuk, N. (1969) 'Personal Influence Networks and Voluntary Association Affiliation', *Sociological Inquiry*, 39 (Spring): 179–88.

Bowler, S., Donovan, T. & Hanneman, R. (2003) 'Art for Democracy's Sake? Group Membership and Political Engagement in Europe', *Journal of Politics*, 65 (4): 1111–29.

Brady, H. E., and Elms, L. (1999) 'Age-Period-Cohort Analysis with Noisy, Lumpy Data', Paper prepared for the Annual Meeting of the Political Methodology Group of the APSA, Texas.

Brady, H. E., Verba, S. & Schlozman, K. L. (1995) 'Beyond SES: A Resource Model of Political Participation', *American Political Science Review*, 89 (2): 271–94.

Bréchon, P. (1999) 'Integration into Catholicism and Protestantism in Europe: The Impact on Moral and Political Values', in L. Halman & O. Riis (eds.), *Religion in Secularizing Society: The European's Religion At the End of the 20th Century*, Tilburg: Tilburg University Press.

Briet, M., Klandermans, B. & Kroon, F. (1987) 'How Women Become Involved in the Women's Movement', in M. F. Katzenstein & C. M. Mueller (eds.), *The Women's Movements in the U.S. and Western Europe: Consciousness, Political*

Opportunity and Public Policy, Philadelphia: Temple University Press.

Brody, R. A. (1978) 'The Puzzle of Political Participation in America', in A. King (ed.), *The New American Political System*, Washington D.C.: American Enterprise Institute for Public Policy Research.

Brown, C. (1991) *Ballots of Tumult: A Portrait of Volatility in American Voting*, Ann Arbor: The University of Michigan Press.

Brulle, R. J. & Jenkins, J. C. (2005) 'Foundations and the Environmental Movement: Priorities, Strategies, and Impact', in D. Faber & D. McCarthy (eds.), *Foundations For Social Change: Critical Perspectives on Philanthropy and Popular Movements*, Lanham: Rowman & Littlefield.

Budge, I. *et al.* (2001) *Mapping Policy Preferences: Estimates for Parties, Electors and Governments 1945–1998*, Oxford: Oxford University Press.

Burbank, M. J. (1997) 'Explaining Contextual Effects on Vote Choice', *Political Behavior*, 19 (2): 113–32.

Burns, N., Schlozman, K. L. & Verba, S. (2001) *The Private Roots of Public Action: Gender, Equality, and Political Participation*, Harvard, MA.: Harvard University Press.

Butler, D. & Ranney, A. (eds.), (1994) *Referendums Around the World: The Growing Use of Democracy?*, Basingstoke: Macmillan.

Castles, F. G. & Mair, P. (1984) 'Left–Right Political Scales: Some "Expert" Judgements', *European Journal of Political Research*, 12 (1): 73–88.

Chong, D. (1991) *Collective Action and the Civil Rights Movement*, Chicago: University of Chicago Press.

Claibourn, M. P. & Martin, P. S. (2000) 'Trusting and Joining? An Empirical Test of the Reciprocal Nature of Social Capital', *Political Behavior*, 22 (4): 267–91.

Clark, P. B. & Wilson, J. Q. (1961) 'Incentive Systems: A Theory of Organization', *Administrative Science Quarterly*, 6: 129–66.

Clark, T. N. & Rempel, M. (1997) *Citizen Politics in Post–Industrial Societies*, Boulder: Westview Press.

Coleman, J. S. (1990) *Foundations of Social Theory*, Cambridge MA: The Belknap Press of Harvard University Press.

Converse, P. E. (1973) 'The Nature of Belief Systems in Mass Publics', in Apter, D. E. (ed.), *Ideology and Discontent*, New York: Free Press.

Conway, M. M. (1989) 'The Political Context of Political Behavior', *Journal of Politics*, 51 (1): 3–10.

— (1991) *Political Participation in the United States* (2nd ed.), Washington DC: CQ Press.

Council of Europe. (1988) *Allocation of Power to the Local and Regional Levels of Government in the Member States of the Council of Europe*, Strasbourg: Council of Europe.

Crepaz, M. M. L. & Lijphart, A. (1995) 'Linking and Integrating Corporatism and Consensus Democracy: Theory, Concepts and Evidence', *British Journal of Political Science*, 25 (2): 281–88.

Curtis, J. E. (1971) 'Voluntary Associations Joining: A Cross-National

Comparative Note', *American Sociological Review*, 36: 860–81.

Curtis, J. E., Baer, D. E. & Grabb, E. G. (2001) 'Nations of Joiners: Explaining Voluntary Association Membership in Democratic Societies', *American Sociological Review*, 66 (4): 783–805.

Curtis, J. E., Grabb, E. G. & Baer, D. E. (1992) 'Voluntary Association Membership in Fifteen Countries: A Comparative Analysis', *American Sociological Review*, 57 (2): 139–52.

Curtis, R. L. & Zurcher, L. A. (1973) 'Stable Resources of Protest Movements: The Multi–Organizational Field', *Social Forces*, 52 (1): 53–61.

Dahl, R. A. (1956) *A Preface to Democratic Theory,* Chicago: The University of Chicago Press.

Dahl, R. A. & Tufte, E. R. (1973) *Size and Democracy*, Stanford, CA: Stanford University Press.

Dalton, R. J. (1996) *Citizen Politics: Public Opinion and Political Parties in Advanced Western Democracies* (2nd ed.), Chatham NJ: Chatham House.

Dalton, R. J., Küchler, M. & Bürklin, W. (1990) 'The Challenge of New Movements', in R. J. Dalton & M. Küchler (eds.), *Challenging the Political Order: New Social and Political Movements in Western Democracies*, Oxford: Polity Press.

Dalton, R. J. & Wattenberg, M. P. (eds.), (2000) *Parties Without Partisans*, Oxford: Oxford University Press.

de Hart, J. D. (2001) 'Religion and Volunteering in the Netherlands', in P. Dekker & E. M. Uslaner (eds.), *Social Capital and Participation in Everyday Life*, London: Routledge.

de Tocqueville, A. (1980) *La Democracia En América*, Madrid: Alianza Editorial. Mansfield, H. C. & Winthrop, D. (2000) *Democracy in America* (H. C. Mansfield & D. Winthrop, Trans.), Chicago: University of Chicago Press.

Dekker, P., Koopmans, R. & van den Broek, A. (1997) 'Voluntary Associations, Social Movements and Individual Political Behaviour in Western Europe', in J. W. van Deth (ed.), *Private Groups and Public Life*, London: Routledge.

Dekker, P. & van den Broek, A. (1998) 'Civil Society in Comparative Perspective: Involvement in Voluntary Associations in North America and Western Europe', *Voluntas: International Journal of Voluntary and Nonprofit Organizations,* 9 (1): 11–38.

— (2004 July 11–14) 'Civil Society in Longitudinal and Comparative Perspective: Voluntary Associations, Political Involvement, Social Trust and Happiness in a Dozen Countries', Paper presented at the 6th International Conference of the International Society for Third-Sector Research, Ryerson University, Toronto.

— (2005) 'Involvement in Voluntary Associations in North America and Western Europe: Trends and Correlates 1981–2000', *Journal of Civil Society*, 1 (1): 45–59.

Della Porta, D. & Rucht, D. (1995) 'Left–Libertarian Movements in Context: A Comparison of Italy and West Germany, 1965–1990', in J. C. Jenkins & B.

Klandermans (eds.), *The Politics of Social Protest: Comparative Perspectives on States and Social Movements*, London: UCL Press.

Diamond, L. & Morlino, L. (2004) 'The Quality of Democracy', *Journal of Democracy*, 15 (4): 20–31.

Djupe, P. A. & Grant, J. T. (2001) 'Religious Institutions and Political Participation in America', *Journal for the Scientific Study of Religion*, 40 (2): 303–14.

Dogan, M. (1994) 'Use and Misuse of Statistics in Comparative Research. Limits to Quantification in Comparative Politics: The Gap Between Substance and Method', in M. Dogan & A. Kazancigil (eds.), *Comparing Nations: Concepts, Strategies, Substance*, Oxford: Basil Blackwell.

Duch, R. M. & Stevenson, R. (2005) 'Context and the Economic Vote: A Multilevel Analysis', *Political Analysis*, 13 (3): 387–409.

Duverger, M. (1955) *La Participation Des Femmes Á La Vie Politique*, Paris: UNESCO.

Ebbinghaus, B. & Visser, J. (2000) *Trade Unions in Western Europe Since 1945*, London: Macmillan.

Eisinger, P. K. (1973) 'The Conditions of Protest Behavior in American Cities', *American Political Science Review*, 67 (1): 11–28.

Elster, J. (1989) *The Cement of Society: A Study of Social Order*, New York: Cambridge University Press.

Erickson, B. H. & Nosanchuk, T. A. (1990) 'How an Apolitical Association Politicizes', *Revue Canadienne de Sociologie et Anthropologie/Canadian Review of Sociology and Anthropology*, 27 (2): 206–19.

Eulau, H. (1986) *Politics, Self and Society: A Theme and Variations*, Cambridge, MA.: Harvard University Press.

Fernández, R. & McAdam, D. (1989) 'Multiorganizational Fields and Recruitment to Social Movements', in B. Klandermans (ed.), *Organizing for Change: Social Movement Organizations in Europe and United States International Social Movement Research*, Vol. 2, Greenwich: JAI Press.

Fillieule, O. (1996) *Police Records and the National Press in France: Issues in the Methodology of Data-Collection From Newspapers* RSC Working Papers: Vol. 96/25, Florence: European University Institute.

Flanagan, S. C. (1987) 'Value Change in Industrial Societies', *American Political Science Review*, 81 (4): 1303–19.

Francisco, R. (1996) 'Coercion and Protest: An Empirical Test in Two Democratic States', *American Journal of Political Science*, 40 (4): 1179–204.

Franklin, M. (1996) 'Electoral Participation', in L. LeDuc, R. G. Niemi & P. Norris (eds.), *Comparing Democracies. Elections and Voting in Global Perspective*, London: Sage.

Franklin, M., van der Eijk, C. & Oppenhuis, E. (1996) 'The Institutional Context: Turnout', in C. van der Eijk & M. N. Franklin (eds.), *Choosing Europe?*, Ann Arbor: The University of Michigan Press.

Franzese, R. J. (2005) 'Empirical Strategies for Various Manifestations of Multilevel Data', *Political Analysis*, 13 (3): 430–46.

Freitag, M. (2006) 'Bowling the State Back in: Political Institutions and the Creation of Social Capital', *European Journal of Political Research*, 45 (1): 123–52.

Gamson, W. A. & Meyer, D. S. (1996) 'Framing Political Opportunity', in D. McAdam, J. D. McCarthy & M. N. Zald (eds.), *Comparative Perspectives on Social Movements: Political Opportunities, Mobilizing Structures, and Cultural Framings*, Cambridge: Cambridge University Press.

Gaskin, K. & Smith, J. D. (1995) *A New Civic Europe? A Study of the Extent and Role of Volunteering*, London: The Volunteer Centre UK.

Gerner, D. J. *et al.* (1994) 'Machine Coding of Event Data Using Regional and International Sources', *International Studies Quarterly*, 38 (1): 91–119.

Giles, M. W. & Dantico, M. K. (1982) 'Political Participation and Neighborhood Social Context Revisited', *American Journal of Political Science*, 26 (1): 144–50.

Goldstein, H. (1995) *Multilevel Statistical Models*, London: Edward Arnold.

Gould, R. V. (1993) 'Collective Action and Network Structure', *American Sociological Review*, 58 (2): 182–96.

Granovetter, M. (1973) 'The strength of weak ties', *American Journal of Sociology*, 78: 1360–80.

— (1983) 'The Strength of Weak Ties: A Network Theory Revisited', in R. Collins (ed.), *Sociological Theory 1983*, San Francisco CA: Jossey–Bass.

Gray, V. & Lowery, D. (1993) 'The Diversity of State Interest Group Systems', *Political Research Quarterly*, 46 (1): 81–97.

Gundelach, P. (1995) 'Grass-Roots Activity', in J. W. Van Deth & E. Scarbrough (eds.), *The Impact of Values*, New York: Oxford University Press.

Halman, L. & Pettersson, T. (1999) 'Religion and Social Capital Revisited', in L. Halman & O. Riis (eds.), *Religion in Secularizing Society: The European's Religion At the End of the 20th Century*, Tilburg: Tilburg University Press.

Hansen, J. M. (1985) 'The Political Economy of Group Membership', *The American Political Science Review*, 79 (1): 79–96.

Harasse, S. (1996) *Engagement Et Désengagement Dans Les Organisations: L'example D'Amnesty International Section Française*. Institut d'études politiques de Paris.

Hardin, R. (1991) 'Acting Together, Contributing Together', *Rationality and Society*, 3 (3): 365–80.

— (2000) 'The Public Trust', in S. J. Pharr & R. D. Putnam (eds.), *Disaffected Democracies. What's Troubling the Trilateral Countries?*, Princeton: Princeton University Press.

Hauser, R. M. (1974) 'Contextual Analysis Revisited', *Sociological Methods & Research*, 2 (3): 365–75.

Hazan, R. Y. (1995) 'Center Parties and Systemic Polarization. An Exploration of Recent Trends in Western Europe', *Journal of Theoretical Politics*, 7 (4): 421–45.

Herreros, F. (2004) *The Problem of Forming Social Capital. Why Trust?*, New York: Palgrave.

Honaker, J. *et al.* (1999) 'Amelia: A Program for Missing Data', electronic document, http://gking.harvard.edu.

Howard, M. M. (2003) *The Weakness of Civil Society in Post-Communist Europe*. Cambridge: Cambridge University Press.

Hox, J. J. (1995) *Applied Multilevel Analysis*, Amsterdam: TT-Publikaties.

Huber, J. & Inglehart, R. (1995) 'Expert Interpretations of Party Space and Party Locations in 42 Societies', *Party Politics*, 1 (1): 73–111.

Huckfeldt, R. (1986) *Politics in Context: Assimilation and Conflict in Urban Neighborhoods*, New York: Agathon Press.

— (2007) 'Information, Persuasion and Political Communication Networks', in R. J. Dalton & H. Klingemann (eds.), *The Oxford Handbook of Political Behavior*, New York: Oxford University Press.

Huckfeldt, R. R. (1979) 'Political Participation and the Neighborhood Social Context', *American Journal of Political Science*, 23: 579–92.

Huckfeldt, R., Johnson, P. E. & Sprague, J. (2004) *Political Disagreement. The Survival of Diverse Opinions Within Communications Networks*, New York: Cambridge University Press.

Huckfeldt, R., Plutzer, E. & Sprague, J. (1993) 'Alternative Contexts of Political Behavior: Churches, Neighborhoods & Individuals', *Journal of Politics*, 55 (2): 365–81.

Huckfeldt, R. & Sprague, J. (1987) 'Networks in Context: The Social Flow of Political Information', *American Political Science Review*, 81 (4): 1197–216.

— (1991) 'Discussant Effects on Vote Choice: Intimacy, Structure and Interdependence', *Journal of Politics*, 53 (1): 122–58.

— (1993) 'Citizens, Contexts, and Politics', in A. W. Finifter (ed.), *Political Science: The State of the Discipline II*, Washington DC: American Political Science Association.

— (1995) *Citizens, Politics, and Social Communication: Information and Influence in an Election Campaign*, New York: Cambridge University Press.

Hug, S. & Wisler, D. (1998) 'Correcting for Selection Bias in Social Movement Research', *Mobilization*, 3 (2): 141–61.

Huntington, S. P. & Nelson, J. M. (1976) *No Easy Choice: Political Participation in Developing Countries*, Cambridge MA: Harvard University Press.

Inglehart, R. (1990) *Culture Shift in Advanced Industrial Society*, Princeton: Princeton University Press.

— (1997) *Modernization and Postmodernization: Cultural, Economic and Political Change in 43 Societies*, Princeton: Princeton University Press.

Inglehart, R. & Norris, P. (2003) *Rising Tide. Gender Equality and Cultural Change Around the World*, Cambridge: Cambridge University Press.

Jackson, E. *et al.* (1995) 'Volunteering and Charitable Giving: Do Religious and Associational Ties Promote Helping Behavior?', *Nonprofit and Voluntary Sector Quarterly*, 24 (1): 59–78.

Jacoby, A. P. (1965) 'Some Correlates of Instrumental and Expressive Orientation to Associational Membership', *Sociological Inquiry*, 35 (Spring): 163–75.

Jenkins, J. C. (1998) 'Channeling Social Protest: Foundation Patronage of Contemporary Social Movements', in W. Powell & E. Clemens (eds.), *Private Action and the Public Good*, New Haven: Yale University Press.

Jenkins, J. C. & Halcli, A. (1999) 'Grassrooting the System? The Development and Impact of Social Movement Philanthropy, 1953–1990', in E. Lagemann (ed.), *Philanthropic Foundations: New Scholarship, New Possibilities*, Bloomington: Indiana University Press.

Jennings, M. K. (1987) 'Residues of a Movement: The Aging of the American Protest Generation', *American Political Science Review*, 81 (2): 367–82.

Jennings, M. K. & van Deth, J. W. (1989) *Continuities in Political Action*, Berlin: Walter de Gruyter.

Johnson, P. E. (1998) 'Interest Group Recruiting: Finding Members and Keeping Them', in A. J. Cigler & B. Loomis (eds.), *Interest Group Politics,* Washington D.C.: Congressional Quarterly Inc.

Jordan, G. & Maloney, W. (1997) *The Protest Business? Mobilizing Campaign Groups*, Manchester: Manchester University Press.

Kaase, M. (1989) 'Mass Participation', in M. K. Jennings & J. W. van Deth (eds.), *Continuities in Political Action*, Berlin/New York: Walter De Gruyter.

— (1992) 'Direct Political Participation in the EC Countries in the Late Eighties', in P. Gundelach & K. Siune (eds.), *From Voters to Participants*, Aarhus: Politica.

Kaempfer, W. H. & Lowenberg, A. D. (1993) 'A Threshold Model of Electoral Policy and Voter Turnout', *Rationality and Society*, 5 (1): 107–26.

Kalyvas, S. N. (1997) 'Polarization in Greek Politics: PASOK's First Four Years, 1981–1985', *Journal of the Hellenic Diaspora*, 23 (1): 83–104.

Katz, R. S., Mair, P. *et al.* (1992) 'The Membership of Political Parties in European Democracies, 1960–1990', *European Journal of Political Research,* 22: 329–245.

Kau, J. B. & Rubin, P. H. (1979) 'Public Interest Lobbies: Membership and Influence', *Public Choice*, 34 (1): 45–54.

Keman, H. & Pennings, P. (1995) 'Managing Political and Societal Conflict in Democracies: Do Consensus and Corporatism Matter?', *British Journal of Political Science*, 25 (2): 271–81.

Kenny, C. B. (1992) 'Political Participation and Effects From the Social Environment', *American Journal of Political Science*, 36 (1): 259–67.

King, D. C. & Walker, J. L. (1992) 'The Provision of Benefits by Interest Groups in the United States', *The Journal of Politics*, 54 (2): 394–426.

King, G. *et al.* (1998) 'Listwise Deletion is Evil: What to Do about Missing Data in Political Science', Unpublished paper, http://gking.harvard.edu.

King, G. & Zeng, L. (1999) 'Logistic Regression in Rare Events Data', Unpublished paper, http://gking.harvard.edu.

Kitschelt, H. (1986) 'Political Opportunity Structures and Political Protest: Anti–Nuclear Movements in Four Democracies', *British Journal of Political Science*, 16 (1): 57–85.

— (1990) 'New Social Movements and the Decline of Party Organization', in R. J. Dalton & M. Küchler (eds.), *Challenging the Political Order. New Social and Political Movements in Western Democracies*, Oxford: Polity Press.

Klandermans, B. (1984) 'Mobilization and Participation: Social Psychological Expansions of Resource Mobilization Theory', *American Sociological Review*, 49: 583–600.

— (1989) 'Interorganizational Networks. Introduction', in B. Klandermans (ed.), *Organizing for Change: Social Movement Organizations in Europe and the United States, International Social Movement Research*, Vol. 2, Greenwich: JAI Press.

— (1997) *The Social Psychology of Protest*, Oxford: Blackwell.

Klandermans, B. & Oegema, D. (1987) 'Potentials, Networks, Motivations, and Barriers: Steps Towards Participation in Social Movements', *American Sociological Review*, 52: 519–31.

Klandermans, B. & Tarrow, S. (1988) 'Mobilization into Social Movements: Synthesizing European and American Approaches', *International Social Movement Research*, 1: 1–40.

Knoke, D. (1982) 'Political Mobilization by Voluntary Associations', *Journal of Political and Military Sociology*, 10 (Fall): 171–82.

— (1986) 'Associations and Interest Groups', *Annual Review of Sociology*, 12: 1–21.

— (1990a) 'The Mobilization of Members in Women's Associations', in L. A. Tilly & P. Gurin (eds.), *Women, Politics and Change*, New York: Russell Sage Foundation.

— (1990b) *Organizing for Collective Action: The Political Economies of Associations*, New York: Aldine de Gruyter.

— (1990c) *Political Networks: The Structural Perspective*, New York: Cambridge University Press.

Knoke, D. & Prensky, D. (1984) 'What Relevance Do Organization Theories Have for Voluntary Associations?', *Social Science Quarterly*, 65 (1): 3–20.

Koopmans, R. (1996) 'New Social Movements and Changes in Political Participation in Western Europe', *West European Politics*, 19 (1): 28–50.

— (1999) 'The Use of Protest Event Data in Comparative Research: Cross-National Comparability, Sampling Methods and Robustness', in D. Rucht, R. Koopmans & F. Neidhardt (eds.), *Acts of Dissent: New Developments in the Study of Protest*, Oxford: Rowman & Littlefield Publishers.

Koopmans, R. & Rucht, D. (1995) *Social Movement Mobilization Under Right and Left Governments: A Look At Four West European Countries,* WZB Working Papers: Vol. FS III 95–106, Berlin: Wissenschaftszentrum Berlin.

Kotler–Berkowitz, L. (2005) 'Linking Diverse Friendship Networks to Political Participation', in A. S. Zuckerman (ed.), *The Social Logic of Politics: Personal Networks As Contexts for Political Behavior*, Philadelphia: Temple University Press.

Kreft, I. & de Leeuw, J. (1998) *Introducing Multilevel Modelling*, London: Sage.

Kriesi, H. (1988) 'Local Mobilization for the People's Petition of the Dutch Peace Movement', in B. Klandermans, H., Kriesi, & S. Tarrow, *From Structure to Action: Comparing Social Movement Research Across Cultures, International Social Movement Research*, Vol. 1, Greenwich: JAI Press.

— (1989) 'The Political Opportunity Structure of the Dutch Peace Movement', *West European Politics*, 12 (3): 295–312.

— (1993) *Political Mobilization and Social Change: The Dutch Case in Comparative Perspective*, Aldershot: Avebury.

— (1996) 'The Organizational Structure of New Social Movements in a Political Context', in D. McAdam, J. D. McCarthy & M. N. Zald (eds.), *Comparative Perspectives on Social Movements*, New York: Cambridge University Press.

Kriesi, H. *et al.* (1995) *New Social Movements in Western Europe: A Comparative Analysis*, London: UCL Press.

Kriesi, H. & van Praag (Jr.), P. (1987) 'Old and New Politics: The Dutch Peace Movement and the Traditional Political Organizations', *European Journal of Political Research*, 15: 319–46.

Kriesi, H. & Wisler, D. (1996) 'Social Movements and Direct Democracy in Switzerland', *European Journal of Political Research*, 30 (1): 19–40.

Kuhnle, S. & Selle, P. (eds) (1992) *Government and Voluntary Organizations: A Relational Perspective*, Aldershot: Avebury.

Lane, J. & Ersson, S. (1990) 'Macro and Micro Understanding in Political Science: What Explains Electoral Participation?', *European Journal of Political Research*, 18 (4): 457–65.

— (1999) *Politics and Society in Western Europe* (4th ed.), London: Sage.

Lane, R. E. (1965) *Political Life: Why and How People Get Involved in Politics*, New York: The Free Press.

Laver, M. (1997) *Private Desires, Political Action: An Invitation to the Politics of Rational Choice*, London: Sage.

Lehner, F. (1987) 'Interest Intermediation, Institutional Structures and Public Policy', in H. Keman, H. Paloheimo & P. F. Whiteley (eds.), *Coping with the Economic Crisis*, London: Sage.

— (1988) 'The Political Economy of Distributive Conflict', in F. G. Castles & R. Wildenmann (eds.), *The Future of Party Government: Managing Mixed Economies*, New York: Walter de Gruyter.

Leighley, J. E. (1990) 'Social Interaction and Contextual Influences on Political Participation', *American Politics Quarterly*, 18 (4): 459–75.

— (1991) 'Participation as a Stimulus of Political Conceptualization', *Journal of Politics*, 53: 198–212.

— (1995) 'Attitudes, Opportunities and Incentives: A Field Essay on Political Participation', *Political Research Quarterly*, 48 (1): 181–209.

— (1996) 'Group Membership and the Mobilisation of Political Participation', *Journal of Politics*, 58 (2): 447–63.

— (2001) Strength in Numbers? *The Political Mobilization of Racial and Ethnic Minorities*, Princeton & Oxford: Princeton University Press.

Leighley, J. E. & Nagler, J. (1992) 'Individual and Systemic Influences on Turnout: Who Votes?', *Journal of Politics*, 54 (3): 718–40.

Lelieveldt, H., Astudillo Ruiz, J. & Stevenson, L. (2007) 'The Spectrum of Associational Activities: From Self–Help to Lobbying', in W. A. Maloney & S. Roßteutscher (eds.), *Social Capital and Associations in European Democracies: A Comparative Analysis*, Oxford: Routledge.

Lelieveldt, H. & Caiani, M. (2007) 'The Political Role of Associations', in W. A. Maloney & S. Roßteutscher (eds.), *Social Capital and Associations in European Democracies: A Comparative Analysis*, Oxford: Routledge.

Lijphart, A. (1975) *The Politics of Accommodation: Pluralism and Democracy in the Netherlands* (2nd ed.), Berkeley CA: University of California Press.

— (1977) *Democracy in Plural Societies*, New Haven CT: Yale University Press.

— (1999) *Patterns of Democracy: Government Forms and Performance in Thirty–Six Countries*, New Haven: Yale University Press.

Lijphart, A. & Crepaz, M. M. L. (1991) 'Corporatism and Consensus Democracy in Eighteen Countries: Conceptual and Empirical Linkages', *British Journal of Political Science*, 21 (2): 235–46.

Lind, J. (1996) 'Trade Unions: Social Movement or Welfare Apparatus?', in P. Leisink, J. van Leemput & J. Vilroks (eds.), *The Challenges to Trade Unions in Europe: Innovation or Adaptation*, Cheltenham: Edward Elgar Publishing.

Maas, C. J. M. & Hox, J. J. (2005) 'Sufficient Sample Sizes for Multilevel Modeling', *Methodology: European Journal of Research Methods for the Behavioral and Social Sciences*, 1 (3): 85–91.

Mabileau, G. *et al.* (1987) *Les Citoyens Et La Politique Locale: Comment Participent Les Britanniques Et Les Français*, Paris: Pedone.

MacKuen, M., Stimson, J. & Erikson, R. (2003) 'Electoral Accountability and Efficiency of Politics in the United States: A Counterfactual Analysis', Draft Manuscript later Published as 'Responsabilité des élus devant l'électorat et efficacité du système politique américain: une analyse contrefactuelle'. *RFSP* 53, 6, 2003.

Madsen, D. (1987) 'Political Self-Efficacy Tested', *American Political Science Review*, 81 (2): 571–81.

Mair, P. & van Biezen, I. (2001) 'Party Membership in Twenty European Democracies, 1980–2000', *Party Politics*, 7 (1): 5–21.

Maloney, W. (1999) 'Contracting Out the Participation Function: Social Capital and Cheque–Book Participation', in J. W. van Deth *et al.* (eds.), *Social Capital and European Democracy*, London: Routledge.

Manin, B., Przeworski, A. & Stokes, S. C. (1999) 'Introduction', in A. Przeworski, S. C. Stokes & B. Manin (eds.), *Democracy, Accountability and Representation*, Cambridge: Cambridge University Press.

March, J. G. & Olsen, J. P. (1984) 'The New Institutionalism: Organizational Factors in Political Life', *American Political Science Review*, 78 (3): 734–49.

Margolis, H. (1982) *Selfishness, Altruism and Rationality*, Cambridge: Cambridge University Press.

Mason, W. M. & Fienberg, S. E. (1985) *Cohort Analysis in Social Research*, New York: Springer/Verlag.

McAdam, D. (1996) 'Conceptual Origins, Current Problems, Future Directions', in D. McAdam, J. McCarthy & M. N. Zald (eds.), *Comparative Perspectives on Social Movements. Political Opportunities, Mobilizing Structures, and Cultural Framings*, New York: Cambridge University Press.

McAdam, D. & Fernández, R. (1990) 'Microstructural Bases of Recruitment to Social Movements', *Research in Social Movements, Conflict and Change*, 12: 1–33.

McAdam, D., McCarthy, J. & Zald, M. N. (1996) 'Introduction: Opportunities, Mobilizing Structures, and Framing Processes – Toward a Synthetic, Comparative Perspective on Social Movements', in D. McAdam, J. McCarthy & M. N. Zald (eds.), *Comparative Perspectives on Social Movements. Political Opportunities, Mobilizing Structures, and Cultural Framings*, New York: Cambridge University Press.

McAdam, D. & Paulsen, R. (1993) 'Specifying the Relationship Between Social Ties and Activism', *American Journal of Sociology*, 99 (3): 640–67.

McFarland, A. S. (1984) *Common Cause: Lobbying in the Public Interest*, Chatham: Chatham House Publishers.

McPherson, J. M. (1981) 'A Dynamic Model of Voluntary Affiliation', *Social Forces*, 59: 705–28.

Milbrath, L. W. (1965) *Political Participation: How and Why Do People Get Involved in Politics*, Chicago: Rand McNally & Co.

Milbrath, L. W. & Goel, M. L. (1977) *Political Participation* (2nd ed.), Chicago: Rand McNally & Co.

Minkoff, D. C. & Agnone, J. (2006) 'The Seeding of Social Movements?: The Consequences of Foundation Funding for Developing Movement Infrastructures', Draft chapter prepared for The Contributions of Foundations to Society Project (UCLA).

Moe, T. M. (1980a) 'A Calculus of Group Membership', *American Journal of Political Science*, 24 (4): 593–632.

— (1980b) *The Organization of Interests: Incentives and the Internal Dynamics of Political Interest Groups*, Chicago: University of Chicago Press.

Morales, L. (2002) 'Associational Membership and Social Capital in Comparative Perspective: The Problems of Measurement', *Politics and Society*, 30 (3): 497–523.

— (2004) *Institutions, Mobilization and Political Participation: Political Membership in Western Countries*. Ph.D dissertation, Madrid: Instituto Juan March de Estudios e Investigaciones.

Morales, L. & Geurts, P. (2007) 'Associational Involvement', in J. W. van Deth, J. R. Montero & A. Westholm (eds.), *Citizenship and Involvement in European Democracies: A Comparative Analysis*, London: Routledge.

Morris, A. (1984) *The Origins of the Civil Rights Movement: Black Communities Organizing for Change*, New York: Free Press.

Muller, E. N. & Opp, K. (1986) 'Rational Choice and Rebellious Collective Action', *American Political Science Review*, 80: 471–87.

— (1987) 'Rebellious Collective Action Revisited (Controversy with G. Klosko)', *American Political Science Review*, 81 (2): 557–64.

Müller-Rommel, F. & Poguntke, T. (eds) (1995) *New Politics*, Dartmouth: Aldershot.

Nanetti, R. Y. (1980) 'From the Top Down: Government Promoted Citizen Participation', *Journal of Voluntary Action Research*, 9: 149–64.

Nedelmann, B. (1987) 'Individuals and Parties. Changes in Processes of Political Mobilization', *European Sociological Review*, 3 (3): 181–202.

Nettl, J. P. (1967) *Political Mobilization: A Sociological Analysis of Methods and Concepts*, London: Faber.

Newton, K. (1999) 'Social and Political Trust in Established Democracies', in P. Norris (ed.), *Critical Citizens*, Oxford: Oxford University Press.

— (September 2001) 'Social Trust and Political Disaffection: Social Capital and Democracy', Paper presented at the EURESCO Conference on Social Capital.

Nie, N. H., Powell, G. B. & Prewitt, K. (1969a) 'Social Structure and Political Participation: Developmental Relationships, Part I', *American Political Science Review*, 63 (2): 361–78.

— (1969b) 'Social Structure and Political Participation: Developmental Relationships, Part II', *American Political Science Review*, 63 (3): 808–32.

Norris, P. (2002) *Democratic Phoenix: Reinventing Political Activism*, New York: Cambridge University Press.

Norris, P. & Inglehart, R. (2004) *Sacred and Secular. Religion and Politics Worldwide*, New York: Cambridge University Press.

Norton, A. (1991) 'Western European Local Government in Comparative Perspective', in R. Batley & G. Stoker (eds.), *Local Government in Europe. Trends and Developments*, London: Macmillan.

— (1993) *The International Handbook of Local and Regional Government. Status, Structure and Resources in Advanced Democracies*, Cheltenham: Edward Elgar Publishing.

O'Brien, D. J. (1974) 'The Public Goods Dilemma and the Apathy of the Poor Toward Neighborhood Organizations', *Social Service Review*, 48 (2): 229–45.

— (1975) *Neighborhood Organization and Interest-Group Processes*, Princeton: Princeton University Press.

Oberschall, A. (1973) *Social Conflict and Social Movements*, Englewood Cliffs: Prentice-Hall.

Oegema, D. (1991) 'The Peace Movement in the Netherlands, 1977–1987', in B. Klandermas (ed.), *Peace Movements in Western Europe and the United States International Social Movement Research*, Vol. 3, Greenwich: JAI Press.

Offe, C. (1988) *Partidos Políticos y Nuevos Movimientos Sociales*, Madrid: Editorial Sistema.

Oliver, J. E. (1999) 'The Effects of Metropolitan Economic Segregation on Local Civic Participation', *American Journal of Political Science*, 43 (1): 186–212.

— (2001) *Democracy in Suburbia*, Princeton: Princeton University Press.

Oliver, P. (1984) 'If You Don't Do It, Nobody Else Will: Active and Token Contributors to Local Collective Action', *American Sociological Review*, 49 (5): 601–10.

Olson, M. (1965) *The Logic of Collective Action*, Cambridge, MA: Harvard University Press.

— (1982) *The Rise and Decline of Nations*, New Haven: Yale University Press.

Opp, K. (1989) 'Integration into Voluntary Associations and Incentives for Political Protest', in B. Klandermans (ed.), *Organizing for Change: Social Movement Organizations in Europe and the United States, International Social Movement Research*, Vol. 2, Greenwich: JAI Press.

Opp, K. & Gern, C. (1993) 'Dissident Groups, Personal Networks, and Spontaneous Cooperation: The East German Revolution of 1989', *American Sociological Review*, 58 (5): 659–80.

Oppenhuis, E. (1995) *Voting Behavior in Europe*, Amsterdam: Het Spinhuis.

Orbell, J. & Dawes, R. M. (1991) 'A Cognitive Miser Theory of Cooperators' Advantage', *American Political Science Review*, 85 (4): 515–28.

Ordeshook, P. (1986) *Game Theory and Political Theory*, New York: Cambridge University Press.

Page, E. C. (1991) *Localism and Centralism in Europe: The Political and Legal Bases of Local Self–Government*, Oxford: Oxford University Press.

Parry, G., Moyser, G. & Day, N. (1992) *Political Participation and Democracy in Britain*, Cambridge: Cambridge University Press.

Pateman, C. (1970) *Participation and Democratic Theory*, New York: Cambridge University Press.

Pattie, C. & Johnston, R. (1999) 'Context, Conversation and Conviction: Social Networks and Voting at the 1992 British General Election', *Political Studies*, 47 (5): 877–89.

Pattie, C., Seyd, P. & Whiteley, P. F. (2004) *Citizenship in Britain: Values, Participation and Democracy*, Cambridge: Cambridge University Press.

Peterson, S. A. (1992) 'Church Participation and Political Participation: The Spillover Effect', *American Politics Quarterly*, 20: 123–39.

Pizzorno, A. (1966) 'Introduzione allo Studio della Partecipazione Politica', *Quaderni di Sociologia*, 15 (3–4): 235–87.

— (1981) 'Interests and Parties in Pluralism', in S. Berger (ed.), *Organizing Interests in Western Europe: Pluralism, Corporatism and the Transformation of Politics*, Cambridge: Cambridge University Press.

Pollock, P. H. I. (1982) 'Organizations As Agents of Mobilization: How Does Group Activity Affect Political Participation?', *American Journal of Political Science*, 26 (3): 485–503.

Popielarz, P. A., McPherson, J. M. & Drobnic, S. (1992) 'Social Networks and Organizational Dynamics', *American Sociological Review*, 57 (2): 153–70.

Popkin, S. (1991) *The Reasoning Voter*, Chicago: University of Chicago Press.

Przeworski, A. (1974) 'Contextual Models of Political Behavior', *Political*

Methodology, 1 (1): 27–61.

Przeworski, A. & Teune, H. (1970) *The Logic of Comparative Social Inquiry*, New York: Wiley Interscience.

Putnam, R. (1993) *Making Democracy Work: Civic Traditions in Modern Italy*, Princeton: Princeton University Press.

— (1995a) 'Bowling Alone: America's Declining Social Capital', *Journal of Democracy*, 6 (1): 65–78.

— (1995b) 'Tuning In, Tuning Out: The Strange Disappearance of Social Capital in America', *Political Science and Politics*, 28 (4): 664–83.

— (2000) *Bowling Alone: The Collapse and Revival of American Community*, New York: Simon and Schuster.

— (2007) 'E Pluribus Unum: Diversity and Community in the Twenty–First Century. The 2006 Johan Skytte Prize Lecture', *Scandinavian Political Studies*, 30 (2): 137–74.

Rochon, T. R. (1988) *Mobilizing for Peace: The Antinuclear Movements in Western Europe*, London: Adamantine Press Limited.

— (1998) *Culture Moves: Ideas, Activism, and Changing Values*, Princeton, NJ: Princeton University Press.

Rodden, J. (2004) 'Comparative Federalism and Decentralization: On Meaning and Measurement', *Comparative Politics*, 36 (4): 481–500.

Rogers, D. L., Barb, K. H. & Bultena, G. L. (1975) 'Voluntary Association Membership and Political Participation: An Exploration of the Mobilization Hypothesis', *The Sociological Quarterly*, 16 (summer): 305–18.

Rohrschneider, R. (2002) 'The Democracy Deficit and Mass Support for an EU-Wide Government', *American Journal of Political Science*, 46 (2): 463–75.

Rokkan, S. & Campbell, A. (1960) 'Norway and the United States of America', *International Social Science Journal*, 12: 69–99.

Roller, E. & Wessels, B. (1996) 'Contexts of Political Protest in Western Democracies: Political Organization and Modernity', in F. D. Weil (ed.), *Extremism, Protest, Social Movements and Democracy Research on Democracy and Society*, Vol. 3, Greenwich: JAI Press.

Rosenau, J. N. (1974) *Citizenship Between Elections: An Inquiry into the Mobilizable American*, New York: The Free Press.

Rosenberg, M. (1954) 'Some Determinants of Political Apathy', *Public Opinion Quarterly*, 18 (3): 350–66.

Rosenstone, S. J. & Hansen, J. M. (1993) *Mobilization, Participation, and Democracy in America*, New York: Macmillan Publishing Co.

Rothenberg, L. S. (1988) 'Organizational Maintenance and the Retention Decision in Groups', *American Political Science Review*, 82 (4): 1129–52.

— (1989) 'Putting the Puzzle Together: Why People Join Interest Groups?', *Public Choice*, 60 (2): 241–57.

— (1992) *Linking Citizens to Government: Interest Group Politics At Common Cause*, New York: Cambridge University Press.

Rucht, D. (1990) 'The Strategies and Action Repertoires of New Movements', in

R. J. Dalton & M. Küchler (eds.), *Challenging the Political Order. New Social and Political Movements in Western Democracies*, Oxford: Polity Press.

— (1996) 'The Impact of National Contexts on Social Movement Structures: A Cross–Movement and Cross–National Comparison', in D. McAdam, J. D. McCarthy & M. N. Zald (eds.), *Comparative Perspectives on Social Movements,* New York: Cambridge University Press.

Rucht, D., Koopmans, R. & Neidhardt F., (eds.), (1999) *Acts of Dissent. New Developments in the Study of Protest*, Oxford: Rowman & Littlefield Publishers.

Rucht, D. & Neidhardt, F. (1999) 'Methodological Issues in Collecting Protest Event Data: Units of Analysis, Sources and Sampling, Coding Problems', in D. Rucht, R. Koopmans & F. Neidhardt (eds.), *Acts of Dissent. New Developments in the Study of Protest*, Oxford: Rowman & Littlefield Publishers.

Rucht, D. & Ohlemacher, T. (1992) 'Protest Event Data: Collection, Uses and Perspectives', in M. Diani & R. Eyerman (eds.), *Studying Collective Action*, London: Sage.

Salamon, L. M., Anheier, H. K. *et al.* (1999) *Global Civil Society: Dimensions of the Nonprofit Sector*, Baltimore: Johns Hopkins Center for Civil Society Studies.

Salisbury, R. H. (1969) 'An Exchange Theory of Interest Groups', *Midwest Journal of Political Science*, 13 (1): 1–32.

Sani, G. & Sartori, G. (1983) 'Polarization, Fragmentation and Competition in Western Democracies', in H. Daalder & P. Mair (eds.), *Western European Party Systems: Continuity and Change*, London: Sage.

Schattschneider, E. E. (1960) *The Semi-Sovereign People*, Hinsdale: Dryden Press.

Schlozman, K. L. (1984) 'What Accent the Heavenly Chorus? Political Equality and the American Pressure System', *Journal of Politics*, 46 (4): 1006–32.

Schlozman, K. L., Burns, N. & Verba, S. (1999) '"What Happened At Work Today?": A Multistage Model of Gender, Employment, and Political Participation', *Journal of Politics*, 61 (1): 29–53.

Schlozman, K. L., Verba, S. & Brady, H. E. (1995) 'Participation's Not a Paradox: The View From American Activists', *British Journal of Political Science*, 25: 1–36.

Schmitt, R. (1989) 'Organizational Interlocks Between New Social Movements and Traditional Elites: The Case of the West German Peace Movement', *European Journal of Political Research*, 17: 583–98.

Schmitter, P. C. (1988) 'La Mediación entre los Intereses y la Gobernabilidad de los Regímenes en Europa Occidental y Norteamérica en la Actualidad'. in S. Berger (ed.) *La Organización de los Grupos de Interés en Europa Occidental. El Pluralismo, el Corporativismo y la Transformación de la Política*, Madrid: Ministerio de Trabajo y Seguridad Social. (Reprinted from *Organizing Interest in Western Europe. Pluralism, Corporatism, and the Transformation of Politics*, 1981, New York: Cambridge University Press)

Schofer, E. & Fourcade-Gourinchas, M. (2001) 'The Structural Contexts of Civic Engagement: Voluntary Association Membership in Comparative Perspective', *American Sociological Review*, 66 (4): 806–28.

Seligson, A. L. (1999) 'Civic Association and Democratic Participation in Central America', *Comparative Political Studies*, 32 (3): 342–62.

Selle, P. & Svasand, L. (1991) 'Membership in Party Organizations and the Problem of Decline of Parties', *Comparative Political Studies*, 23 (4): 459–77.

Sharpe (ed.), L. J. (1993) *The Rise of Meso-Government in Europe*, London: Sage.

Siaroff, A. (1999) 'Corporatism in 24 Industrial Democracies: Meaning and Measurement', *European Journal of Political Research*, 36 (2): 175–205.

Siegfried, A. (1995) *Tableau Politique De La France De L'Ouest Sous La IIIè Republique*, Paris: Imprimerie nationale.

Sigel, R. S. & Hoskin, M. B. (1981) *The Political Involvement of Adolescents*, New Brunswick, NJ: Rutgers University Press.

Skocpol, T. (2003) *Diminished Democracy: From Membership to Management in American Civic Life*, Norman: University of Oklahoma Press.

Skocpol, T., Ganz, M. & Munson, Z. (2000) 'A Nation of Organizers: The Institutional Origins of Civic Voluntarism in the United States', *American Political Science Review*, 94 (3): 527–46.

Smidt, C. (1999) 'Religion and Civic Engagement: A Comparative Analysis', *Annals of the American Academy of Political and Social Sciences*, 565 (September): 176–92.

Smith, B. C. (1985) *Decentralisation: The Terrritorial Dimension of the State*, London: Allen & Unwin.

Smith, T. W. (1990) 'Trends in Voluntary Group Membership: Comments on Baumgartner and Walker', *American Journal of Political Science*, 34 (3): 646–61.

Sniderman, P., Brody, R. A. & Tetlock, P. (1991) *Reasoning and Choice*, New York: Cambridge University Press.

Snijders, T. A. B. & Bosker, R. J. (1999) *Multilevel Analysis: An Introduction to Basic and Advanced Multilevel Modeling*, London: Sage.

Snow, D. A., Zurcher, L. A. & Ekland–Olson, S. E. (1980) 'Social Networks and Social Movements: A Microstructural Approach to Differential Recruitment', *American Sociological Review*, 45: 787–801.

Solt, F. (2008) 'Economic Inequality and Democratic Political Engagement', *American Journal of Political Science*, 52 (1): 48–60.

Sprague, J. (1982) 'Is There a Micro Theory Consistent with Contextual Analysis?', in E. Ostrom (ed.), *Strategies of Political Inquiry*, Beverly Hills: Sage.

Stinchcombe, A. L. (1965) 'Social Structure and Organizations', in J. G. March (ed.), *Handbook of Organizations*, Chicago: Rand McNally.

Stoker, G. (1991) 'Introduction: Trends in Western European Local Government', in R. Batley & G. Stoker (eds.), *Local Government in Europe: Trends and Developments*, London: Macmillan.

Stokes, S. C. (1999) 'What Do Policy Switches Tell Us About Democracy?', in A. Przeworski, S. C. Stokes & B. Manin (eds.), *Democracy, Accountability and Representation*, Cambridge: Cambridge University Press.

Stolle, D. & Lewis, J. (2002) 'Social Capital. An Emerging Concept', in B. Hobson, J. Lewis & B. Siim (eds.), *Contested Concepts in Gender and Social Politics*, Cheltenham: Edward Elgar Press.

Stolle, D. & Rochon, T. R. (1998) 'Are All Associations Alike? Member Diversity, Associational Type, and the Creation of Social Capital', *American Behavioral Scientist*, 42 (1): 47–65.

Tarrow, S. (1977) *Between Center and Periphery: Grassroots Politicians in Italy and France*, New Haven CT: Yale University Press.

— (1994) *Power in Movement: Social Movements, Collective Action and Mass Politics in the Modern State*, Cambridge: Cambridge University Press.

— (1996) 'Making Social Science Work Across Space and Time: A Critical Reflection on Robert Putnam's Making Democracy Work', *American Political Science Review*, 90: 389–97.

— (1999) 'Studying Contentious Politics: From Event-Full History to Cycles of Collective Action', in D. Rucht, R. Koopmans & F. Neidhardt (eds.), *Acts of Dissent: New Developments in the Study of Protest*, Oxford: Rowman & Littlefield Publishers.

Taylor, M. (1976) *Anarchy and Cooperation*, London: John Wiley.

Taylor, M. & Herman, V. M. (1971) 'Party Systems and Government Stability', *American Political Science Review*, 65 (1): 28–37.

Teorell, J. (2006) 'Political Participation and Three Theories of Democracy: A Research Inventory and Agenda', *European Journal of Political Research*, 45 (5): 787–810.

Teorell, J., Sum, P. & Tobiasen, M. (2007) 'Participation and Political Equality: An Assessment of Large-Scale Democracy', in J. W. van Deth, J. R. Montero & A. Westholm (eds.), *Citizenship and Involvement in European Democracies: A Comparative Analysis*, London: Routledge.

Tilly, C. (1978) *From Mobilization to Revolution*, New York: Random House.

Tingsten, H. (1937) *Political Behavior: Studies in Election Statistics*, London: P.S. King.

Topf, R. (1995) 'Beyond Electoral Participation', in H. Klingemann & D. Fuchs (eds.), *Citizens and the State*, New York: Oxford University Press.

Torcal, M. & Montero, J. R. (1999) 'Facets of Social Capital in New Democracies. The Formation and Consequences of Social Capital in Spain', in J. W. van Deth *et al.* (eds.), *Social Capital and European Democracy*, London: Routledge.

Truman, D. B. (1951) *The Governmental Process: Political Interests and Public Opinion*, New York: Alfred A. Knopf.

Uleri, P. V. (1996) 'Introduction', in M. Gallagher & P. V. Uleri (eds.), *The Referendum Experience in Europe*, London: Macmillan Press.

Uslaner, E. M. (2001) 'Volunteering and Social Capital: How Trust and Religion

Shape Civic Participation in the United States', in P. Dekker & E. M. Uslaner (eds.), *Social Capital and Participation in Everyday Life*, London: Routledge.

van Deth, J. W., Montero, J. R. & Westholm, A. (2007) *Citizenship and Involvement in European Democracies. A Comparative Analysis*, London: Routledge.

van Deth, J. W. (1997) 'Introduction: Social Involvement and Democratic Politics', in J. W. van Deth (ed.), *Private Groups and Public Life: Social Participation, Voluntary Associations and Political Involvement in Representative Democracies*, London: Routledge.

— (1998) 'Equivalence in Comparative Political Research', in J. W. van Deth (ed.), *Comparative Politics: The Problem of Equivalence*, London: Routledge.

— (2001) 'Studying Political Participation: Towards a Theory of Everything?', Paper presented at the ECPR Joint Sessions, Grenoble.

— (2003) 'Measuring Social Capital: Orthodoxies and Continuing Controversies', *International Journal of Social Research Methodology*, 6 (1): 79–92.

van Deth, J. W. & Elff, M. (2000) *Political Involvement and Apathy in Europe, 1973–1998 MZES Arbeitspapiere: Vol. 33*, Mannheim: Mannheimer Zentrum fur Europaische Sozialforschung.

van Deth, J. W. & Kreuter, F. (1998) 'Membership of Voluntary Associations', in J. W. van Deth (ed.), *Comparative Politics: The Problem of Equivalence*, London: Routledge.

van Egmond, M., de Graaf, N. D. & van der Eijk, C. (1998) 'Electoral Participation in the Netherlands: Individual and Contextual Influences', *European Journal of Political Research*, 34 (2): 281–300.

van Sickle, A. & Dalton, R. J. (March 2005) 'The Roots Of Political Protest: A Contextual Analysis Of Protest Behavior', Paper presented at the Annual Meeting of the International Studies Association, Honolulu.

Verba, S., Burns, N. & Schlozman, K. L. (1997) 'Knowing and Caring About Politics: Gender and Political Engagement', *The Journal of Politics*, 59 (4): 1051–72.

Verba, S. & Nie, N. H. (1972) *Participation in America: Political Democracy and Social Equality*, New York: Harper & Row.

Verba, S. *et al.* (1973) 'The Modes of Participation: Continuities in Research', *Comparative Political Studies*, 6 (2): 235–50.

Verba, S., Nie, N. H. & Kim, J. (1971) *The Modes of Democratic Participation: A Cross-National Comparison*, Beverly Hills: Sage.

— (1978) *Participation and Political Equality: A Seven–Nation Comparison*, New York: Cambridge University Press.

Verba, S., Schlozman, K. L. & Brady, H. E. (1995) *Voice and Equality: Civic Voluntarism in American Politics*, Harvard: Harvard University Press.

— (2000) 'Rational Action and Political Activity', *Journal of Theoretical Politics*, 12 (3): 243–68.

Verba, S. *et al.* (1993) 'Citizen Activity: Who Participates? What Do They Say?', *American Political Science Review*, 87 (2): 303–18.

Verba, S., Schlozman, K. L. & Burns, N. (2005) 'Family Ties: Understanding the Intergenerational Transmission of Political Participation', in A. S. Zuckerman (ed.), *The Social Logic of Politics: Personal Networks As Contexts for Political Behavior*, Philadelphia: Temple University Press.

Vetter, A. (2002a) 'Local Political Competence in Europe: A Resource of Legitimacy for Higher Levels of Government?', *International Journal of Public Opinion Research*, 14 (1): 3–18.

— (2002b) *Lokale Politik Als Ressource Der Demokratie in Europa? Lokale Autonomie, Lokale Strukturen Und Die Einstellungen Der Bürger Zur Lokalen Politik*, Opladen: Leske + Budrich.

Walker, J. L. (1991) *Mobilizing Interest Groups in America: Patrons, Professions and Social Movements*, Ann Arbor: University of Michigan Press.

Warren, M. E. (2001) *Democracy and Association*, Princeton & London: Princeton University Press.

Wessels, B. (1997) 'Organizing Capacity of Societies and Modernity', in J. W. van Deth (ed.), *Private Groups and Public Life*, London: Routledge.

Whiteley, P. F. (1995) 'Rational Choice and Political Participation: Evaluating the Debate', *Political Research Quarterly*, 48 (1): 211–33.

Wiarda, H. J. (1997) *Corporatism and Comparative Politics: The Other Great 'Ism'*, Armonk, NY: M.E. Sharpe.

Widfeldt, A. (1995) 'Party Membership and Party Representativeness', in H. Klingemann & D. Fuchs (eds.), *Citizens and the State*, New York: Oxford University Press.

Wielhouwer, P. W. & Lockerbie, B. (1994) 'Party Contacting and Political Participation, 1952–1990', *American Journal of Political Science*, 38 (1): 211–29.

Wilson, J. Q. (1995) *Political Organizations*, Princeton: Princeton University Press.

Wuthnow, R. (1994) *Sharing the Journey*, New York: The Free Press.

— (1999) 'Mobilizing Civic Engagement: The Changing Impact of Religious Involvement', in T. Skocpol & M. P. Fiorina (eds.), *Civic Engagement in American Democracy*, Washington, DC: Brookings Institution.

Wuthnow, R. E. (1991) *Between States and Markets: The Voluntary Sector in Comparative Perspective*, Princeton: Princeton University Press.

Zipp, J. F. & Smith, J. (1979) 'The Structure of Electoral Political Participation', *American Journal of Sociology*, 85: 167–77.

Zuckerman, A. S. (ed.) (2005) *The Social Logic of Politics: Personal Networks As Contexts for Political Behavior*, Philadelphia: Temple University Press.

index